HOW TO USE
PSYCHOLOGICAL
RESEARCH

HOW TO USE
PSYCHOLOGICAL
RESEARCH

A GUIDE FOR THOSE NEW TO STUDYING PSYCHOLOGY

AMANDA MORRIS
TRACEY ELDER

S Sage

1 Oliver's Yard
55 City Road
London EC1Y 1SP

2455 Teller Road
Thousand Oaks
California 91320

Unit No 323-333, Third Floor, F-Block
International Trade Tower
Nehru Place, New Delhi 110 019

8 Marina View Suite 43-053
Asia Square Tower 1
Singapore 018960

Library of Congress Control Number: 2024933128

British Library Cataloguing in Publication data

A catalogue record for this book is available from the British Library

Editor: Janka Romero
Editorial Assistant: Hanine Kadi
Production Editor: Neelu Sahu
Marketing Manager: Camille Richmond
Cover Design: Wendy Scott
Typeset by: TNQ Tech Pvt. Ltd.

ISBN 978-1-5296-2622-3
ISBN 978-1-5296-2621-6 (pbk)

Amanda: to my husband, Rob, who supports me in all my endeavours, and to my two wonderful children, Jett and Harrison – I am so proud of everything you both do.

Tracey: to my wonderful son, Aidan, who is so kind and warm-hearted, and to my husband, Adam, who is always so patient and supportive – I cannot thank you enough. To my other boy, Dexter, our black Labrador, who never fails to make me smile. And finally, to my parents and my sister, whose lifetime support has meant so much.

1

PSYCHOLOGICAL RESEARCH – WHY ALL THE FUSS?

Key goals for this chapter

- Understand psychology as a discipline.
- Understand the importance of conducting research in psychology.
- Understand core research methods used to conduct research in psychology.

WELCOME TO PSYCHOLOGY

Congratulations on deciding to study psychology, great to see you here. Whether you have decided to study psychology for the first time or you are coming back for more, you are very welcome. The aim of this book is to help you through. We can remember what it feels like when you have an assignment, and you find yourself staring at a blank page. You have been told to use psychological research in your essay or report, but you have very little idea of how to do that and where to start. It feels intimidating, too difficult, too academic and suddenly any other task seems more enjoyable (vacuuming, cleaning the car, tidying the kitchen). This is where we come in. We hope to demystify, simplify and demonstrate how you can use research in your work to the best effect so that it becomes second nature to you. Despite what you may think, this is a skill to develop and not something you should be expected to know; like any skill it needs to be taught, modelled and practised and this book will help you to do that (and more). We have structured this book in a way that means you can dip in and out grabbing what you need to help you on your way. We will now get started and where better to start than by exploring the importance of research in psychology.

PSYCHOLOGY AS A RESEARCH-LED DISCIPLINE, BEYOND THE ARMCHAIR AND INTO THE UNIVERSITIES

It may not surprise you to learn that psychology is an evidence-based discipline. The evidence comes from research that has used a wide range of methods including experiments, observations, questionnaires, interviews and case studies (and these are just the more popular ones). You will learn about these methods later in this chapter. Without this emphasis on research and evidence, psychology would not be an academic discipline but a collection of ideas. The evidence is needed to support the ideas and to be taken seriously as a discipline; to help you to understand this, let us introduce to you the difference between opinions, claims and most importantly evidence-based claims.

Claims

If you are new to psychology, you may be wondering what we mean when we refer to 'claims' and how they are different from opinions.

Consider the following statement, 'We think computer games are boring'. This is not a claim, it is an opinion. Opinions cannot be right or wrong; they are subjective to the person who they belong to. In this example, whilst we may state that computer games are boring, our sons would strongly disagree with us and protest that 'We think computer games are amazing'. Neither of us are factually correct nor incorrect, we are simply sharing our opinion. Opinions are not useful in academic writing, as someone can simply offer an alternative opinion, for example:

Person A: 'I think dogs make the best pet'.

Person B: 'I prefer cats'.

Person A: 'No way, I think cats are boring, they just sleep all day'.

Person B: 'It is nice that they sleep a lot, as I like when my cat sleeps on my lap whilst I watch television'.

This highly exciting exchange about cats and dogs could continue with each person presenting their opinion about their favourite pet and what they like about it. Claims differ to opinions as a claim is not opinion based and are therefore not influenced by subjective experiences. For example, 'Owning a cat or dog helps to reduce stress'. This is a claim and not an opinion, as it is not internal to someone's beliefs. Instead, it is being presented as fact, as though it were true.

━━━━━━ Think 1.1 ━━━━━━

Now, before you rushed out to buy a cat or dog to help you to manage stress, would you want any additional information? Is this claim enough to convince you that the statement is true? If you would like further information, what kind of information would you want? Where could you find this information?

Whilst claims are integral to your writing in psychology, a claim that is a simple statement and nothing else is of no more use than an opinion. In fact, we could simply rephrase our own opinion to present it as a claim.

'We think computer games are boring' becomes 'computer games dull creativity in gamers.'

The claim sounds much more convincing, however without any evidence to support this claim it is unsubstantiated and anecdotal, offering us no more than an opinion. If we had evidence to support our claim, suddenly it becomes a lot more convincing. For example,

Person A: 'Computer games dull creativity in gamers', – An unsubstantiated claim.

Person B: 'Actually, there is evidence which found creativity increased in 16–17-year olds after playing a digital game in one of their classes for 27 weeks', – This claim has evidence to back it up (Yang, 2015).

━━━━━━ Key tip 1.1 ━━━━━━

One quick way to check if you have backed up a claim with evidence is to check that you have an in-text citation alongside each claim you make.

The claim that is evidence based provides a stronger argument and this is integral to your psychological writing and is in fact the key purpose of this book! This book aims to aid you in developing how you use research in your writing, but before we get to that part it is important you understand why research is so important in psychology.

━━━━━━━━ **Stop 1.1** ━━━━━━━━

Remember, claims that you make in your academic writing for psychology must be backed up with evidence.

The Goals of Psychology

To begin to understand *why* research is important in psychology, you first need to be familiar with the goals of psychology which are to describe, explain, predict and to control.

Describe

The first step in studying human behaviour is to notice that a particular behaviour is occurring. For example, when mobile phones became a regular feature in our daily lives' researchers noticed how phones were being used and described this behaviour.

> Some people seem to be always using their phone, even when in a face-to-face conversation with someone else. Often people walk around holding onto their mobile phone even if they are not using it.

Explain

Once we can describe a particular behaviour, as psychologists, we want to understand what is causing that behaviour and seek to explain the cause.

> Some people may have **nomophobia**, which are feelings of **anxiety** or fear of being away from their mobile phone.

Predict

If our explanations of what is causing a particular behaviour are correct, we should be able to predict future behaviour.

> Individuals who have higher levels of nomophobia will be more likely to use their mobile phone regularly, even when they are in a face-to-face interaction with another person, than those who do not have nomophobia.

Control

When we speak about 'controlling' behaviour, we are referring to implementing strategies and interventions which seek to improve behavioural outcomes. This is important in psychology as these changes can make a significant impact on people's well-being.

Treatments can be implemented for the anxiety that nomophobia creates. These treatments could include **cognitive behavioural therapy** or **exposure therapy**.

━━━━━━━━━━ Think 1.2 ━━━━━━━━━━

Where does the collection of evidence come in this cycle? At what point would we want to start backing up our ideas/claims with evidence?

Why Is Research Important?

As you have just learnt, one of the goals of psychology is to be to *explain* behaviour. Thinking back to what you know about claims, any explanations as to what is causing specific behaviours need to be evidence based. If not, any claims made are meaningless and literally anyone could give any reason to explain behaviour. There would be no need to study psychology, we could say whatever we wanted as our suggestions would be as valid as anyone else's as they would all be anecdotal. However, with the addition of *evidence* this separates an anecdotal claim from a claim which is now more than opinion and has some support for its truth.

Having evidence is crucial if we are to implement interventions to support changes in behaviour. Imagine you are feeling ill and go to see your general practitioner (GP) to see if they can give you anything to help you to feel better. Your GP suggests that you spin in a circle for three minutes a day to treat your illness. This sounds strange to you (it is!) and you ask the GP if they are sure this will work; the GP replies that they think it will work but there is no evidence that has tested it. Based on this interaction, it would be unlikely that you would want to try the 'circle treatment'; however, if the GP told you that there were numerous studies that had tested its effectiveness, and the GP could explain how the treatment worked you may be more willing to try it. This is the same in psychology; if we are going to make suggestions to individuals and organisations about how to encourage positive behaviours, we need to have evidence to ensure we are not wasting people's time and to encourage people to engage with the suggestions.

For example, exercise has been suggested to both prevent and treat mild to moderate **depression**. For someone who is depressed asking them to engage in regular exercise will require a level of motivation, something that an individual who is depressed will be likely to lack. If we have evidence to support the positive impact exercise has on depression, it may be easier for someone with depression to begin an exercise programme than it would be if it was simply our opinion.

━━━━━━━━━━ Stop 1.2 ━━━━━━━━━━

Evidence is important to back up claims and to allow us to develop effective interventions that build on explanations for behaviour.

It is important to recognise that the ideas psychologists have come from the society around them and as such psychology is a dynamic and fluid discipline that moves with society. Psychology as a discipline would not be useful to society if it occurred in a vacuum that was immune from the outside world. This presents challenges and opportunities. If you think about the rise of the internet and the use of smart phones and smart technology, this has changed the way we interact with each other and how our children develop socially. It may also influence children's brain and physical development. Psychology can help answer important questions in this area and can use a variety of techniques and methods to do so. These techniques and methods have also progressed through the development of technology with the use of **brain scanning, eye-tracking, computer simulation** and **video conferencing** to name just a few. So, you can see how there is a strong desire in psychology to understand real-life behaviour. But it is important to recognise that whilst conducting research provides us with answers, it also conjures up additional questions that need answering and so a researcher's work is never done (you will learn more about the research cycle in Chapter 3).

■■■■■■■■■■■ Think 1.3 ■■■■■■■■■■■

Having established that psychology uses research to provide evidence to support researchers' ideas, the next question is how do researchers disseminate their findings to others? How do we know that the research is to be trusted and is reliable?

These are important questions as we always need to be critical when we are assessing research and that should start by looking at who has conducted the research, where has the research been published and who has funded the research. Researchers often work at universities, and they will often want to publish their research in **peer-reviewed journals** in their field. Research can also be published in book chapters and psychologists are now making increasing use of tools such as Facebook, Twitter, Research Gate, LinkedIn and blogs to share their research. This enables their findings to reach a potentially wider audience. We will be exploring how research is disseminated in more detail in Chapter 3.

There are many other ways to find psychology research but do consider the credibility and reliability of the information. Often when watching television or online we will be presented with the statement 'research in psychology has shown...' and this could lead you to consider – 'What research?' 'Who did it?' 'What are their credentials?' 'How did they carry out their research?' 'What analysis did they do?' It is only by asking these types of key questions that will you be able to see whether the claims being made can be accepted or not.

The increase in social media means that research claims are made and spread so quickly and often without the appropriate scrutiny. If it is being shared multiple times and you see the same message across your socials, it can lead you to accepting the 'research' as 'truth'. As psychology is a relevant and engaging subject, the interest in the subject is strong and attracts attention and as a psychology student you need to be discerning. This is part of the critical thinking that we will be exploring in more detail in Chapter 6 but will be a common theme running through this book.

Now you are aware of how psychology functions as a discipline, we can turn to exploring how psychologists conduct research.

APPROACHES TO RESEARCH

You now have an idea of why we collect evidence in psychology. The process however becomes more complex when we begin to think of *how* we can collect evidence and what type of data that may give us.

There are multiple ways we can collect evidence, but before we address these (which we will do later in the chapter) we need to go back a step and consider what type of approach we are taking to our data collection. Most researchers tend to take one of two approaches, either **nomothetic** or **idiographic.** A nomothetic approach to conducting research aims to discover general laws of behaviour that we can apply to most people. This usually involves gathering **quantitative** data in numeric form (American Psychological Association, 2023a). An idiographic approach aims to understand one person in detail and their unique experiences without seeking to apply what is found to everyone. This usually involves gathering **qualitative** in-depth data (American Psychological Association, 2023b).

Neither approach is 'better' than the other; they are simply different ways to explore and understand behaviour. What is important to keep in mind is that the approach we take to our data collection will influence our choice of method and how we interpret the findings. Due to the richness of qualitative data, when analysed, different people can draw different **(subjective)** interpretations. This is less likely to happen with quantitative data as it is analysed using complex mathematical formulas rather than individual interpretation, making it **objective**.

RESEARCH METHODS IN PSYCHOLOGY

In Chapter 3, you will learn about the principles of science and the features in psychology which fit into a scientific discipline. When you read Chapter 3, think about the methods described below and whether they fit with scientific principles. Keep in mind that not all studies in psychology are designed to be rigorously scientific. A nomothetic approach which is seeking to discover generalisable laws of behaviour will follow the principles of science more closely than researchers taking an idiographic approach.

With this in mind, the approach to research that is taken will influence *how* the research is conducted and the method used. Having some understanding of the methods used in psychological research is important as it will assist you in being able to think critically about the research that you engage with during your studies. Crucially, as you progress through this book, you will begin to appreciate the importance of thinking critically about the research that you bring into your assignments. We will come back to this later, but for now we will introduce some of the most commonly used methods in psychological research. It is important to be aware that this is a very basic introduction to the methods used and often psychological research uses a mix of methods as well as methods not covered here.

Experiments

An **experiment** seeks to establish a causal relationship between two variables: an independent variable and a dependent variable. A variable is something that varies, for example hair colour can vary and be brown, blonde, ginger or even pink if you dyed it. An **independent variable** is one that varies between groups of people and as researchers we are interested in the effect that this has on the **dependent variable**. A dependent variable is one that we measure to see if it *depends* on the independent variable.

An independent variable can either be manipulated by the researcher or it may be pre-existing in participants. If we were interested in whether height affects how helpful someone is, height would be our independent variable as this is what is varying between groups. Our dependent variable is level of helpfulness. In this example, the researcher cannot manipulate the independent variable as height is not something that researchers can change. Height is already pre-existing in research. Let's consider another example whereby we want to know whether eating chocolate increases happiness. In this example, the independent variable would be the amount of chocolate eaten and the dependent variable is level of happiness. Here, it is possible for the researchers to manipulate the independent variable as we can vary the amount of chocolate that our participants eat. We could use a **between participants design** and have different participants complete different levels of the independent variable. One group of participants eats 10g of chocolate, another group eats 15g of chocolate and a third group does not eat any chocolate. In this example, our independent variable has three levels, 10g, 15g and no chocolate. The inclusion of having a group that does not consume chocolate provides us with a control group. When the researcher can manipulate the independent variable, a true experiment will include a control group and participants will be randomly allocated to one of the levels of the independent variable. A control group is necessary as it gives us a baseline measure to compare to. **Random allocation** means that which level of the independent variable each participant takes part in is selected randomly, removing bias from the study. Having different participants in each level of the independent variable can be problematic. If we consider the chocolate example, it is possible that by chance the participants who are given 15g of chocolate to eat are generally happier than the participants given 10g of chocolate to eat. If our results show higher happiness levels in the 15g of chocolate group, it may therefore not be the chocolate causing happiness but instead *individual differences* between the participants in the three groups. An alternative way to test this could be to use a **within-participants design** where all participants take part in all levels of the independent variable. Thus, participants' happiness is measured after eating no chocolate, a week later participants return and eat 10g of chocolate and their happiness is measured and finally another week passes, and the same participants consume 15g of chocolate and have their happiness measured again. This way, if some participants are generally happier this will be spread across all conditions of the independent variable.

To allow researchers to conclude that the independent variable has *caused* the dependent variable, researchers will try to control any factors other than the independent variable which might influence the dependent variable. In our chocolate study, the type of chocolate could influence our outcome. Therefore, all participants would have to consume the same brand of chocolate with the same amount of cocoa. Other potential controls would be what other food the participants have eaten that day, the time of day the chocolate is eaten, what liquids (if any) are consumed with the chocolate and where participants eat the chocolate. This list is not exhaustive, and you may be able to think of other factors, as the researcher you would need to control as many of these factors as possible to ensure that the only thing that is influencing the dependent variable is the independent variable. Table 1.1 covers some general strengths and limitations of experiments.

Table 1.1 Strengths and limitations of experiments

Strengths	Limitations
Experiments by their design seek to establish cause and effect between an independent variable and dependent variable. The high levels of control that are put into place in a true experiment, allow for cause and effect to be established. Other methods do not allow for such strict controls of all other factors that might influence our outcomes.	Due to the researcher manipulating the key variables in the study, they are usually narrowly defined to be made measurable. This is problematic due to this strict manipulation; it means the variables are unlikely to truly reflect the behaviour in question as it occurs in everyday life. Everyday life is messy and full of complex interactions which highly controlled experiments do not reflect.
Due to the high levels of control in experiments, it means that every decision is recorded, and the study is conducted following a strict protocol. The benefits of this are that it allows other researchers to reproduce and replicate the study to see if the same findings are found.	Experiments usually require that participants are aware that they are participating in psychological research. They are often conducted in psychology laboratories at universities and as such, participants may respond in a way that is not a natural reflection of their behaviour. Participants in psychological research have given up their time to participate in research and subsequently can be keen to 'please' the researcher and give them the results they think the researcher wants. These **demand characteristics** can leave us with an inaccurate measure of the independent variable on the dependent variable.

Correlation

Unlike an experiment, a **correlation** does not allow us to establish cause and effect between variables. A correlation does measure variables, but there is no manipulation of the variables and no comparison of different levels of the variables across groups. Instead, a correlation measures covariables to see if there is a relationship between these variables. The researcher simply needs access to already measured data or a way of measuring constructs which gather quantitative data.

We could use a correlation to measure the relationship between chocolate consumed and happiness. In this example, we would not be comparing the different (pre-specified) amounts of chocolate across groups instead we would be looking at the relationship between *the amount* of chocolate consumed and *the amount* of happiness. We could give participants a

survey (more on these in a minute) to measure how much chocolate participants have eaten in the past week and that asks how happy they have felt on average in the previous week. This would give us two scores for each participant, a happiness score and a chocolate consumption score. Imagine we have 100 participants who complete this survey; we could then see whether across these 100 participants there is a relationship between chocolate consumption and happiness. To work this out we would use a statistical analysis where we would input both scores for all 100 participants and end up with a number called the **correlation coefficient**. This is a number between −1 to +1. The positive and negative tell us whether the correlation is positive or negative. A **positive correlation** occurs when as one variable increases, so does the other, in our example as chocolate consumption increases happiness also increases. A **negative correlation** occurs when as one variable increases, the other decreases. In our example, increased chocolate consumptions occur alongside decreased levels of happiness.

A positive correlation ranges from 0.001 to 1, a negative correlation ranges from −0.001 to −1. The number tells us the strength of the correlation, the closer to 1 the stronger the relationship. However, even if a correlation is strong and close to 1 this only tells us that there is a relationship between two variables. It does not tell us if one variable *causes* the change in the other variable, it is possible that the relationship happens by coincidence (you can see some examples of coincidental correlations here https://www.tylervigen.com/spurious-correlations). Another possibility is that there is another variable that is causing a change in the variables being measured. In our chocolate example, it is possible that stress is an additional (not measured) variable that influence both chocolate consumption and happiness. Higher stress levels may lead to higher consumption of chocolate as a form of emotion focused coping, higher stress levels may also reduce levels of happiness. Table 1.2 covers some general strengths and limitations of correlations as a research method.

Table 1.2 Strengths and limitations of correlations

Strengths	Limitations
As there is no manipulation of variables, there is less chance of **researcher bias** occurring in the process. The researcher simply measures the variables as they occur naturally.	As previously mentioned, correlations only tell us the strength and direction of the relationship between variables. We cannot determine cause and effect and if this is what we are seeking to find, we would need to follow up a correlation with an experiment.
An additional benefit of the researcher not manipulating any variables is that we are able to measure behaviours that may not be possible on a practical and/or ethical level to manipulate in an experiment.	A correlation only gives us meaningful information if any relationship between variables is a linear one. Not all relationships are linear such as attention levels and time of day. In the morning we may find a positive relationship between attention levels and time of day. However, in the afternoon the relationship might be a negative one. A correlational analysis would not allow us to accurately measure this non-linear relationship as the two opposite relationships would cancel each other out and suggest nothing is happening, when there is a pattern to the data.

Observation

An **observation** involves the researcher observing the behaviour of the participants. Participants may be observed in a controlled setting that has been set up for the purpose of the research (a **controlled observation**), or they may be observed in their normal everyday environment (a **natural observation**). There is usually no manipulation of variables, even if the setting is controlled. However, it is possible to conduct an experiment whereby the data for the dependent variable is collected via an observation. Thus, an observation can be a method in its own right or used as a means to collect data in an experiment. In Chapter 2, you will explore in more detail a study by DeLoache et al. (1998) who tested whether nine-month-old infants could distinguish between real and drawn objects. In this example an experiment was conducted, and an observation was used to collect the data for the dependent variable, the number of times the infant tried to explore the object.

In psychological research, the researcher is not usually involved in the interaction being observed; they observe from afar (a **non-participant observation**). Or more commonly in a controlled observation, the observation is recorded, and the researcher can go through the recording at a later time. In some circumstances the researcher may join the interaction being studied, a **participant observation**. This is less commonly used in psychological research as the researcher's presence will change the dynamics of the interaction.

Another feature of observations is whether the participant is aware they are being observed or not. If the observation is taking place in a controlled setting, the participant will know they are being observed (an **overt observation**). If the observation occurs in the participant's natural environment, they are unlikely to be aware that they are being observed for psychological research (a **covert observation**). Due to ethics, you can only observe someone covertly in a situation where they would expect their behaviour to be seen by members of the public. You could therefore observe someone in a restaurant or a park, but you could not peer through people's windows to observe them in their own homes! That is not to say you cannot conduct observations in the home, but they would need to be overt and with the participants consent.

■■■■■■■■■ Think 1.4 ■■■■■■■■■

We have used the example of studying chocolate and happiness for both an experiment and a correlation. Would it be possible to also study this using an observation? When you are thinking about the answer to this question, think about all of the different types of observation, controlled, natural, participant, non-participant, overt and covert. Would any of these types of observations be suitable for *this* study?

In answering the previous question, you may have struggled to think of exactly how you could measure chocolate and happiness with an observation. One of the main reasons for this is because happiness is not a trait which lends itself well to an observation. We can observe someone who is smiling, but this does not mean they *feel* happy. Happiness is an internal feeling and whilst there are some external signs which can signal happiness, we can only truly measure happiness by asking the individual how they feel. This is something that is important to recognise with regards to research, which method is selected to conduct the research depends on what we are trying to find out. If we want evidence which gives us information on social interactions, an observation would be the most suitable method.

Let's say we are interested in the interactions between romantic partners and '**phubbing**'. Phubbing is when someone uses their phone during a social interaction, thus snubbing their social partner. We might be interested in whether romantic partners do 'phub' their partner during social interactions, how often this occurs, how long the phone is used and how the other person responds when their partner uses their phone. We would be able to observe and see these behaviours via an observation. This would need to be a non-participant observation, so that the interaction is not disrupted by the researcher. A natural or controlled observation could be used with this study, but in a controlled environment participants may be less likely to behave naturally and may not use their phone, demonstrating socially desirable behaviour. Table 1.3 covers some general strengths and limitations of observations as a research method.

Table 1.3 Strengths and limitations of observations

Strengths	Limitations
If the observation is covert it allows us to get a true representation of behaviour as participants will not behave in a **socially desirable** way. They will also not exhibit demand characteristics and behave in a way to please the researcher.	Covert observations are limited as we can only observe what participants would be expected to be observed by others in a public setting due to ethical considerations. This restricts what we can observe using this method and we may never observe behaviours that are not censored in some form.
A controlled observation ensures that all participants are observed in the exact same environment. This means that any differences in the behaviours observed are unlikely to be due to any differences in the environment. It also allows the observation to be **replicated** by other researchers.	Controlled observations are not the participants' natural environment, which means the behaviour observed is unlikely to truly reflect how the participants behave in their everyday lives. This is problematic as it means any behaviour we observe may be valid in the controlled environment but it does not necessarily tell us much about natural behaviour.

Self-Report: Survey

Self-report techniques differ from other methods in that these methods ask the participants to report on their own behaviour rather than observing/recording the behaviour from the researcher's perspective. They are usually used to gather data on people's beliefs, attitudes or feelings as these are constructs which we can only measure by asking someone as we cannot observe them.

It is likely you have completed a survey before and will be familiar with their structure. They are a written set of questions that the participant can complete either within the researcher's presence or alone. Surveys can be completed via pen and paper, but the more common approach is to distribute them online.

The questions included in a survey can be open or closed. Open ended questions are those which allow the respondent to write their responses without having to select from a set of prescribed options. Whereas closed ended questions are those where there are either a set of options to select from, or you may give your response on a Likert Scale, e.g. 'strongly agree' to 'strongly disagree'.

Key to a successful survey is that questions are not ambiguous in any way, as this leaves the respondent to interpret what the question is asking. Leading questions also need to be avoided, otherwise responses will be bias.

If we think back to our previous example of phubbing in romantic relationships, one way to investigate this (as previously stated) is to observe interactions in romantic relationships. It is possible to also investigate this behaviour using a survey. We could ask participants questions as to how they feel when their partner uses their phone and they are with them. We could use open questions where participants explain how this makes them feel or we could ask them to respond on a Likert Scale in relation to specific questions such as 'I feel frustrated when my partner uses their phone when I am with them'. When deciding whether to use an observation or a survey to investigate this behaviour, the researcher would need to decide whether they wanted to know how often the behaviour happened and how people respond behaviourally or whether they want to know people's attitudes or feelings towards phubbing. Table 1.4 covers some general strengths and limitations of surveys as a research method.

Table 1.4 Strengths and limitations of surveys

Strengths	Limitations
Questionnaires have the benefit of being able to be distributed to a large sample with relative ease. Once the questions have been designed, the URL can be shared online and participants can complete in their own homes with minimal effort from both the researcher and the participant. This increases the likelihood that a larger sample can be gathered.	Whilst surveys are easy to distribute, the response rate is low. Even when reminder emails are sent to potential respondents in the target population, participants may forget to complete the survey or not have the time to. Thus, we may end up with a biased sample who are more motivated, interested or willing to help than those who do not completed the survey making generalising results difficult.
As the researcher does not need to be present when the participant completes the survey, it means participants will be unaffected by the **interpersonal variables** from the researcher such as friendliness, gender. It also means the participant is less likely to respond in a socially desirable way as the researcher does not see who answers the question. Taken together, we are more likely to receive genuine responses from participants.	As surveys tend to be distributed online without the researcher present, it is hard to know that the person completing the survey does meet the criteria for the target population. There is a problem with bots auto completing online surveys, which means you could have a high response rate but not all of these are of genuine people. This is particularly problematic if there is an incentive for completing the survey, which often there is due to the low response rate.

Self-Report: Interviews

As a self-report method, **interviews** are also used when you want to find out about someone's opinions, attitudes or feelings. An interview is essentially a conversation between two people, but with one person directing the conversation to focus on a specific research question. As the interviewer is asking questions and can follow up on questions, this allows for a more flexible approach to data collection and provides the opportunity to gather in-depth data.

There are different ways that interviews can be conducted, and which approach is chosen often depends on what is already known on the topic and the types of likely answers to be given. A **structured interview** involves the interviewer having a list of predetermined question on the topic of interest and asking all participants the same questions in the same order. It is therefore similar to a questionnaire, except that the questions are being asked verbally and are usually open to allow for more detail in the responses. A **semi-structured interview** has a list of predetermined questions but includes the flexibility to ask additional questions to follow up on the interviewee's responses. This allows for a more natural interaction, to clarify responses and to explore new lines of enquiry. An **unstructured interview** does not have any predetermined questions; the interviewer raises the topic of interest and lets the interviewee lead the direction of the discussion.

We can apply these three types of interviews to our earlier example of phubbing during a social interaction with a romantic partner. The interview technique would allow us to explore in more depth how an individual feels when their partner uses their phone and why they feel that way. It is possible that how one feels is dependent on the context of the situation such as what their partner is doing on their phone, where the couple are. For example, during a date night one may be more upset by their partner's phone use than they would be if they are both sat on a train together. An interview would allow us to explore these intricacies and understand why they occur. Table 1.5 covers some general strengths and limitations of interviews as a research method.

Table 1.5 Strengths and limitations of interviews

Strengths	Limitations
The nature of a face-to-face interaction is that it allows for a rapport to build up between the interviewee and interviewer. As this develops the respondent may feel more comfortable in opening up with their responses and being honest about how they feel. The face-to-face element also allows for the participant to ask for clarification if they do not understand a question, which helps to ensure they are answering the question raised.	However, a face-to-face interaction is likely to be influenced by interpersonal variables between the interviewer and participant. Characteristics such as age, gender, race or even attractiveness can all influence the interaction and subsequently how the participant answers the questions.
Interviews provide us with in-depth qualitative data. This is unlike most of the other methods presented so far in this chapter. Even in a questionnaire that has open questions, the respondent may not want to go to the effort of writing out their feelings/opinions/beliefs. This allows us to understand the 'why' behind the responses.	In-depth data is difficult to analyse, as it requires the researcher to go through every word and utterance to explore themes in the responses. This can lead to subjectivity in the analysis of the data, as different researchers may identify different information to be relevant to the research question.

Self-Report: Focus Groups

A **focus group** is similar to an interview, but rather than the interview being between the interviewer and one interviewee the interview is conducted with a small group of participants at the same time. There is no fixed group size, but the average is around 6–8 participants. A group that is too large may become difficult to manage and to hear everyone speak and share information. The participants for a focus group are selected based on a set of demographics that are relevant to the research question. For example, in our investigation on phubbing we would want participants in our focus group who are in a romantic relationship where their partner uses their phone. It would be of no benefit to have participants who are not in a romantic relationship, as this would not help to answer our question of interest.

The aim with focus groups and interviews is not usually to apply the findings to everyone in the target population of interest, but instead to find out detail about this specific group of individuals.

Unlike an interview where the researcher controls and directs the conversation, in a focus group the researcher acts more as a facilitator to the discussion. Thus, the researcher is on the outskirts of the discussion rather than central to it. A focus group may take place across three or four sessions to allow an in-depth exploration of the topic of interest. Table 1.6 covers some general strengths and limitations of focus groups as a research method.

Table 1.6 Strengths and limitations of focus groups

Strengths	Limitations
Due to multiple group members in the discussion, it can lead to participants building on each other's responses and giving additional information that may not have been gathered in a one-to-one interview setting.	Unlike an interview, as the focus group involves a number of people the participants' responses are likely to be influenced by the group dynamics. One group member may dominate the discussion, giving biased data. **Groupthink** can occur, where group members maintain the same viewpoints to keep the consensus of the group stable.
Similarly to interviews, focus groups provide the researcher with rich in-depth data that is not possible to gather with other methods.	Whilst the researcher does not ask the questions, they need to have suitable communication skills in order to move the discussion along. They also need to have enough knowledge on the subject to encourage discussion, but also able to come across with some level of naivety to encourage participants responses.

■■■■■■■■ Stop 1.3 ■■■■■■■■

There is no one 'perfect' way to conduct research in psychology. The method used depends on the question that needs to be answered. All methods are prone to limitations, it is therefore important to look at studies that have employed different methods to test the same construct. This is because the method used can impact the results gathered.

┌─────────────────── Explore further ───────────────────┐

In the previous explanations of the different methods, we returned to the example of phubbing in interactions between a romantic couple. Whilst the examples given were hypothetical, this is an area of research which has utilised different methodology.

Below are the references for published research on the topic, which have used a different method. If you put the title of the article into your university library search engine, you should have access to the paper via your institution. If this is not the case, then read the abstract as this will give you some idea of what the researchers did.

For each of the studies below, answer the following:

1 What method was used in this study?
2 What information in the study informs you that this method was used?
3 What are the benefits of using this method in the context of *this* study?
4 What are the limitations of using this method in the context of *this* study?
5 For one of these limitations, consider how the study could be improved to overcome this issue.

Aagaard, J. (2020). Digital akrasia: A qualitative study of phubbing. *Ai & Society, 35,* 237–244. https://doi.org/10.1007/s00146-019-00876-0

Chotpitayasunondh, V., & Douglas, K. M. (2018). The effects of 'phubbing' on social interaction. *Journal of Applied Social Psychology, 48*(6), 304–316. https://doi.org/10.1111/jasp.12506

Vanden Abeele, M. M., Hendrickson, A. T., Pollmann, M. M., & Ling, R. (2019). Phubbing behaviour in conversations and its relation to perceived conversation intimacy and distraction: An exploratory observation study. *Computers in Human Behaviour, 100,* 35–47. https://doi.org/10.1016/j.chb.2019.06.004

└──┘

KEY TAKEAWAYS

This chapter has introduced you to the importance of gathering research in order to present evidence-based arguments, as opposed to simply presenting our opinion. Whilst researchers take differing approaches to their data collection, which is informed by the exact purpose of their research and what questions they are seeking to address, what is common across all areas of psychology is that claims are evidence based.

Differing research methods have been introduced in this chapter to raise awareness of some of the ways that evidence can be gathered in psychology. Identifying some of the strengths and limitations of each method hopefully reinforces that no method is 'perfect' and each comes with its own limitations. A researcher will be aware of these limitations when designing their study and will weigh up the methods against each other when deciding which to use.

You may be wondering why any of this is relevant to you; you may have no intention of moving into research after your psychology studies. The reason we have added this chapter to the book is that this book has been written to help you to make more effective use of research in your psychological writing. The first step in this process is understanding why research is important in psychology and why it is necessary to draw on psychological research in your assignments. Having an understanding of the different methodologies is necessary when weighing up the value of the research you present in your writing in addressing the question set.

2
CORE PERSPECTIVES IN PSYCHOLOGY

--- Key goals for this chapter ---

- Understand some of the key perspectives in psychology with examples.
- Understand how key perspectives contradict or complement each other.

In the first chapter you were introduced to psychology as a discipline and the importance of having evidence to support any claims we make. The purpose of this book is to help you to not only understand the importance of psychological research but also to support you in using this understanding to develop the use of research in your academic writing. To assist with this, it is important that you understand the different perspectives in psychology. It may surprise you to know that different researchers seek to understand and test behaviour and psychological processes in different ways, depending on their perspective. Developing your understanding of these differing perspectives will help you with interpreting and analysing research, both of which are crucial to use research effectively in your writing.

THE PERSPECTIVES IN PSYCHOLOGY

Following the framework provided by the British Psychological Society (BPS), degrees in psychology cover a broad range of content with a focus on four main perspectives: biological, cognitive, developmental and social psychology. These four areas are the core content. There are additional areas that form part of the degree which are conceptual/historical issues, individual differences and research methods. If you are studying an accredited degree in the United Kingdom then you will be studying these areas. Outside of the United Kingdom, equivalent bodies have a broadly similar framework.

We will be focusing now on introducing you to the four core perspectives as they are a useful framework for studying psychology.

Biological Psychology

Biological psychology is concerned with looking at the influence of physical, physiological processes such as genetics, hormones and neurotransmitters and the structure of the brain on behaviour.

All our behaviours can be seen as rooted in biology, from sleeping to cognitive processes such as memory. The development of brain scanning techniques is being used to map the brain so that the structures involved in our thinking and behaviours can be identified. One branch of biological psychology - neuropsychology - uses scanning studies to help understand how a person's cognition and behaviour are related to the brain and the rest of the nervous system. If an individual sustains an injury to their brain through disease or trauma, they may experience a corresponding change in their cognition (i.e. their memory, thought, etc.), emotions (low mood, anxiety, etc.) or their behaviour. For example, following a stroke, scanning studies can help identify lesion sites and different pathways of neural communication. Neuropsychology has become one of the most exciting areas of science due to the advancements in technology and one that will continue to expand in years to come.

There have also been developments in the understanding of genes and their influence on our behaviour. There is mounting evidence that genes play a role in behaviours such as personality and intelligence, as well as our susceptibility to psychological disorders. The genetic basis of behaviour has used twin studies to explore whether psychological characteristics have a genetic basis. In these studies, researchers look at the **correlation** (relationship) between the scores of a pair of twins on a specific variable, known as the concordance rate. As monozygotic (identical) twins are genetically identical there should be a higher concordance rate than dizygotic (non-identical) twins who share around 50% of their genes. An example would be Miguel et al. (1997) who found a concordance rate of between 53% and 87% for obsessive-compulsive disorder (OCD) in monozygotic twins compared with between 22% and 47% for dizygotic twins. So, this suggests there is potentially a genetic component to OCD as the concordance rate is higher for monozygotic compared to dizygotic twins. However, as the concordance rate for OCD was not 100% for monozygotic twins this also suggests that environmental factors are involved in the development of OCD.

Biological psychology is also concerned with the neurochemical basis of behaviour. Neurochemistry refers to the action of chemicals in the brain. Our thoughts and behaviours are a direct result of chemical transmissions in the brain which occur using neurotransmission. An imbalance of neurochemicals is implicated in mental health conditions such OCD and **schizophrenia**. Specifically, low levels of serotonin (a **neurotransmitter**) have been implicated in the development of OCD and depression, whilst overproduction of dopamine (another neurotransmitter) has been related to schizophrenia. By identifying the impact of neurotransmitters on the brain, it is possible for drugs to be developed that may alter the balance of these chemicals to relieve symptoms. However, it is important to remember that whilst neurotransmitters are implicated in some conditions, they are not the whole story which is why drug treatments that impact neurotransmitters are limited in their effectiveness. An example of this is the use of antidepressants which increase levels of the neurotransmitter serotonin at synapses in the brain. These drugs have been associated with a decrease in depressive symptoms but in Cipriani et al.'s (2018) large scale review of 522 studies they demonstrated that although antidepressants were more effective than placebos, they only described the effect of the drugs as 'mostly modest'.

Having explored some of the areas that biological psychology covers, it is worth mentioning the research methods this perspective uses. Biological psychology commonly uses more scientific methods when conducting research. As mentioned above, these can include scanning techniques such as functional Magnetic Resonance Imaging (fMRIs) and electroencephalogram (EEGs) (measure activity in the brain). The benefit of fMRIs is that it produces maps showing which parts of the brain are involved in specific activities. Participants will usually have their brain activity measured when resting and then again when completing different tasks as this allows a comparison of brain activity. This allows researchers to identify the parts of the brain dedicated to different activities, such as the production of speech. Other methods used include experiments, observations, questionnaires and case studies. The data collected via these methods tend to produce quantitative data (numbers) and as such they are normally analysed using statistical software.

Cognitive Psychology

Cognitive psychology is concerned with the mental processes through which we perceive, think and reason about the world around us. These cognitive (thinking) processes cannot be seen, although we may be able to guess what people are thinking through their behaviour.

This idea of inference is whereby cognitive psychologists draw conclusions about mental processes based on observed behaviour. As such, cognitive psychologists use theoretical models to help them understand internal mental processes. These models of behaviour take the form of interconnected 'boxes in the brain' which attempt to identify how incoming information is processed. By doing so, these models can help to identify where the issue may be for individuals struggling to process information.

An example of a theoretical model is the multi-store model of memory suggested by Atkinson and Shiffrin (1968) which explains information processing occurring through distinct stages. Information enters from the environment, which is the input, and it goes through a sequence of key processes that includes attention and rehearsal. There are distinct storage systems and the information flows through the stages and illustrated using a flow diagram. This way of presenting cognitive processes, using computer terminology such as inputs and outputs, is popular with cognitive psychologists as it generates predictions that can be tested using controlled laboratory experiments. In the case of the multi-store model (see Figure 2.1), each feature of the model can be tested, especially the idea of there being different stores.

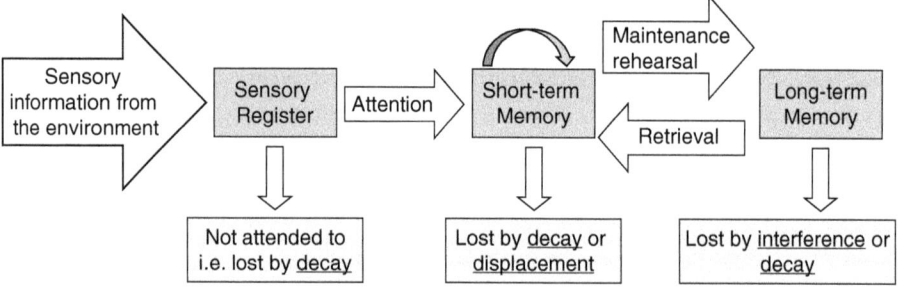

Figure 2.1   The multi-store model of memory (Atkinson & Shiffrin, 1968)

The figure shows the multi-store model of memory. There is a flow diagram that shows information going through a series of stages. The first stage that is shown is information from the environment going to the sensory register. If attended to, that information goes to the short-term memory. If not, the diagram shows the information is lost due to decay. In the short-term memory if information is rehearsed, using maintenance rehearsal, then it enters long-term memory, if not it is lost due to decay or displacement. The diagram shows that information can be lost in long-term memory due to interference or decay. There is also an arrow in the diagram showing that information can be retrieved from long-term memory so that it enters the short-term memory.

Alongside memory, cognitive psychologists are interested in the study of attention, perception, learning, language, consciousness and cognitive neuropsychology. These are the more prevalent topics but there are others. Some areas are still developing, and the intro-duction of **cognitive neuroscience** in relatively recent years is one such area. This is an area of research that brings together work in the field of cognitive psychology with the work of neuroscience (and others). It is interesting to note that the *Journal of Neuroscience* aims to develop a cross-disciplinary approach as they invite contributions that integrate research in neuroscience, neurobiology, cognitive psychology, linguistics and computer science. You will learn more about journals in Chapter 3.

Having read about cognitive psychology, it is probably not surprising for you to learn that the cognitive psychologists tend to favour more objective, scientific research methods. Probably the most common method used by cognitive psychologists is experiments as they are often wanting to manipulate variables in controlled conditions to enable cause and effect to be established. Cognitive psychologists have also used eye-tracking which has enabled researchers to identify where participants are focusing their attention but may fail to process the incoming visual information. Eye-tracking studies using a simulator have been useful to explore what happens when drivers try to dual-task.

Other allied areas of cognitive psychology, cognitive neuroscience, as mentioned above, use brain imaging techniques such as fMRI and Positron Emission Tomography (PET) to enable them to systematically observe and describe the neurological basis of mental processes. For example, thinking back to the multi-store model of memory, Squire et al. (1992) carried out brain scans and found that the hippocampus was more active when using long-term memory, whereas areas in the prefrontal cortex are more active for short-term memory tasks. This study was used to support the multi-store model of memory as it demonstrates that long-term memory and short-term memory are two separate memory stores and can work independently of each other by using different parts of the brain.

Developmental Psychology

Developmental psychology explores the changes that occur across the lifespan, from early infancy through to later life. It helps us to understand how humans learn, mature and adapt. Developmental psychologists study aspects of human growth and development across the lifespan including physical, cognitive, social, intellectual, perceptual and emotional growth. These changes can occur due to biological, individual and environmental influences. Many influential psychologists have suggested that human development goes through set stages. For example, Piaget, a Swiss psychologist, suggested that intellectual development goes through a series of stages which he outlines in his theory of cognitive development (see Piaget, 1932). Each stage has a series of steps that a child must go through before continuing to the next step and each stage builds on the last stage. Whilst Piaget himself was not prescriptive as to what age the child must be at each of these stages, subsequent studies have suggested when these cognitive abilities need to be mastered. Kohlberg (1958) built on Piaget's work but focused on moral development from a justice perspective. These stages of moral development were not solely focused on children's development but could be seen across an individual's lifespan. An individual will move from basing their reasoning on rewards and punishment connected to one's actions (pre-conventional moral reasoning), to those based on the rules and conventions within society from a hierarchical and authoritarian perspective (conventional moral reasoning). In the last stage, an individual will see those rules and conventions as being subjective and context based rather than hard lines (post conventional moral reasoning). How individuals move through these stages will largely depend on their biological, individual and environmental influences which lay at the core of developmental psychology.

Developmental psychologists employ a wide variety of research methods with the most common being observational studies, experiments, psychological testing, longitudinal studies and correlational studies. So, for example observational studies when looking at babies and young children may involve repeated observation of the same baby over time. Parents or caregivers may be asked to record or describe several aspects of development. These are often called baby diaries or baby biographies. These are not without their obvious drawbacks when it comes to generalisations, but they can offer detailed accounts of subtle changes in behaviour due to the knowledge of the child. This can then lead to creation of theories that can be then more systematically tested using other methods like experiments later. Experiments can also be conducted on babies and young children but although there can be a clear manipulation of the independent variable (IV) in these experiments, the measurement of the dependent variable may be partly through observation due to the limitations of babies' responses. This is quite different from experiments in say cognitive psychology where the dependent variable (DV) in studies of memory is clearly a more objective measure such as numbers of words recalled in a memory experiment. An example is when DeLoache et al. (1998) wanted to test whether nine-month-old infants would be able to distinguish between real and drawn objects. The IV was the extent to which the object in the picture looked like the real thing and the DV was the number of times the infants tried to explore the object. They manipulated the IV by having four conditions ranging from the most to the least realistic – colour photograph/black and white photograph/coloured line drawing/black and white line drawing. The results showed what was expected, those that were most convincing as a visual representation the more the infant try to explore it and vice versa. So, although the IV was clearly manipulated, the DV was measured using observations of the infants' behaviours, suggesting an indirect and less objective measure than most 'true' experiments. But this reflects the nature of studying infants' behaviours within develop-mental psychology where direct measures are not often possible. Both experiments and observations are important tools for developmental psychologists and sometimes, as this example demonstrates, a blurring between the two is needed.

Another important research method for developmental psychologists is the use of **longitudinal studies** as it allows behaviours over time to be studied. Longitudinal research is where researchers measure the same variables at different points in time on the same individuals. For example, Rutter et al. (2011) followed a group of 165 Romanian orphans across many years as part of the English and Romanian adoptee study (ERA). These Romanian children had been adopted from orphanages by families in the United Kingdom following the 1989 Romanian revolution. They had been subjected to very poor care in the Romanian orphanages. Therefore, Rutter and colleagues wanted to see whether experiencing good care in the United Kingdom could make up for the poor previous care. When they arrived in the United Kingdom, the children showed delayed intellectual development and were severely malnourished. When they were tested at age 11 the extent of their recovery differed according to the age at which they were adopted. The younger they were at adoption (i.e. before six months) the less impact on their intellectual and social development later. Longitudinal studies like this provide critical insights into the lasting impact of early childhood experiences on later life and through this type of research recommendations concerning when children should be adopted can be made. This evidence-based approach can ensure that children have the best chance to succeed.

Social Psychology

Social psychology is interested in developing an understanding of how people navigate the complexities of their relationships with others and their surrounding social environment. The topics that are covered include group processes and intergroup relations, close relationships, attribution, social cognition and more. These are challenging topics particularly as when studying social aspects of behaviour any number of factors are at play simultaneously including mood, attitude, values, culture, stress levels, the temperature, etc. Trying to isolate these factors to assess their impact is not easy.

Within social psychology there are two 'camps' or divisions. The first, often called *mainstream social psychology*, would describe social psychology as a scientific discipline that uses the scientific method to collect data by empirically testing theories about human behaviour. Here, the idea is that human nature is universal or at least guided by general principles. That is not to say that social psychologists in this camp deny the notion that people from different cultures or with different experiences may behave differently, just that they believe even these differences follow general principles. As such, these social psychologists believe that as a scientific discipline that should obey the principles of scientific enquiry (see Chapter 3). However, not all social psychologists believe human nature should be subjected to the application of universal laws. These *critical social psychologists* argue that because of the ever-changing contexts it is impossible to have universal principles. The word critical here is referring to the term that is found in sociology called critical theory which is about the examination and critique of society and culture.

As you can see, the two camps of social psychology are quite different and most social psychologists identify themselves as either mainstream or critical social psychologists and are deeply entrenched in the approach and methods they use. It will not be surprising to learn that mainstream social psychologists favour the use of research methods that will produce quantitative data which is more objective and can be analysed using statistics, such as experiments, questionnaires and surveys.

An example of research from mainstream social psychology can be seen in the topic of persuasion. One of the factors that can influence how the effectiveness of a message is whether the argument is presented as one-sided or two-sided. Werner et al. (2002) wanted to see if a one-sided (persuasive) or two-sided (persuasive with counterargument) would lead to increased recycling. On a university campus rubbish bin, a note was placed with students being asked to not bin the cans but to take them to the recycling bin located upstairs (persuasive). When the message was presented alongside recognition of the inconvenience this caused (counterargument) recycling was measured at 80%, which was significantly higher than in the persuasive only condition. The use of a **field experiment** here has provided some research evidence to demonstrate how acknowledging and validating a counterargument may serve to make persuasion more effective. This research evidence is important because it can be applied to other settings such as marriage counselling and customer service environments to offer support that acknowledging and validating the other person's viewpoint can reduce defensiveness and increase the likelihood of a resolution.

However, critical social psychologists, who do not believe in establishing universal laws regarding human behaviour, tend to favour research methods that produce qualitative data such as interviews and observations where behaviour is not focused on aspects of behaviour that can be counted. The aim is to emphasise the variation and complexity of human experience rather than discover 'rules' or 'laws' of behaviour.

This means that mainstream and critical social psychologists may explore similar social psychological phenomenon using very different methods. One thing that all social psychologists can agree on it that at our most fundamental level, human behaviour cannot be fully understood without the appreciation of the relational, situational, cultural and political contexts in which we reside.

Different Perspectives in Psychology: Do They Contradict or Complement?

It is clear to see that the different perspectives offer quite varying explanations of who we are and what makes us who we are. Biological psychologists would think about us as being physical entities made up of brain tissue, genes, hormones, neurons, etc. and this biological makeup determines who we are and our behaviour. Contrast this with social psychologists who would argue that you cannot reduce our behaviour down to our biological compositions as our individual behaviours are a result of our social structures and connections to others. Therefore, these different perspectives offer quite explanations for why we think, feel and behave as we do. For example, a social psychologist could explain prejudice as a function of group dynamics and intergroup conflict whilst a biological psychologist would focus on the brain structures that are involved in processing particular emotional and behavioural responses (e.g. fear) in response to social stimuli (e.g. skin colour).

So, it may seem that the four main perspectives contradict one another, suggesting an element of conflict. We are now going to explore whether this apparent conflict is an issue for psychology or whether these perspectives can complement one another and thereby further the discipline of psychology to the benefit of society.

It is possible to see that the four different perspectives can answer different questions about a topic and take different approaches to psychological research. For example, taking a topic such as aggression, it can be explored from a biological perspective (e.g. the parts of the brain that are involved in aggression), a social perspective (e.g. the influence of intergroup relations and cultural norms on aggression), a developmental perspective (e.g. a longitudinal study on how early exposure to violence impacts aggression in adulthood) or cognitive perspective (e.g. ways of processing and storing information related to aggression). As aggression involves an understanding of all these aspects, it is important to integrate the insights these different perspectives provide to fully understand the topic. Whilst the different perspectives are answering different questions, they can complement each other to give us a better understanding of aggression. By specialising in different aspects of a topic it extends our psychological knowledge of the topic and leads to psychologists building concepts and methods to address the different research questions effectively.

Attempts to work across the different perspectives to produce integrative accounts of psychological phenomenon can produce useful insights. For example, cognitive neuropsychology, social cognition and developmental neuroscience are examples of blending the different perspectives to answer research questions. Social cognition, the blend of social and cognitive psychology, is concerned with explaining social psychological phenomena by investigating the cognitive processes that underlie them. The areas of interest for social cognition include social influence, attitudes, attribution theory, personal perception and moral judgements.

You may then wonder why integration across the perspectives is not the preferred way of advancing psychology. It is important to remember that specialisation is often advantageous. As an example, if you think about biological psychology, the focus on neurological processes and creating specialist equipment to explore brain structures and functions has enabled us to fully understand areas such as visual perception which is an area of little interest to other perspectives such as social psychology. So specialisation is definitely worthwhile and has allowed a depth of understanding that may not have been gained had the focus not been on specific perspectives. But at the same time, we want to highlight the importance of thinking about topics across the boundaries of these different perspectives so that you can appreciate the way other perspectives may be able to answer important questions in psychology.

■■■■■■■ Stop 2.1 ■■■■■■

Studying psychology according to the different perspectives is a helpful way to understand psychology and how it functions as a discipline. It also helps you understand why specific research methods are used. However, it is also important to think across the boundaries of each perspective and appreciate the contribution of other perspectives to answer different questions on the same topic.

Explore further

For each of the topic areas listed below, there are references for published studies that are from two different perspectives. If you put the title of the article into your university library search engine, you should have access to the paper via your

(Continued)

(Continued)

institution. If this is not the case, then read the abstract as this will give you some idea of what the researchers did.

For each study answer the following questions:

- What perspective is this study from?
- What was the aim of the study?
- What were their results and conclusion?
- What are the advantages and disadvantages of studying the topic (i.e. empathy or schizophrenia) from one perspective?

Topic 1: Empathy

Jackson, P. L., Meltzoff, A. N., & Decety, J. (2005). How do we perceive the pain of others: A window into the neural processes involved in empathy. *NeuroImage, 24,* 771–779. https://doi.org/10.1016/j.neuroimage.2004.09.006

Riva, P., & Andrighetto, L. (2012). 'Everyone feels a broken bone, but only we can feel a broken heart': Group membership influences perceptions of targets' suffering. *European Journal of Social Psychology, 42,* 801–806. http://dx.doi.org/10.1002/ejsp.1918

Topic 2: Schizophrenia

Berry, K., Barrowclough C., & Wearden A. (2008). Attachment theory: A framework for understanding symptoms and interpersonal relationships in psychosis. *Behaviour Research and Therapy, 46*(12), 1275–1282. https://doi.org/10.1016/j.brat.2008.08.009

Tienari, P., Wynne, L. C., Sorri, A., Lahti, I., Läksy, K., Moring, J., Naarala, M., Nieminen, P., & Wahlberg, K. E. (2004). Genotype-environment interaction in schizophrenia-spectrum disorder. Long-term follow-up study of Finnish adoptees. *British Journal of Psychiatry, 184,* 216–222. https://doi.org/10.1192/bjp.184.3.216

KEY TAKEAWAYS

This chapter has introduced to you the four different perspectives in psychology – biological, cognitive, developmental and social. You explored the key assumptions and core focus of each perspective alongside some of the key research methods used by each perspective. Examples of research were included so that you could see how topics and research methods were used to answer some important questions within each perspective.

You then considered how the different perspectives can be integrated to fully understand a topic as each perspective was able to examine the topic from a different angle. In the case of aggression, the biological perspective could explain the brain structures involved in aggression, the social aspects could explore the role of the media in aggression, from the developmental perspective an understanding of the long-term effects of growing up in violent household and from the cognitive perspective the processes involved in processing and recalling aggression. This served to highlight how psychology as a discipline can work together to integrate knowledge to fully understand a psychological issue such as aggression and violence whilst still maintaining the benefits of specialisation.

3

HOW IS PSYCHOLOGY RESEARCH CONDUCTED AND DISSEMINATED?

Key goals for this chapter

- Understand psychology as a science and the research cycle.
- Identify key features of science.
- Understand the structure of research papers.
- Understand the peer review process.
- Understand contemporary issues within research including the replication crises, open science, Western domination in research and attempts to decolonise research.

EXPLORING PSYCHOLOGY AS A SCIENCE AND THE RESEARCH CYCLE

When you think of psychology you may not think about it as a science. The word science may conjure up memories from school of using Bunsen burners and of making electricity circuits. Whilst you are unlikely to find these kinds of experiments in psychology, psychology does share many of the same features as physics, chemistry and biology, the more traditional sciences. However, psychology differs to these more traditional sciences as we are humans studying humans. This makes things a little trickier and can mean that the process of collecting data can be prone to bias. As you have already read, psychology researchers can take different approaches to gathering evidence. A nomothetic approach tends to be more scientific, whereas an idiographic approach does not adhere so rigidly to the features of science as the aim is not to generate laws but to understand.

This raises the question as to whether psychology can truly be classed as a science and indeed whether it should be. This discussion is beyond the scope of what we are aiming to support you with in this book; however, it is something to be aware of. For now, it is sufficient to understand that regardless of how scientific psychology is deemed to be and what approach researchers take, that the collection of evidence is necessary to take our arguments from opinions to claims. The process of collecting evidence follows a framework often referred to as the **research cycle.** This process varies slightly depending on whether an idiographic or nomothetic approach has been taken; we outline to general process in Figure 3.1.

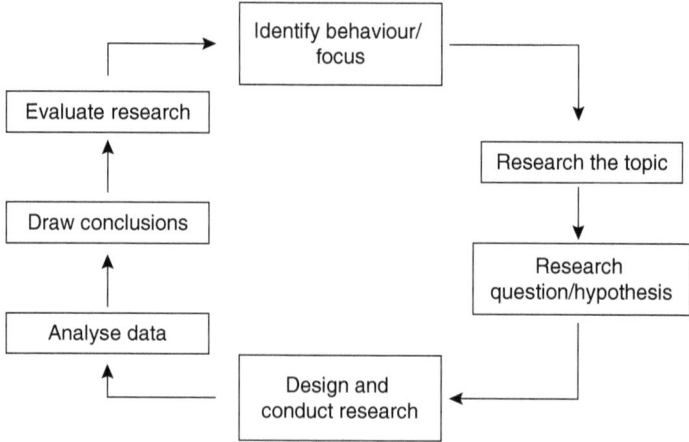

Figure 3.1   The research cycle

In this figure you can see seven boxes presented in a cyclical pattern with arrows connecting them in a clockwise direction. The starting box states 'identify the behaviour/focus' and this is then linked to the next box called 'research the topic'. The next box is 'research question/hypothesis' and this is then linked to 'design and conduct research' which is at the bottom of the cycle. Following on from this is 'analyse data' then this leads to 'draw conclusions' with the final box called 'evaluate research'. From this you then return to the start of the cycle.

The first stage in gathering evidence is finding a behaviour of interest and deciding what it is that you want to gather data about. You may decide on a behaviour or interest because it is something you have noticed in your everyday life and are interested in it, or you may read the findings and conclusions of other research which leads you to want to explore this further. Before designing your research and focusing on the exact element you are interested in, you need to know what is already out there. This is important as it is useful to know what has already been found on a topic as this can identify what is known and what other directions you might want to take the research in. Once you have an idea of previous findings you can narrow down and identify your research question and if relevant the **hypothesis** (prediction) you will test. When you have a more defined idea of what it is you are testing, you are in a position to design your study to be focused on exactly what it is you are interested in. After the data is collected it needs to be analysed and this analysis will allow you to draw conclusions in line with your research question and hypothesis (if applicable). The process of gathering evidence is an ongoing one and no study ever gives us a definitive answer. How we design and conduct our research is never perfect, more on this in Chapter 6, and therefore as a researcher we need to think about the limitations of the evidence gathered which can in turn lead to designing further research. This is one reason why you should never use the word 'prove' in your writing. A study does not prove anything, it simply tells us that when we test a construct in a specific way with a set of people, that is what we find. All research is limited in its ability to draw any firm conclusions. Think of research as one extremely large puzzle, each set of findings are a piece of the puzzle but do not give much information in isolation. Table 3.1 shows a fictional example of the research cycle.

Table 3.1 The research cycle (fictional example)

The research cycle	Explanation	Example
Identify behaviour/ focus	Identify a specific behaviour that you want to explore in your study.	You notice that one of your housemates drinks a lot of energy drinks. The same housemate is also very good at playing the guitar. You wonder if there is a link between energy drink consumption and musical ability.
Research the topic	Explore the already published literature on the topic to see what is already known and where the gaps are in the field.	You carry out a literature search and discover some links between energy drink consumption and reaction time, memory and sport performance. However, you cannot find anything specifically exploring energy drink consumption and musical ability.
Research question/ hypothesis	Narrow down and identify the focus of the research	You decide to take a nomothetic approach and therefore have a specific hypothesis that you would like to test. Based on previous research, you

(Continued)

Table 3.1 The research cycle (fictional example) *(Continued)*

The research cycle	Explanation	Example
	question and the hypothesis (if applicable).	predict that consumption of an energy drink will result in less error made when playing a piece of music on a guitar compared to individuals who do not consume an energy drink.
Design and conduct research	Plan how you will conduct the study in order to align with the research question and then carry out the study to collect the data (evidence).	As you are interested in musical ability, you decide the participants in your study should already be able to play the guitar to a certain standard. If this was not considered, then your findings may be influenced by musical ability rather than the energy drink. In your study you will have half of the participants drink a can of energy drink, whilst the other half do not drink anything. All participants will then be taught a short piece of music that they are not familiar with. After a specified period of time to practise (e.g. 20 minutes), all participants will be asked to perform the piece. Their performance will be recorded and watched back to count how many mistakes were made during the performance.
Analyse data	Depending on the way in which you have collected data, this will influence how you analyse the data.	In this study, you have collected quantitative (numerical) data as you are counting the number of mistakes. This means you need to conduct a statistical analysis (we will not cover that in this book, but you will need to understand how to analyse data as you progress through your studies).
Draw conclusions	The results from the data analysis are interpreted in line with what the research was aiming to test and find out.	After analysing the results of the study, the statistics show no difference between the two groups in relation to the number of mistakes made in their musical performance. You conclude that consumption of energy drinks does not affect musical performance.
Evaluate research	An analysis of how the study was conducted considering what the limitations are and how future research may address this.	In your study, you only focused on playing the guitar as a measure of musical ability. It is possible the results may differ with different musical instruments. You also only gave participants one brand of energy drink at one time point. Any effects may occur from the regular drinking of energy drinks (like your housemate) rather than a one-off drink.

▬▬ Key tip 3.1 ▬▬

When you read research, do not interpret the study in isolation. Research is purposefully kept simple to allow researchers to focus on specific aspects of behaviour. Remind yourself that this one study is one piece of the puzzle when trying to understand the behaviour in question.

FEATURES OF SCIENCE

We mentioned earlier in this chapter that there is some debate over whether psychology is a science. We are not here to answer this debate, but it is important that you are aware of the features of science; these features are not unique to psychology but instead underpin the basic principles of all sciences. This will allow you to form your own opinion on whether psychology is a science or not.

━━━━━━━━━ Think 3.1 ━━━━━━━━━

Using what you already know about science from previous experience and any psychological knowledge you have to date, think about what features we would expect to be present in a discipline that is considered a 'science'. One of which we have already addressed in this chapter is the need for evidence.

As humans we are prone to making numerous errors in the way that we think and make sense of information. These are errors which are inbuilt into our cognitive processing system (and no doubt you will learn or have already learnt about some of these in your psychology lectures). We do not want these biases to influence the process of how we design, conduct and analyse research; therefore one of the key underlying principles of a science is to prevent against bias as much as possible. One of these biases that science tries to protect against is **confirmation bias** (Lilienfeld, 2010). Confirmation bias is the tendency to seek out information that supports what we already believe and disregard information that does not align with our already held beliefs. This can be problematic when conducting research as it could lead to us not testing factors which may provide evidence that our hypothesis is wrong. This may sound counterintuitive, but falsifiability is a key feature of science.

Falsifiability is the notion of seeking out evidence which can disprove our hypothesis and was suggested by Popper as a key feature of science (Veronesi, 2014). Imagine that you carry out your study on energy drink and musical ability on multiple musicians who play different instruments across 20 studies and all studies found that there was no difference in musical performance between those who do and do not drink energy drinks. Even though we have a lot of studies which have all found the same thing, we can still not say with certainty that consumption of energy drinks has *no* effect on musical ability. Indeed, all it would take is one study which *did* find a difference in musical ability between those who did and did not drink energy drinks to disprove that the suggestion that energy drinks have *no* effect on musical ability. Therefore, a key feature of science is to design our research in such a way that there is always the possibility that our findings can disprove our hypothesis. **Pseudoscience** is beliefs or practices that claim to be scientific, but lack the key features of science. Pseudoscience is problematic because it lacks the protection against confirmation bias and the emphasis of the research is often on confirmation rather than falsification (Lilienfeld, 2010). Particularly problematic is that on the surface and to the untrained eye, pseudoscience can appear to be scientific and do not follow the 'rules' of science (Lilienfeld & Landfield, 2008).

What exactly are these 'rules' of science that pseudoscience lacks beyond falsifiability? Whilst the rules of science may vary depending on which science you are working in, there are some general points which are key to taking a scientific approach.

Objectivity – An objective perspective is one that is free from bias. A researcher's own opinions and beliefs should not influence the research process in any way. This includes in the design of the study, carrying out the study and when analysing the data and making conclusions.

True objectivity is difficult in research as humans are prone to numerous biases (such as confirmation bias which we mentioned earlier). Researchers should seek to minimise these biases as much as possible throughout the research process.

Empirical evidence – We need to base our conclusions on evidence that we have collected through the research process. This evidence may come from surveys, interviews, experiments or observations (more on these methods later). Key here is that we have evidence that has been collected rather than basing any conclusions on beliefs or assumptions.

You might believe that less than five hours per night impairs concentration the following day, but we would want evidence to support this. We could collect this data by giving participants a concentration task to do after having slept less than five hours the previous night. To have a comparison, we would also want the participants to complete a concentration task after having slept for more than five hours.

Control – Whilst collecting empirical evidence is important, evidence is not all equal and how you collect the evidence impacts on the types of conclusions we can make based on the evidence. Depending on the question we are asking, the way in which we collect our evidence and the conclusions we seek to draw from it will differ. A more scientific approach will want to ensure that no other factors are influencing what we are measuring, other than the variables of interest. In our previous example, there are factors other than the number of hours of sleep that could affect levels of concentration such as what the individual has eaten, the specific concentration task that has been given and how long after waking the concentration task is given. If one participant completes the concentration task within an hour of waking, whilst another completes it five hours after waking, it is likely that we might find differences due to the difference in time frame. Anything that might influence the variable being measured that can be controlled by the researcher should be controlled. In this example, the researcher could ask participants to complete the concentration task after being awake for x number of hours. The important part being that the time is held constant for all participants.

Reproducibility – The findings we gain from one study does not allow us to draw any firm conclusions about what we have measured. In our sleep example, if our study found that concentration was impaired when people have fewer than five hours of sleep a night this would not be enough for us to conclude that lack of sleep definitely causes impaired concentration. It is possible that our findings were a one off, to check this we need to be able to reproduce research in the exact same way to see if we achieve the same results. This means care needs to be taken in how research is conducted to ensure that it is systematic and able to be repeated in the same way again by other researchers.

Ethical – Ethics are important in psychology as we need to ensure that our participants are protected. This is important from the perspective of respecting our participants and treating them with dignity. From a scientific perspective, ethical research is important in several ways. Firstly, if participants are protected in psychological research, then future participants will be more likely to want to participate (without participants we cannot collect evidence). Secondly, if research is unethical then future researchers will be unable to replicate the research to check for **reliability**, as ethical approval will not be granted. In addition, if psychological research is not ethical it is unlikely to be accepted by the scientific community or the general public and could damage the reputation of psychology as a discipline.

━━━━━━━ Stop 3.1 ━━━━━━━

A scientific approach is one that minimises the role that human biases can play in the design of research, the collection of data and when analysing data.

DISSEMINATING RESEARCH

Once the research has been conducted and analysed it is then the job of the researcher to write it up so that the findings can be added to the growing body of psychology evidence, much of which is published in academic journals (see later). The way that this is done is standardised for research papers so that readers know where to look for the information that they need. This is what we are going to explore in more detail next.

Structure of Research Papers

Writing, or even reading, a research paper can feel like a daunting task. We both remember our first time reading a research paper and thinking that it was like reading a foreign language at times, especially if you make our mistake of thinking the results would be a good place to start. In fact, some of the results are written using Greek symbols/letters! It can feel intimidating. But this is where we come in. We are going to take you through the structure of research papers, so you know what to expect from each section and how to find the information you need, with some top tips and reassurances along the way.

Firstly, the papers you will encounter in your reading will follow a very similar format, which helps you to locate what you need quickly and also means that if you are writing a paper, you will know what goes where. There are some variations depending on the journal and if it is a qualitative or quantitative report, but these impact the subsections within the main sections so not really an issue.

The aim of a research report is to clearly explain the topic area that the research examined, what they were trying to find out, how they went about conducting their research, what they found and some interpretations of what their results mean.

Here is a list of the different sections of a research report:

- Title
- Abstract
- Introduction
- Method/Methodology (depending on whether quantitative or qualitative)
- Results/Analysis (depending on whether quantitative or qualitative)
- Discussion
- References
- Appendix

Now we will take each section in turn and explain the purpose of each section and some top tips for reading and writing these sections.

Title – this is where the researchers (authors) summarise the content of the study. It is normally around 15 words or less and needs to be clear and accurate. If it is not, then readers will skip over the study not even reaching the abstract. Some researchers try to come up with an attention grabbing title, but be careful if you try to do this as sometimes it means that the title does not fully capture the content of the study. If it can do both then that is great, but if there is a compromise to be made then best to have a clear title that summarises the research rather than one that just sounds catchy.

Abstract – this is an important section as it should clearly and concisely summarise the research. It is normally 150-200 words long. The Abstract should include details of what the research is about, what method was used, the results obtained and some interpretation of the results. If you want to know whether a study is relevant for your essay or report and whether to read the whole report, then this is the section to read (more about how to decide in Chapter 4). This is an important skill because with approximately 3,000 psychology journal articles published every month (Adair & Vohra, 2003), you need to be able assess their suitability quickly. Reading abstracts is a great way of deciding whether the article is relevant for your argument and needs to be read in full or not. The great news is that abstracts are accessible via large databases that can be searched for using keywords in just a few seconds (see Chapter 4).

If you are writing an abstract for your own report, always factor in more time than you were expecting it to take, especially if you struggle to write concisely. Due to the tight word count for this section, it can take time to select what information is critical and therefore should be included. You will then inevitably need a while to do some editing.

Introduction – the introduction involves summarising theories and studies that are relevant to the research. Following this, a rationale for the research should be provided. This is where the gap in the knowledge is identified which the research will fill. One of the ways to think about this is like a funnel where it is wide at the top (outline of the topic area) getting narrower at the bottom (stating the research question or hypothesis). Whether the introduction ends with a research question or a hypothesis will depend on the method used. For example, if it is an experiment the introduction will end with a precise prediction about the outcome of the experiment. This prediction is called a hypothesis.

Key tip 3.2

It is important when outlining the topic area at the start of the introduction that you don't go too wide. To give an example, if you were exploring the effects of caffeine on exam performance you would not want to start by discussing an overview of all stimulants and their effects. Instead, you would probably want to focus on what caffeine is and the effects it has on performance before then discussing what effects have been found on academic performance before presenting a rationale for your study and the novel aspect of your study that fills the gap in the current literature. As this study is likely to be an experiment, you would then end your introduction with a clear hypothesis. It is important that the hypothesis (or research question) flows logically from the rationale for your study and does not just appear as a statement tagged on at the end.

Method – this section describes *what* was done in the study and *how*. The main purpose is to provide sufficient detail to enable **replication**. You should be able to pick up a method section and use the information just in this section to recreate the study. It is a bit like a recipe in a cookbook with details of what you need (ingredients) and how to make it (from gathering your ingredients to serving up). This enables you to produce a dish that should look and taste the same to that produced in the cookbook (well, that is the theory at least).

As you can imagine, there is quite a bit of detail needed in the method section, so this is why this section is often broken down into subsections. How this section is broken down depends on the journal but often there are different subsections for design, participants, materials (apparatus) and procedure. Even if this section is not presented as subsections, researchers will still include the detail needed to enable replication.

Key tip 3.3

Whilst it is important that there is enough detail for replication, certain trivial details can be omitted as they are not particularly relevant, or it may be assumed. For example, students often like to state that a pen and piece of paper is needed or a desk when they write up their reports. Whilst that may be true, we can probably assume this information and it is not particularly specific or relevant to their study.

What is needed in this section is a step-by-step guide that outlines what happened in the study. This should be written in chronological order and take the reader from the recruitment of participants to when participants complete the study. So, it should include all the ethical information too, including information regarding how consent was gained, if any deception was involved and how participants were debriefed. All this information normally goes in the procedure subsection.

Results – this section contains what the research has found. This section will provide a summary of the data rather than the raw data. The type of data reported will depend on whether the research was a qualitative or a quantitative study. If the study was quantitative then you would expect to see **descriptive statistics** such as **measures of central tendency** (i.e. means, medians or modes) alongside measures of **dispersion** (i.e. standard deviations or range). These could be presented in tables or graphs. This section will also contain details of other analysis that was carried out on the data, so for quantitative research this may be inferential statistics. For qualitative data this section will contain descriptions and summaries (e.g. themes) alongside illustrative examples such as the use of quotations.

━━━━━━━━━ Key tip 3.4 ━━━━━━━━━

This section can be the most difficult to read and understand as a student. If it is a quantitative study, it is likely to include some **inferential statistics** that at this point in your studies is going to be completely alien to you. Don't panic, skim read it and skip the complicated statistics. If there are means (averages) presented or a graph, you can just get a sense of the data and where the differences or the patterns are emerging. The start of the next section, the discussion, is where you can go to if you want a summary of the findings and what they mean.

Discussion – this section starts with a summary of the findings; the 'take home' message. The Discussion is all about explaining what the results mean. As the research has not been conducted in isolation it is important here to place the results in the wider context, so reference to the literature reviewed in the introduction is needed. It is important to consider if the results are consistent with previous studies and if not, why that may be. There may be an explanation for the differences and/or inconsistencies that need explaining. It is also important for the researchers to explore any limitations in their study and what questions may remain. It may be that the results are just the start, and more studies are needed to fully explore the topic (see research cycle earlier), so in the Discussion the researchers will explore what research should come next.

References – the reference list is where all the citations included in the report are listed in alphabetical order. As we have already mentioned in Chapter 1, it is essential that we provide evidence for any claims we make so referencing signals where the evidence is from, and the reference list provides the required details of where that reference can be found. This means that the reader can then obtain the source of that information if they want to. Providing references adds weight to the claims being made. References are also important because it acknowledges where the ideas have come from and provides the original authors with the appropriate credit. If you do not provide a citation then you are suggesting that the point you are making is your own point rather than someone else's. It also suggests that you do not have evidence to support that point. Do remember that psychology research can impact people's lives and so providing evidence to support any claims made is very important. It is good academic practice to reference and producing a long reference list is quite satisfying too!

Key tip 3.5

Make sure that your reference list matches the references in your report. Check that each citation in your report is then listed in your references and once you have ticked them off, make sure that there are no references in your list that have not been ticked off. When you are creating your reference list you can use different tools to help (see Chapter 9) but do make sure that you are consistent with your formatting and that the style is right (check your institutions guidance for details).

Appendices – in general, an appendix is not used when you are looking at reports in journals (the plural of appendix is appendices). However, when you are writing up your own report, it is very common to use appendices. This is because an appendix is used to provide examples of the materials used in the research. Therefore, you may find copies of images used in an experiment, a list of interview questions or other relevant information.

Key tip 3.6

When writing up a quantitative report, it is likely you will be asked to include SPSS output and/or your raw data in the appendices so that the person marking your work can see what you have done. For qualitative reports, such as a thematic analysis, you may be asked to provide an annotated transcript to show how you went from initial coding to your themes. Don't be tempted to put these in your results section.

PUBLICATIONS

Journal Articles

In the previous section, we have mentioned about writing up research into a report style and these reports normally appear in journals. You may be wondering what a journal is and why they seem to be so popular. As we have mentioned quite a lot, research in psychology can have wide-ranging impact on people's lives. It may influence how people are taught in schools, how roads are designed, how we help people with mental health difficulties, where we put healthy food in the supermarket and the list goes on. If research can have such an impact, then it is important that the research is both reliable and valid. To ensure that this is the case, the research needs to be published in places where others in the field can read about it and evaluate it. It is important that the method of publication can be trusted and this is where academic journals play an important part. Academic journals are where researchers publish their research using a report structure as outlined above. It is a way to get their research out into the field and where others with similar research interests can engage and build on that research. This is why journals are quite specialist in that they are focused on specific disciplines or sub-disciplines in psychology. For example, mainstream social psychologists, as outlined in Chapter 2, will often look to publish in the *Journal of Experimental Social Psychology* or the *European Journal of Social Psychology* amongst others.

Psychology researchers are normally academics that work at universities such as lecturers and professors or are experienced researchers hired specifically on research contracts. For academics that are not on teaching only contracts, it is part of their contracts that they conduct and disseminate their research. The number and quality of their publications, particularly their journal publications, will impact academics' promotional prospects. However, not all publications carry the same kudos. Getting published in peer reviewed journal articles is the aim but in addition, being published in certain peer reviewed journals is seen as more prestigious than others. The more prestigious the journal, the more difficult it is to get published in that journal as they set the standard higher than for other journals. When deciding where to publish researchers will first consider publications that are relevant for their sub-discipline (e.g. experimental social psychology) and they will know what types of research and methods are typically published in that journal. They are looking for a good fit between their paper and the journal's remit. They will also consider the journals reputation in their decision. Researchers will submit their paper (report) to the journal and then their work will be subject to the peer review process.

What Is Peer Review?

Peer review is the process by which psychological research papers, before publication, are subjected to independent scrutiny by other psychologists working in a similar field. These experts will consider the research in terms of its **validity**, significance and originality. Due to their specialist knowledge, they can judge the importance and significance of the research in a wider context. Research will only get published if it makes an important contribution to the scientific field, and the research process has been methodologically and ethically sound. It also helps to prevent the dissemination of irrelevant or unjustified findings, personal views or deliberate fraud.

The Peer Review Process

At the start of the process, the Editor of the journal is sent the report and they will initially assess the suitability of the research for the journal. If the Editor is concerned about the research or the fit of the research in the journal, they can reject the paper before even sending it for review, known as a desk rejection. They will explain to the author(s) why the paper has been rejected. If the paper passes this initial consideration, they send the paper on to appropriate experts in that field. These reviewers carefully read the report, assessing the appropriateness of the method and design used. Each reviewer then sends it back to the editor with comments which may suggest that the paper is either: suitable for publication; accepted after some revisions; rejected, but offer revisions and a resubmission; or rejected for publication. The editor makes the final decision whether to accept or reject the research report based on the reviewers' comments. Peer review helps to ensure that the research in the scientific and public domain is of the highest quality and can be taken seriously by fellow researchers and the public.

It can take several months before the Editors replies with the comments from the reviewers and their overall judgement. This is because those reviewing will be busy with their own deadlines. If revisions are necessary, it can take years before the research is published as it goes back and forth, delaying publication of potentially important findings.

Other Ways to Disseminate Research

There are other ways in which research can be disseminated but these are not subject to peer review in the same way that journal articles are. Researchers can publish their work in edited books where several researchers will write different chapters along a common theme. They may also decide to go to a conference to present their work so that they can engage with other researchers who have a common interest. Conference presentations not only allow researchers to get their work known amongst their peers but also provide a great opportunity to receive feedback on their work. This feedback may include ideas for future work and even future collaborations with researchers from other universities.

Once researchers have completed a comprehensive collection of work, they may decide to publish a book; this is particularly the case if their work is applied and may have a wider audience. If they are pitching their work to a non-specialist audience then they need to write in a way that summarises their work ensuring that it can be easily digestible by a non-specialist audience. One of the key skills here is that researchers can 'sell' their work to the public so that they can see the relevance and importance of what they are doing. This is also the case for other types of media such as blogs, podcasts and even television.

There are several psychologists that have become well known due to the engaging way that they can communicate their research. Daniel Kahneman, Elizabeth Loftus, Richard Wiseman, Carol Dweck and Steve Pinker are just a few examples of psychology researchers that have gained popularity amongst the public. Many have presented TED talks that have amassed millions of views and have had books in the Times best sellers list.

CONTEMPORARY ISSUES WITH RESEARCH

Replication Crises

Relatively recently in psychology there has been a great deal of discussion around the idea that there is a 'replication crises'. Replication is crucial in science as it allows us to see if we get the same findings across time, samples and situations. Attempts to replicate *some* of the key findings in psychological research have been unsuccessful. For example, Aarts et al. (2015) conducted replications of 100 studies, using papers published in 2008 in three high-ranking psychology journals. They wanted to assess whether the replication and the original experiment yielded the same result according to several criteria. They found that 97% of the original studies found significant effects, but only 36% of replicated studies found significant effects. This means that 61% of the studies that were replicated were unable to produce the same findings as the original studies. The authors discuss the issue that replicating existing studies is not as exciting as creating and executing new studies. When you create new studies there is a sense and perception of being innovative, whereas replication is seen as old news. This means that studies are less likely to be replicated. However, Aarts et al. (2015) argue that replication can offer certainty when the findings are reproduced and can also lead to innovation when they are not, because understanding the reasons why opens up the debate.

It is also important to remember that there may be reasons why replication was not achieved. For example, in the studies discussed in Aarts et al. (2015) they were more likely to replicate studies that were less resource intensive which means that their selection of studies was biased. Further, in each article only one study was replicated so this means that we don't know if the other studies could have been successfully replicated in the article. Also, in each study only one statistical result was tested for replication so it may be that other results may have been replicated.

There are issues when researchers fail to replicate the findings of studies, and this is something that needs careful consideration when assessing the reliability of the research. It is often the case that researchers replicate their own research when they are looking at creating variations of their original study and this increases the likelihood that the findings are robust. But do be on the lookout for findings that are quite fragile, such as only just reaching statistical significance and/or the effect size being small.

Replication is particularly important to expose fabricated data. Diederik Stapel was an eminent Dutch social psychologist who was exposed for having fabricated data in numerous studies. Stapel's research had been published in a number of publications over the years and was a highly regarded researcher, so to expose his record of fabrication shocked everyone in the field of social psychology. Whilst this may be an exception, the case did highlight the need for greater scrutiny of claims made by psychologists and the need to fund research that aims to replicate previous studies even if doing so may be less interesting or regarded as less prestigious than coming up with new studies.

As a result of the replication crisis and concerns over falsified data or data that is analysed in such a way that it finds significant findings, where there may not be any genuine results (a concept called p-hacking), psychology is moving towards **open science**. Open science involves transparency at all stages of research, this includes in the design and planning of the study as well as data collection and analysis. By researchers being 'open' and allowing the academic community access to their analysis plan, data and materials it allows other researchers to more accurately replicate research and to check the data and how it has been analysed.

At the initial stages, researchers pre-register their study before any data collection takes place. This includes stating the procedure and materials to be used in the study, as well as the hypothesis/research question and the planned data analysis. By doing this, researchers are not able to manipulate the research process or data in any way to try to 'encourage' positive findings. Once the study has been conducted, researchers put any relevant materials or data on an open science repository such as https://osf.io/ and https://www.cos.io/ where other researchers (and the general public) can access them.

This transparency has also begun to move into the publication process. You will learn in Chapter 4 how universities subscribe to research databases to access published research. Research which is published as open access does not require any form of payment to read or access the paper. Some journals are fully open access whereas others publish some open access papers. This allows research to be disseminated to a wider audience and not only to those with a university affiliation.

■■■■■■■■■ Think 3.2 ■■■■■■■■■

Go to the following open science repository https://osf.io/. In the search box, type in a topic or author that you are familiar with. Browse through the materials available to give you an idea of the types of resources that are shared to allow for a transparent research process. You may want to try this with a few topics/authors to allow you to see a range of material.

Dominance of Western Research

There is a dominance of research conducted in Western industrialised countries. In fact, Arnett (2008) analysed publications in the top psychology journals between 2003 and 2007 and found that 96% of all samples were taken from Western industrialised countries, with 68% of participants from the United States. This led to the term 'WEIRD' introduced by Henrich et al. (2010). WEIRD stands for Western, Educated, Industrialised, Rich and Democratic societies. In their study, they found that approximately 80% of participants in psychology research were taken from a sample of the world that represents roughly 12% of the whole human population. This has important implications for the generalisation of research. It is difficult to draw universal conclusions about human behaviour from samples that do not represent a range of cultures. Even when cross-cultural research is conducted it tends to stem from Western research paradigms that are then applied and tested in other countries (Iyengar et al., 1999). This means that we are taking our own culture as the 'norm' and viewing other cultures through that lens, forgetting that this western norm is influenced by our own culture, heritage and societal conditions.

This has led to calls for the decolonisation of psychology (e.g. Bhatia & Priya, 2018). The aim of this movement is to embrace greater diversity and different perspectives in how we study human behaviour. Cross-cultural psychology is critical here. As Segall et al. (1998, p. 1102) argued, 'what cross-cultural psychology is called is not nearly as important as what it does – to ensure the broadest range of psychological topics be explored within the broadest possible spectrum of ethnicity and culture and by diverse methodologies'.

It is important to also remember that you, psychology students, are culturally diverse and there is a need to represent your culture and reality in the psychology you are being taught. This issue is not restricted to psychology but is a problem across higher education and has initiated several university-led initiatives dedicated to decolonising the UK curriculum.

Explore further

TED talks are a great watch. If you go to the TED website (www.ted.com/talks) and search for the psychologists listed below you will see how they engage the audience with their research:

Elizabeth Loftus, Daniel Kahneman, Dan Gilbert, Carol Dweck, Oliver Sacks and Philip Zimbardo.

Your task:

Watch Elizabeth's talk about reliability of memory: https://www.ted.com/talks/elizabeth_loftus_how_reliable_is_your_memory

and read one of her papers, for example:

Loftus, E. F. (2005). Planting misinformation in the human mind: A 30-year investigation of the malleability of memory. *Learning & Memory, 12*(4), 361–366. https://doi.org/10.1101/lm.94705

Both the paper and the TED talk contain a review of research and investigations in the area of the malleability of memory. When reading and watching consider the following questions:

- How do the talk and the paper differ in terms of the way research is presented?
- Why do you think these differences exist?
- What are the benefits of disseminating research via TED talks and other sources such as Podcasts?

You may want to repeat the same exercise with another of the researchers listed above.

KEY TAKEAWAYS

The focus of the first part of this chapter was to help you understand how important evidence is and how that evidence is gathered using the research cycle. We explored whether psychology is a science, considering how to avoid confirmation bias by seeking out evidence which can disprove our hypothesis (falsifiability). Other features of a science-based approach were considered including the need to be objective, where we don't allow our opinions and beliefs to influence any aspects of the research process, which is not particularly easy given that as humans we are, by definition, biased. Issues such as control and reproducibility were also explored as they help us to be sure that our results and conclusions are both valid and reliable, key factors when you are striving to be scientific in your approach.

The second half of this chapter explored how once the research has been conducted; it then needs to be written up, and this is when we covered the sections of a research paper (report). We then explored the different places you can disseminate research including journal articles and the peer review process researchers experience to get their research published in journals. We also explored other ways to disseminate research that go beyond the psychology community into the wider community. Finally, we explored some more contemporary issues with research including the replication crises and the dominance of western research.

4

PSYCHOLOGICAL RESEARCH – WHERE DO I FIND IT?

―――――――― Key goals for this chapter ――――――――

- Understand where you can find psychological research.
- Understand how to assess the relevance of psychological research.
- Understand other factors you need to consider when searching for psychological research.

HOW TO FIND PUBLISHED PSYCHOLOGICAL RESEARCH

Hopefully from reading the first three chapters you now appreciate the value of psychological research. *Understanding* the research is great, but when you are writing essays and reports in psychology you will need to not just understand but also be able to *use* research. To do this effectively, you need to be able to find research that is relevant to the essay/report that you are writing. You will no doubt be introduced to studies in your lectures and module materials and of course you can and should use these studies where they are relevant. However, there are at least two reasons why you will still need to know where to find psychological research. Firstly, when you are reading about a study via lecture materials or a textbook you are reading someone else's interpretation of the study rather than the original write up of the study. One issue with this is that you are then relaying information third hand, which allows more opportunities for mis-understandings. Additionally, you learnt in Chapter 3 how research is disseminated in reports. These reports are extremely detailed, and this level of detail cannot be replicated in textbooks or lecture materials. The second reason that you will need to find additional research is because you will be expected to engage in critical thinking and higher level analysis. This will require reviewing a range of research and going into depth on a topic. Lectures and textbooks usually introduce you to a topic, but the expectation is that you as an independent learner will build on this.

Databases

In your day-to-day life you are likely to be in the habit of 'Googling' something that you want to find out. Google is a search engine that searches all information available publicly on the internet. Unfortunately, this is not the most effective way to find research. This is partly because access to published journals is not publicly available and costs money to access. Fortunately, you are not expected to have to pay for each individual study you wish to access, instead your university library will subscribe to various subscription databases. These databases will give you access to different journals; you learnt about journals in Chapter 3. Remember there are many different journals relevant to psychology and it is these journals which publish research. It is important to keep in mind that there are thousands of journals that publish psychological research, and each database will not have access to all these journals. Therefore, there may be times where you cannot access a study that you would like to read.

Different institutions will have access to different subscription databases, the best place to find out which databases your university subscribes to is to check with the university library. Some of the commonly subscribed databases relevant to psychology are APA PsycINFO, APA PsycARTICLES and Web of Science.

Aside from subscription databases you can search for academic sources via free databases such as Google Scholar and Semantic Scholar.

It is usually a good idea to use more than one database when you are searching for research, to give yourself the best chance of accessing a broad range of available research.

━━━━━━━ Stop 4.1 ━━━━━━━

Remember, to find peer-reviewed academic sources you must search an academic database rather than use a generic search engine.

Searching for Sources

As it is not possible for us to know which subscription databases that your institution has access to, the examples that are used in this section are all taken from Google Scholar (https://scholar.google.co.uk/) as everyone has access to this. If you want advice on how to search in a specific database, you can find guides on the internet as well as tutorial videos on YouTube. Rather than step-by-step instructions of how to use Google Scholar, this section aims to give you a general overview of how you can search for academic papers.

Search Terms

As with Google, Google Scholar makes use of search terms. The search terms you use can make a vast difference in the results that you receive.

In Chapter 1, we used the concept of phubbing to illustrate some of the concepts of research. We will continue with that example here. Let's imagine you have been set the following essay question 'Discuss the relationship between phubbing and mental health'. You have been given some relevant research from your lecture, but you need to find more research to allow you to generate a sustained discussion. You decide that your first stop is Google Scholar!

━━━━━━━ Think 4.1 ━━━━━━━

What search terms would you want to include to help you to find relevant research?

It is important that you use search terms that maximise the chances of finding studies that are relevant to the question you are trying to answer. If we simply typed 'phubbing' into Google Scholar, at the time of writing this would provide us with 6,100 results! Nobody has the time or patience to read this many research papers to decide which are relevant.

Let's try to be a bit more precise, remember our essay question is 'Discuss the relationship between phubbing and mental health'. It would therefore make sense to add 'mental health' to our search term. Searching with 'phubbing and mental health' provides us with 3,050 results (at the time of writing). This is good, we have halved the amount of potentially relevant studies, but this is still an unmanageable number.

We could make the search more precise by focusing on specific elements of mental health, e.g.,

Phubbing and depression = 2,620 results
Phubbing and anxiety = 2,820 results
Phubbing and **OCD** = 190 results

We imagine that many of you reading are thinking 'OCD looks the best option, as there are fewer studies'. This is not necessarily the case as just as when you search on Google, many of the results will not be relevant. Thus, part of your job is being able to decide relatively quickly if a study is relevant or not (we will come to this in a minute).

An alternative way to narrow your search is to be more precise with the term 'phubbing'. Phubbing can occur in any social interaction; therefore, you may want to focus your essay on specific types of interactions to help to focus it, e.g.,

> Parent phubbing and depression = 1,660 results
> Partner phubbing and depression = 1,280 results
> Peer phubbing and depression = 1,330

If two terms are important to appear together, you can put speech marks around them, e.g.,

> 'Parent phubbing' and depression = 56 results
> 'Partner phubbing' and depression = 666 results
> 'Peer phubbing' and depression = 43 results

Not only is this a useful practice to help to search in a more refined way, but it is also useful in helping you to think about your writing and what focus you want it to take. It is not possible in one piece of academic writing to cover an entire topic; part of your job is to decide which elements of a topic you will focus on.

Another way you can refine your search is to narrow down the year of publication. You may decide you only want research published after a certain time-period. For example, mobile phones and how they are used changed quite significantly with the introduction of smartphones. Therefore, for this essay you may want to limit your search term to studies published after this date as any research prior to this may be testing something quite different from contemporary mobile phone use.

Cited By

Some databases have a 'cited by' function. This function allows you to see which other publications have referenced each source identified by the search engine. Therefore, you first need to refine your search terms before using this function. As journal articles refer to other studies that have researched similar topics to themselves, 'cited by' allows you to see which other studies have referred to the source. Of course, many of these will not be relevant but you are likely to find additional papers that you did not find with your search terms. As this function is constantly updated, you will also be able to see the most recent publications that have cited the paper which can give you an indication of the direction that more recent research is exploring. On Google Scholar, it also tells you how many times the study has been cited which can give you an indication of how impactful the study has been (Figure 4.1).

[HTML] **Partner phubbing** and **depression** among married Chinese adults: The roles of reltionship satisfaction and relationship length

X Wang, X Xie, Y Wang, P Wang, L Lei - Personality and Individual ..., 2017 -Elsevier

... in married adults' **depression**, it is less clear whether **partner phubbing** can undermine ... of **depression**. The current study investigated the indirect effect of **partner phubbing** on **depression** ...

☆ Save 99 Cite Cited by 246 Related articles All 3 versions

Figure 4.1 A screenshot of Google Scholar results showing a paper that has been cited 246 times

In this figure, you can see the result of a search in Google Scholar. This includes the title of the research paper, which is 'Partner Phubbing and depression among married Chinese adults: The roles of relationship satisfaction and relationship length'. The screen shot also lists the authors of the paper, the name of the journal, the year of publication and the publisher which owns the journal. There is a small excerpt from the paper, as well as the number of times that this paper has been cited.

Reference Lists

When you select relevant sources and read the paper, at the end of the paper you will find a reference list. The reference list will include information on each of the sources that the study you are reading has cited. If the study you are reading is relevant to the topic you are researching, then many of the references in the reference list may also be relevant. You will need to read the introduction of the paper carefully to identify which sources are potentially relevant and then use the reference list to give you the information to find them. You do not want to be aimlessly searching for every source on the reference list, as this would not be productive.

Below is an extract from the introduction section of the paper by Wang et al. (2017).

> To our knowledge, there are only two studies that have tested the effects of partner phubbing and technoference on depression (McDaniel & Coyne, 2016; Roberts & David, 2016). Technoference, which is similar to partner phubbing, is defined as everyday intrusions or interruptions in couple interactions or time spent together that occur due to technology including cell or smart phones (McDaniel & Coyne, 2016). They both found that partner's frequently engaging in phubbing behaviours or overuse of technology can directly and significantly affect individual's depression.

Here you can see that the authors refer to two other studies that have investigated partner phubbing and depression:

- McDaniel and Coyne (2016)
- Roberts and David (2016)

You may feel you would like to know more about these studies; to find the original publications, you would need to look to the reference list. The reference list is usually in alphabetical order; you will need to search the reference list until you find the authors you are looking for. In this case:

McDaniel, B. T., & Coyne, S. M. (2016). 'Technoference': The interference of technology in couple relationships and implications for women's personal and relational well-being. *Psychology of Popular Media Culture*, 5(1), 85–98.

We will cover referencing in more detail in Chapter 9, but briefly all references for journal articles will include the authors, the year of publication, the title of the article, the title of the journal, as well as the volume, issue, and page numbers. If you wish to find the original article, you can copy and paste the title of the article into either a free or subscription database.

Assessing the Relevance of Psychological Research

When you have a list of 'hits' from your database search, or papers via the 'cited by' function, your next task is to decide which of these research papers may be of relevance to the essay/report that you are writing.

Using the Title to Assess the Relevance of Research

In the previous section we looked at how to search in academic databases; you will recall that searching databases can give you thousands of results which you will not be able to read. Even if you only get a few hundred results, this is still too many research reports to read. You may be wondering how you are expected to identify which results could be relevant to your topic if you are unable to read each source. Do not panic, there are strategies you can use to quickly decide how relevant a research paper is likely to be to your topic.

The first of these strategies is to read the title. Titles are extremely important as they are written with the aim to inform a naïve reader as to the key focus of the study. Therefore, you should be able to make a reasonably informed decision about the relevance of a research paper from the title.

■■■■■■ Think 4.2 ■■■■■■

Below are some titles from one of our earlier searches *'Partner phubbing' and depression*. Read each title and decide whether each appears relevant to our essay question. As a reminder, our essay question is 'Discuss the relationship between phubbing and mental health'.

1 Partner phubbing and relationship satisfaction: Self-esteem and marital status as moderators.
2 Partner phubbing: Why using your phone during interactions with your partner can be detrimental for your relationship.
3 Phubbing: A literature review of the technological invasion that has changed lives for the last decade.
4 Phubbing in romantic relationships: Cell phone use, couple satisfaction, psychological well-being and mental health.
5 Mobile phone addiction, phubbing, and depression among men and women: A moderated mediation analysis.
6 Daily technology interruptions and emotional and relational well-being.

We will look at some examples and then come back to these titles so you can see how your thoughts match up with ours.

You learnt about the title in a research report in Chapter 3. Titles give a clear and concise description of the focus of the research and will usually make it clear whether qualitative or quantitative data was gathered and possibly the method used to gather these data. This is useful to us whilst we are searching for research, as it means we can have a reasonably good idea of what the study is about without reading the study. Let's look at an example of two titles which have collected different types of data.

- **Digital akrasia: a qualitative study of phubbing**
  This title quite clearly states that a qualitative approach has been taken, we do not know *how* the qualitative data has been gathered but the title is limited as to what it can tell us.
- **Phubbing Behavior: Is There a Gender Difference in College Students?**
  Whilst this title does not explicitly state a quantitative approach has been taken, it does identify that a *difference* has been tested. If we are looking for a difference, the research is likely to have an independent variable (IV) (see Chapter 1).

Let's have a look at some more examples of titles and what information these can give us with not very many words. We will keep with our previous example and fictional essay question of 'Discuss the relationship between phubbing and mental health'. For the following example, we will use the search terms 'parental phubbing' and **addiction**. Using these search terms gives us some of the following titles.

- **Why parental phubbing is at risk for adolescent mobile phone addiction: A serial mediating model.**
  The title here suggests that the paper is looking at the reasons *why* parental phubbing can lead to mobile phone addiction in adolescents. The part of the title that says 'a serial mediating model' tells us that the statistical analysis explored more than one factor that might mediate the relationship between mobile phone addiction in adolescents and parental phubbing. Thus, we can tell a quantitative approach has been taken.

  However, the title also leaves us with some questions. For example, we do not know how parental phubbing was measured. It is likely that parents were asked about their phone use around their child; it is important to know this, as how the variable was measured will influence the results found. We also do not know what potential mediating factors were measured. This is important as we might want to build our discussion around what other factors are involved and how this compares to the mediating factors involved in other aspects of mental health.
- **The relationship between parental phubbing and short-form videos addiction among Chinese adolescents.**
  This title makes it clear that a relationship was measured rather than testing for cause and effect or exploring qualitative data. The relationship being measured is between parental phubbing and a specific type of addiction – short-form videos (e.g. TikTok). We also have some detail on the sample that was studied, both their age (adolescence) and their culture (China).

  We do not however know how short-form videos were operationalised. It may be only one platform was considered or multiple platforms. We also do not know what constitutes an addiction and how long the adolescents needed to spend watching these videos to be classed as addicted.

- **Parental phubbing and internet gaming addiction in children: Mediating roles of parent-child relationships and depressive symptoms.**

  The focus in this title is parental phubbing and a specific type of addiction in children - internet gaming. The title also informs us that a mediation model was measured, and the researchers have explored whether the relationship between parental phubbing and internet gaming addiction in children is indirect and instead parental phubbing affects parent-child relationships and depression, which in turn affects internet gaming.

  What we do not know from this title, is the age range of the children who were studied. Childhood is a broad age group and could include children from 5-18-years old. This could be important as we may want to focus our discussion on a specific age group. There are further details on the sample we do not know, including the culture and socioeconomic status. It would also be pertinent to know how parental phubbing was measured and how internet gaming addiction was measured. It is likely that a survey was used, but we do not know if the children were asked, or the parents, or both. It is also possible other measures were used, e.g. an app (or similar) to measure the amount of time spent on internet games.

- **How is father phubbing associated with adolescents' social networking sites addiction? Roles of narcissism, need to belong and loneliness.**

  From this title we can decipher that this study has only focused on the phubbing behaviour of fathers, not mothers. This could be useful for the essay, as it may be that the phubbing behaviour of each parent has a different effect. Although to build a discussion on this, we would want to also look at research which has specifically focused on mothers so we can generate a discussion.

  The title also informs us that the study is focused on addiction but a specific type of addiction, social networking sites. In the earlier titles we looked at, some of these also examined specific types of addiction, this could be something we would want to explore in our essay and we may wish to follow up on different types of addiction.

  A final thing this title tells us is that it has explored how three other factors, narcissism, need to belong and loneliness, are involved in the relationship between parental phubbing and social networking addiction.

  However, as with all titles we are left with questions. We do not know the sample that was used in the study, neither do we know how the variables in the study were measured or whether they were measured at one time point or across multiple time points.

============ Stop 4.2 ============

Whilst the title is informative, we cannot make a fully informed decision as to whether the research is relevant or not without reading the paper in more detail to assess its usefulness to our needs.

━━━━━━━ Think 4.3 ━━━━━━━

Below are the titles you were asked to review in an earlier activity to consider their potential relevance to our essay question 'Discuss the relationship between phubbing and mental health'. We have added our thoughts on the potential relevance underneath each title.

1 **Partner phubbing and relationship satisfaction: Self-esteem and marital status as moderators.**
   There is no specific focus on depression or mental health in the title. Instead, the focus is on relationship satisfaction and which factors may mediate the relationship between partner phubbing and relationship satisfaction. Therefore, this title does not seem particularly relevant to our question.

2 **Partner phubbing: Why using your phone during interactions with your partner can be detrimental for your relationship.**
   The title is focused on phubbing, but there is no mention of depression or mental health. The outcome being the impact on the relationship rather than mental health. Therefore, this is not very relevant to our question.

3 **Phubbing: A literature review of the technological invasion that has changed lives for the last decade.**
   This title tells us that the publication is not a research report instead it is a literature review. In a literature review rather than writing up one study, the author instead reviews key studies in the field to come to a general conclusion on what research has told us on a topic. Literature reviews can be very useful as they essentially do a lot of the hard work of finding papers for you. With this literature review, it is not clear whether mental health is covered but it would be a source we would recommend reading to see what is covered.

4 **Phubbing in romantic relationships: Cell phone use, couple satisfaction, psychological well-being and mental health.**
   This paper appears potentially relevant as the title refers to phubbing and mental health, so would be worth exploring further.

5 **Mobile phone addiction, phubbing, and depression among men and women: A moderated mediation analysis.**
   This paper is focused on depression and phubbing; note that it also includes mobile phone addiction. Addiction is relevant to mental health, therefore reading this paper could give us further ideas on which aspects of mental health we wish to cover.

6 **Daily technology interruptions and emotional and relational well-being.**
   This research sounds potentially relevant, whilst the title does not explicitly mention 'phubbing' daily technology interruptions are a similar concept albeit broader and extending to technology other than the phone. However, to build a discussion it is important to look at other lines of argument. Possibly, any technology interruption could have the same effect as phubbing, if this is the case it could be discussed in the essay.

Using the Abstract to Assess the Relevance of Research

Chapter 3 introduced you to what an abstract is. Once we think we have found a research paper that is potentially relevant based on the title, we need to find out more information to allow us to understand the research further. Not every title that we think is relevant will end up being research that we decide to use in our work. But reading the title will help us to reduce the number of abstracts we need to read, and, in turn, reading the abstract will allow us to identify which papers we want to read in full.

To allow you to see some other topics, let's move away from our phubbing example and move to an example you were introduced to in Chapter 2 from cognitive psychology. You will recall that cognitive psychology is focused on our internal mental processes, one of these that you were introduced to in Chapter 2 is memory. Let's imagine you have been studying cognitive psychology and have been given the following essay question 'Discuss the role that exercise has on memory'. You have used a database to search for relevant research and as explained earlier, you have also reviewed the titles that the search returned. You now want to read the abstract of some of these papers that you have identified as potentially relevant to the question. Please read the first one below, taken from Loprinzi, Loenneke and Storm (2021), titled *Effects of acute aerobic and resistance exercise on episodic memory function.*

Accumulating research provides suggestive evidence that acute aerobic exercise may, potentially, enhance episodic memory function post-exercise. Limited research has evaluated whether acute resistance exercise may also enhance episodic memory post-exercise. Furthermore, whether these two exercise modalities have a differential effect on post-exercise episodic memory is relatively unknown. To address these research questions, three experimental studies were conducted ($N = 104$) among young adults (18–25 years). The experiments implemented acute bouts of aerobic or resistance exercise for 15 min. Episodic memory was comprehensively evaluated post-exercise with a list-learning paradigm and a computerised assessment of what-where-when aspects of episodic memory. Various manipulations (e.g. between vs. within-group) of the study design were implemented across the experiments. Across these three experiments, we failed to find consistent evidence of either type of acute exercise affecting episodic memory performance post-exercise.

Think 4.4

Read the abstract from Loprinzi, Loenneke and Storm (2021) and identify the following:

1 How many studies were conducted?
2 What type of method was used?
3 Who was studied?
4 What happened in the study?
5 What was found?
6 What relevance does this study have for the essay question?

From this abstract, we can identify that three studies were conducted, and the method used was an experiment. You will recall from Chapter 1 that an experiment involves IV and dependent variables (DV). In this study, the IV is the type of exercise, aerobic or resistance. The abstract states that various between and within participants designs were employed, which suggests the experiments may have been a little more complicated than this. The DV is memory, specifically **episodic memory**, after the exercise was completed. Episodic memory is our long-term memory for events which are personal to us. The sample studied was 18–25-year olds and there were 104 of them. The findings suggest that neither type of exercise was beneficial for episodic memory. Upon reading the abstract, this study could be relevant to the essay. It is useful to include null findings that do not show an effect because it helps to build an argument around the conditions necessary for exercise to benefit memory.

We will now look at another abstract which has been selected with the same essay question in mind. The abstract is from a research paper by Klaming et al. (2017), which is titled *Episodic memory function is affected by lifestyle factors: a 14-year follow-up study in an elderly population.*

Understanding the relationship between memory function and lifestyle offers great opportunities for promoting beneficial lifestyle choices to foster healthy cognitive ageing and for the development of intervention programs for older adults. We studied a cohort of older adults (age 65 and older) enroled in the Longitudinal Ageing Study Amsterdam, an ongoing prospective population-based research project. A total of 1,966 men and women participated in an episodic memory test every 3 years over a period of 14 years. Lifestyle habits were repeatedly assessed using self-report measures. Physical activity, light-to-moderate alcohol consumption, difficulties staying asleep and social engagement were associated with better memory function over the course of 14 years. In contrast, smoking and long sleep duration were associated with worse memory function. These findings suggest that certain lifestyle factors can have long-term protective or harmful effects on memory function in ageing individuals.

Think 4.5

Read the abstract from Klaming et al. (2017) and identify the following:

1 What was being tested?
2 What type of method was used?
3 Who was studied?
4 What happened in the study?
5 What was found?
6 What relevance does this study have for the essay question?

Klaming et al. (2017) were researching which factors in people's lifestyles influenced their memory functioning. The method used was a longitudinal study, which means that participants were followed up over a period of time. In this study participants were followed up every 3 years for 14 years. The study had a specific sample of adults aged 65 and over as the researchers wanted to use their findings to give advice on how to promote cognitive functioning in older age. To gather the data, participants completed self-report measures. Self-report measures include surveys and interviews and the abstract does not specify which method was used in this study; you would need to read the full report to find that out. At each time point, participants reported on various lifestyle factors including physical activity, alcohol consumption, sleep, smoking and social engagement. It is likely that other factors were also measured, and the abstract only states those which were found to be associated with memory functioning. Specifically, physical activity, little alcohol, difficulties staying asleep and social engagement were all related to better memory functioning. This study is useful to our essay as it allows us to consider the effects of exercise beyond a one-off exercise session; it could also allow us to build some critical thinking around factors other than exercise which influence memory.

Hopefully now you are beginning to see how you can read the abstract to decide whether the research paper is likely to be useful. Let's look at one last example using a study conducted by Loprinzi et al. (2020) titled *The Effects of Acute Exercise on Retroactive Memory Interference.*

Purpose:
Retroactive interference involves the disruption of previously encoded information from newly learned information and thus may impair the consolidation of long-term memory. The objective of this study was to evaluate whether acute exercise can attenuate retroactive memory interference.

Design:
Three experimental studies were employed. Experiment 1 employed a between-subject randomized control trial (RCT) involving moderate-intensity walking (15 minutes). Experiment 2 employed a between-subject RCT involving high-intensity jogging (15 minutes). Experiment 3 employed a within-subject RCT involving moderate-intensity walking (15 minutes).

Setting:
University setting.

Participants:
One hundred twelve young adults.

Measures:
After exercise, memory interference was evaluated from an episodic word-list memory task, involving the recall of two word lists.

Results:

The pooled effect size (standard difference in means: −0.35; 95% confidence interval: −0.64 to −0.06) across the three experiments was statistically significant (P = 0.01).

Conclusion:

We provide suggestive evidence that acute, short-duration exercise may help attenuate a retroactive memory interference effect. Implications of these findings for exercise to improve memory and attenuate memory decay are discussed.

Think 4.6

Read the abstract from Loprinzi et al. (2020) and decide whether you think this is relevant to our essay question 'Discuss the role that exercise has on memory'. You will need to break down the study, this time you have not been given questions to help you to do this. However, you can use the same questions here if you need to.

You will notice that this abstract is structured a little differently, as it has subheadings. You will find this in some journals, but regardless the structure will be the same. Thinking about this paper, memory was measured, and the researchers focused on a specific type of forgetting; **retroactive interference**. Retroactive interference occurs when we learn new information; we struggle to recall previously learnt information as the new information interferes with it. In this study, participants were given two word lists to learn, if retroactive interference occurs the second word list will interfere with recall of the first word list. The abstract tells us that three different studies are covered in the publication, all of which were experiments. Importantly, the manipulation in each experiment centred around exercise and each study manipulated a different type of exercise, moderate-intensity jogging, high-intensity jogging and moderate-intensity walking. The sample used was quite narrow, as only university students were studied; this would create questions over the extent to which we can generalise the findings to older populations. The findings show a difference in all three experiments between each exercise manipulation and what we have to assume was the control group. However, the abstract does not specify explicitly there was a control group in each experiment.

Thinking about our essay question, this study seems potentially relevant. We may want to structure our essay around different aspects of memory, e.g. episodic, semantic. If so, then this study would be highly relevant as we could focus on forgetting as an aspect of memory. If we were to do this, we would need further research into retroactive interference and exercise, ideally with a broader sample of participants. We may also want studies that have look at exercise over a prolonged period of time, e.g. weekly exercise sessions as opposed to one 15-minute session.

━━━━━━━ **Key tip 4.1** ━━━━━━━

Taking the time to read the titles and then selecting carefully which abstracts to read can allow you to only select the most relevant papers to read in full.

Other Factors to Consider

We have looked at using the title and the abstract to decide whether a source could be useful for your work; however, there are other factors to consider that we will now briefly explore.

Credibility of the Source

Not all sources are equal. If you wanted some advice on how to build muscle, who would you ask? Would you take the advice differently depending on who gave it? It is likely that you would value the advice from a qualified personal trainer more than you would value the advice of a delivery driver. This is because the personal trainer is a more credible source on that topic. If you wanted advice on the quickest route to take, you are more likely to value the information from the delivery driver over the personal trainer.

Research also varies with regards to how much value you should place on it and how credible the source is. You might be wondering how someone who is new to studying psychology is able to assess the creditability of a source. Luckily there are some quite simple strategies you can employ to assist you with this.

Place of publication: Where a piece of research has been published, will give you some indication of the credibility of the source. You learnt about the peer-review process in Chapter 3; whilst many journals only publish academic papers that have been peer-reviewed, this is not the case for all journals. If you are not sure whether the paper has been published in a peer-reviewed journal, you can simply search for the journal to find out. Studies that are not published in a peer-reviewed journal are less credible because they have not been checked by experts. Many studies do not make it through the peer-review process, or they require many amendments before being accepted for pub- lication. If you read about a study via a website or blog, unless the source is summarising a study published by someone else in a peer-reviewed journal, you cannot be confident about the credibility of the source.

Publication bias: Another consideration is that you should try to find research that has found null results and has not supported the hypothesis being tested. This can be difficult, as research which does not support the hypothesis tends to be less likely to be published. A phenomenon known as the 'file drawer effect', with negative findings remaining unpub- lished in the researcher's file drawer. Of course, you cannot change the file drawer effect, and this is an issue that journals need to work on. However, you can make a conscious effort to try to find research which has reported a range of different findings.

Non-WEIRD research: The concept of WEIRD was introduced to you in Chapter 3 and is an acronym for research that has been conducted in Western, Educated, Industrialised, Rich and Democratic societies. Much of the research conducted in psychology has been conducted in these types of societies, which is problematic as it does not give us a true understanding of behaviour. When you are searching for research, you should keep this in mind and try to seek out research which has been conducted outside of Western societies, or with less educated participants. If we are going to have an informed discussion, we need to include cross cultural research, which has ideally been conducted by researchers from that culture who have an understanding of the norms in that culture.

Methodology: In Chapter 1, we gave you a very brief overview of some of the more common methods used in psychological research. You will recall that each method has its strengths and limitations, and you should keep these in mind when you are selecting research studies. Think carefully about the method used and the potential limitations of that method in relation to the hypothesis/research question being tested. It can be a good idea to find research that has utilised different methods where possible, because if the same findings are similar across studies using different methods it suggests the conclusions are more likely to be valid.

Explore further

To further develop your skills in finding and selecting relevant research, you will be given a new hypothetical essay question. Your task is to search for research papers that could potentially be helpful in answering the question.

For this activity our essay question is 'To what extent does the use of screen time before bed affect the sleep of adolescents?'

Your task:

Using at least one academic database (you can use more), do the following:

1 Identify at least four different search terms that you can type into the database.
2 Using these search terms, identify at least six titles that could be potentially relevant to assist you in answering this question.
3 Read the abstract of each of the six research papers you have selected, and when reading the abstract identify the following:
   - What was being tested?
   - What type of method was used?
   - Who was studied?
   - What happened in the study?
   - What was found?
   - What relevance does this study have for the essay question?

KEY TAKEAWAYS

The focus of this chapter has been making you aware of how you can search for and find further research beyond the lectures, textbooks and reading lists you are given as part of your modules. Whilst these should form the beginnings of your research, in order to develop a more sophisticated line of argument in your writing, you will need to draw on multiple sources beyond these.

The main way you were advised to search for research is via databases, either those your institution subscribe to or free databases. It is important you use these databases as these will return academic published sources, as opposed to 'Googling' to find research which will give you content from anywhere on the internet including many non-peer-reviewed sources.

This chapter also introduced you to strategies to make sifting through the results you receive quicker, primarily reading the title to assess the relevance and, if deemed relevant, continuing to read the abstract.

The focus of this book is to support you in using psychological research effectively in your academic writing, and being able to find and select relevant studies is the first step in this process.

5

THINKING CRITICALLY ABOUT RESEARCH IN PSYCHOLOGY

─── Key goals for this chapter ───

- Understand what critical thinking is and how it is defined.
- Develop critical thinking as a skill.
- Understand the importance of critical thinking in psychology.
- Explore examples of critical thinking in psychology.

WHAT IS CRITICAL THINKING?

A key theme throughout this book is concerned with reading, thinking and writing critically. We have discussed the importance of thinking about psychology as being a research focused discipline that relies on evidence to support any claims that are being made in Chapter 1. The discussion of the publication process and peer review in Chapter 3 highlighted the importance of critical analysis by academics working in the field to ensure only high-quality research is disseminated. Chapter 4 also included some discussion about assessing the relevance and quality of different papers. All of these chapters have been addressing critical thinking, albeit in a less direct and obvious way compared to the next two chapters. In this chapter we are going to explore critical thinking in great detail, alongside examples so that we can demystify this elusive concept. The following chapter will then demonstrate and apply your newly acquired critical thinking skills to journal articles in a practical and hands-on way. We are sure that by the end of these two chapters you will be more confident about demonstrating critical thinking.

Critical thinking is a difficult skill to define precisely and concisely. It is about the ability to analyse arguments or evidence, synthesise them (put together multiple pieces of evidence) and evaluate them (Moseley et al., 2005). It is not about negative thinking as it also includes an appreciation of the strengths too. Critical thinking is a skill that we use in our everyday life. It is so much a part of our decision-making processes that it has become automatic, and we don't even recognise it as critical thinking. This means that when we are asked to think critically it stops us in our tracks as it sounds academic and possibly a bit intimidating. However, as we have mentioned, it is something you are doing all the time, so you just need to apply it to your academic work and hone your skills. That is where we come in.

Take an example like deciding where to go on holiday. It can be confusing when you put your search parameters into a holiday booking site and you get back an array of choices to make. How do you make that decision? This is where you apply your critical thinking. You look at the options and assess the positives and negatives. This one is near the beach but the pool looks a bit small and possibly a struggle to get a sunbed. But this other one is a bit of a walk to the beach but has a great pool and a spa. The rooms in the first one look bigger and one has Wi-Fi included in the price but the other has a daily charge. You then start to assess how important each of those factors are to you and your enjoyment of the holiday. This is an example of thinking critically. You are weighing up the different aspects, drawing on your previous experiences, and then coming to a decision.

Critical thinking skills are important for life and for your academic success. They are vital when reading, writing and when you are working in groups with other students. Critical thinking is about taking an idea or suggestion, examining against what you already know and evaluating its merit. When critically evaluating in your academic life, you want to stay objective by weighing up all sides of an argument and then assessing the strengths and weaknesses. It is important that when you are looking at the different sides of an argument that you explore the soundness of the claims and evidence presented. How you do this will depend on the context and what you are trying to achieve. In this chapter, and the next chapter, we will be expanding on this.

THE IMPORTANCE OF CRITICAL THINKING

Critical thinking means that the reader can assess the evidence and spot potentially spurious and/or illogical reasoning. Developing your critical thinking means you will be able to compare theories, methods, concepts and perspectives. It will also help you in your own writing as your argument will be stronger and more convincing. You will be able to present evidence to support your arguments and be able to synthesise your thoughts with those of other researchers.

It is important to recognise here that critical thinking is directly associated with critical reading, both will be addressed in this chapter and the next chapter. When students are provided with feedback that they are not demonstrating critical thinking in their writing, what is really being said is that they have not demonstrated that they have read the original sources critically. So, if you are reading with a critical mindset, you can then make notes to ensure that you record your critical thinking, and this then will feed through into producing assignments that include critical writing. You can see how critical thinking is not something that can be 'tacked on' but must be present throughout the process of completing your work. Just like everyday critical thinking, this academic critical thinking becomes second nature after a while.

What Is an Argument?

To be able to think critically you are often asked to consider the argument that the researcher or writer is putting forward. An argument in an academic sense is not bickering. It is the message that is being conveyed and this can be through speech or writing. A researcher should be putting forward an argument that is clear, free from bias and supported by evidence.

Toulmin (1958) came up with a model for analysing arguments. His model identified three basic parts of an argument: the claim, the data and the warrant. We explored claims and evidence in Chapter 1, and we are going to take some time to expand on those concepts here in relation to building an argument.

- Claim

  i) This is the main thrust of the argument. It can be thought of as a statement that is 'true'.

Example of a claim: Schools should ban sugary drinks from their premises.

- Evidence

  ii) This is the grounds for the claim. In psychology this would normally be evidence from research that has been undertaken. The evidence needs to support the claim being made or if it doesn't fully then there will need to be an acknowledgement of the qualifications (see later).

Example of evidence: Studies have shown a positive correlation between sugary drink consumption and rates of obesity.

- Warrant

    iii) This is the assumption on which the claim and the evidence depend. In other words, it is the general principle that the evidence is based upon. As the warrant is the link between the data and the claim it means if this warrant is not valid, the argument falls apart. As the warrant links evidence and claim it doesn't have to be last, it could come first.

Example of a warrant: Poor diets lead to health problems in children.

In addition to the three main parts of an argument, there are also three other elements Toulmin identified.

- Qualifier

    i) This is a statement that considers how strong the claim is. It is quite usual for researchers to qualify their claims as there are often other causes for behaviour. Researchers may, for example acknowledge the limitations of correlational studies or in experimental studies they may acknowledge something is the most significant cause but not the only cause. Do remember from Chapter 1 that evidence only supports and does not prove.

Example of a qualifier: Whilst there is a positive correlation between sugary drink consumption and obesity, we cannot state that sugary drink consumption leads to obesity.

- Rebuttal

    ii) This is an exception to a claim. In other words, there are counterarguments where the claim is problematic in some way or may not hold true.

Example of a rebuttal: Banning children from drinking sugary drinks in school won't prevent children from consuming sugary drinks outside of school.

- Backing

    iii) As mentioned earlier the warrant can be an integral and important part of the argument. It can be the case that the warrant is not accepted or understood by others, the researcher may need to defend the warrant by using reasons to support the warrant.

Example of backing: Schools should provide a healthy and positive environment for children, and they do this in many other ways such as PE lessons and pastoral support, so banning sugary drinks should be part of an overall well-being strategy.

Figure 5.1 summarises the Toulmin's model of argumentation, so you can visually see the different elements of an argument and how they interact.

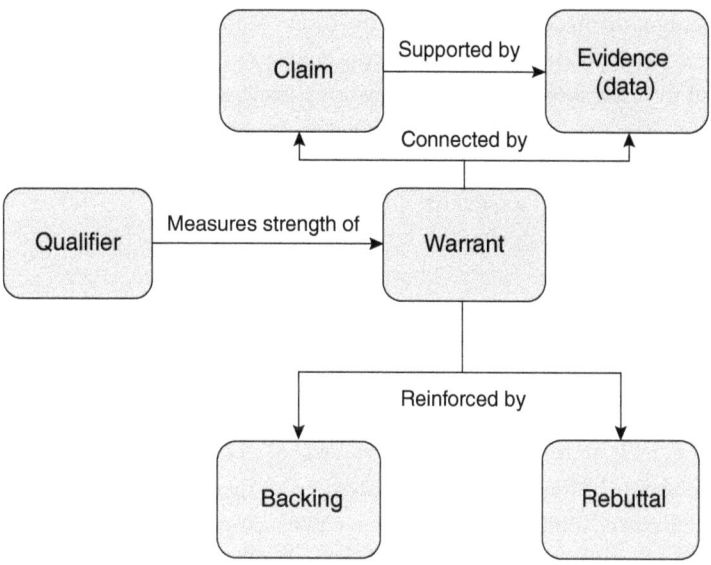

Figure 5.1 Toulmin's model of argumentation

In the figure you can see seven boxes, each with a word related to Toulmin's model of argumentation. The figure shows how the claim is supported by evidence (data) and that the claim and the evidence are connected by the warrant. The qualifier measures the strength of the warrant and the warrant is subsequently reinforced by backing and rebuttal.

━━━━━━━━ Think 5.1 ━━━━━━━━

Critically think about this argument for banning sugary drinks in schools by considering the following questions (there are others):

- What else could be contributing to obesity in children?
- What is it about sugary drinks that have an impact? Does it lead to cravings for other sugary drinks and food?
- Will banning sugary drinks in school lead to a decrease in consumption or just change where they are consumed?

THE PROCESS OF THINKING CRITICALLY

There is no one definitive way to think critically but there are some steps you can take before you start to analyse and evaluate the material.

1 Identify the main line or thrust of the argument.

When reading the material think about the thrust of the information that is being presented. Here you are just trying to define and be aware of the subject matter. It may be useful to think about the main claims being made, the evidence used and the conclusions reached. This mirrors Toulmin's model.

2 Examine and interrogate the material used in the argument.

Ask yourself the following questions:

- Where is the argument situated in relation to other theories/research and the wider picture?
- Is the argument relatively recent? Do they use up-to-date evidence?
- Is the argument balanced? Or is the author not considering other perspectives or aspects so that they can advance their own argument?
- Is the material presented in the argument clear and comprehensive? If not, do you need to look for other material that will help to understand their line of argument?

3 Thinking about the implications and application of the argument.

- Weaknesses or limitations of the argument when applied to real-life situations
- The implications of the theory or evidence on other theories or evidence
- Limitations in scope and coverage – do you need to refer to other theories or evidence to gain a complete understanding?

Identifying Flaws in an Argument

One of the most important concepts to appreciate when thinking critically is the concept of a **fallacy**. A fallacy is defined as an incorrect conclusion or a mistaken belief that is based on faulty or no evidence. Avoid these fallacies in your own arguments and keep an eye out for them in the arguments of others.

Slippery Slope

This is where a conclusion is based on the premise that if A occurs then eventually through a series of small steps, through B, C, D... through to X and Y, Z will happen too. By doing so you are equating A and Z. As a result, the suggestion is that if we don't want Z to occur then A must not be allowed. Whilst sometimes Z may happen, these arguments are not discussed through the exploration of probability. Therefore, although the argument presented may be possible, they are not probable and this where the argument loses its strength.

Using an example, following the pandemic there has been a great deal of discussion about flexible working and changing the traditional work pattern. Here is an example of the slippery slope fallacy in this context:

- Changing to a four-day working week from five days will mean employees will have more time to spend with their families. Spending time with their families will mean employees will be happier and more productive at work.

Whilst this may be true, this is an example of a slippery slope argument because of the assumption that the initial change will lead to a specific result through a series of steps. Let us examine each of the assumptions. Firstly, changing to a four-day week could mean employees will spend more time with their families but that may not be where they choose to spend their time. They may decide to take on more work elsewhere instead to fill up that day and raise their income. This may then mean that they are not happier and not more productive, the reverse could be true. Alternatively, they may end up spending more time with their families but that may not be what makes them happy. Also, even if spending more time with their family does make them happier that does not necessarily lead to greater productivity. Can you see how there several assumptions built into the argument above that need to be examined carefully. This sends our 'evidence radar' off – we are screaming 'where's the evidence for any of these assumptions'? When examining arguments, you need to consider the evidence for the link between A and B, B and C and so on and then think about the probability of each link happening. It is not that the argument is illogical; the key is the likelihood or probability that the initial event will lead to the result claimed. Be on the lookout for those pieces of writing that weigh up the likelihood and alternatives in their line of argument, as stronger writing will explicitly consider these factors.

Post Hoc Ergo Propter Hoc (Latin for 'After This, Therefore Because of This')

This is the notion that because two things happen together that one causes the other. Psychologists are aware of not confusing correlation with **causation** (see Chapter 1), but we want to pause here to consider this fallacy in more detail. To do so, we need to discuss necessary and sufficient conditions. Necessary conditions are those that must be present for the event to occur. In other words, if B happens then A must have been present. However, just because A is present it doesn't mean that B will happen. For example, if A is sitting an exam and B is passing the exam, you cannot pass the exam without sitting it, so sitting the exam is a necessary condition. However, just because you sit the exam does not mean you will pass the exam.

A sufficient condition is when A is present means that B will happen but also that something else might have caused B. In other words, B can occur without A but when you have A you can expect B. So, for example you know that if you achieve an overall grade of 70% on all of your psychology modules you have studied you will get a first class in psychology. However, getting a first-class degree in psychology does *not* necessarily mean that you achieved a first in all of your psychology modules.

False Dilemma or False Binary Opposition

It is the fallacy of presenting only two choices, outcomes or sides as the only possibilities when more are available. This often occurs as we have a need to simplify the world around us and create clear distinctions. Alternatively, these false dilemmas can be presented in political situations to manipulate the audience so that they are distracted from other choices and coerce them into selecting the 'correct' choice. This can include the use of divisive language such as you are 'with us or against us'.

In psychology, it is normally the case that we are a cautious bunch and would often avoid making binary statements such as depression is caused by a chemical imbalance in the brain or criminal behaviour is caused by social factors. Instead, we would suggest that it is a range of factors and influences that determine our thoughts and behaviour and would use evidence to support those factors. In your reading, be on the lookout for clear distinctions that are being made to see if those distinctions are real or just being imposed.

Evaluating an Argument

Whenever you are reading academic material, try to be focused on forming a judgement based on the validity of the argument being presented. It is easy to get swept up by what is being written and to take it at face value, but it is good to be sceptical and questioning. It can also be helpful to be thinking about the coherence of the argument and the supporting evidence when you are reading material such as journal articles or academic books (see the next chapter).

Coherence

Here you are on the lookout for a clear, coherent and logical line of argument that progresses sensibly. If the argument manages to do that then it is more likely to be a valid argument. Remember to be considering whether there are flaws in the argument that have been presented above.

- Have the researchers used evidence to support their claims and if so, is the evidence convincing?
- Is there any bias in the claims made and supporting arguments?
- Are there assumptions made? Are those reasonable or a step too far?
- Is the claim an opinion or based solely on evidence?
- Does the claim and the evidence fit together?
- What about the conclusions drawn, are they supported by the claims made in the argument and are these valid?

Supporting Evidence

You should not just accept the evidence provided. Instead, you need to examine it carefully and compare it with other evidence. It is useful to be thinking as you are reading, and these questions can help you to assess the validity of the evidence:

- Does the evidence support *all* the claims being made and not just some of them?
- Is the evidence appropriate and related to the argument directly? It can be the case that when researchers are citing other researchers' work and conclusions, they can be selective in what they report and provide the wrong impression – try to hunt down the original evidence to verify.

- Are there issues with the methodology used in the collection of the evidence that could then impact the appropriateness and usefulness of the evidence?
- Is the evidence relatively recent and if not, does this matter?

Don't Forget to Take Notes as You Read

When you are reading and considering the coherence and evidence contained in the materials, it is a good idea to make notes. These notes can be answers to the questions or could be general impressions, or even notes for further action such as obtaining the original sources. The exact nature of your considerations should be driven by what you are trying to achieve. For example, if you are writing an assignment that is asking you to consider the strengths and limitations of a theory then you will need to be making notes centred on those requirements.

Explore further

Imagine you have been asked to 'critically evaluate whether primary school children should have mobile phones' – what do you need to consider here?

Using Google Scholar and/or other search engines, find peer reviewed articles exploring the effects of mobile phone use on primary school children. Once you have found some articles, consider the following questions:

- Does the evidence support *all* the claims being made and not just some of them?
- Is the evidence appropriate and related to the argument directly? It can be the case that when researchers are citing other researchers' work and conclusions, they can be selective in what they report and provide the wrong impression – try to hunt down the original evidence to verify
- Are there issues with the methodology used in the collection of the evidence that could then impact the appropriateness and usefulness of the evidence?
- Is the evidence relatively recent and if not, does this matter?

CRITICAL THINKING IN PSYCHOLOGY

It is worth noting here that critical thinking is a psychological variable that can be measured (e.g. Ku, 2009). It is probably not surprising to learn that as you become more educated you become more skilled at critical thinking, especially when you are encouraged to do so as part of your studies.

To be able to think critically, it is often said that you need to be able to use your imagination. Specifically, it is useful to be able to imagine alternative interpretations or explanations when examining results and theories. Another way to think imaginatively is to consider if a researcher was to run their study differently or use a different situation or context, would the results differ and if so how and why? This is a great source of critical evaluation.

Applying Critical Thinking to the Main Perspectives in Psychology

We discussed the main perspectives in psychology in Chapter 2. We are going to return to each of those perspectives to apply some critical thinking to these overarching perspectives.

Biological Psychology

This is the perspective where many students would feel apprehensive about applying critical thinking as the language can be complicated and if it is biological, it feels like it must be too 'sciency' to be criticised. But remember that each perspective comes with a set of overarching principles and those need to be carefully scrutinised. For example, biological psychologists focus on the notion that our brains tend to work in very similar ways so damage to certain parts of the brains will lead to predictable changes in behaviour or experience irrespective of someone's culture or life experiences. It should also mean that any recovery after damage should follow a predictable trajectory. But is that really the case? Do all stroke victims who have similar damage have the same recovery of function? Remember that in Chapter 2 you learned that biological psychologists believe that all our behaviours can be seen as rooted in biology. However, is it not the case that our brains and our subsequent behaviour are influenced by several factors, so whilst a single explanation for behaviour is attractive it is often not entirely plausible. It is true that most biological psychologists would acknowledge that other explanations are possible and even probable, it is important to look for times when they make a strong case for an explanation that goes beyond the data.

To provide a concrete example, research has supported the idea that chemical imbalances in the brain are linked to depression. However, it is not the case that one single chemical or even a range of chemicals being too high or too low causes depression. This is for several reasons. Firstly, correlation is not causation so whilst there may be a link between certain chemicals in the brain and depression, we don't know whether that the chemical imbalance causes depression or is the result of depression. This is complicated by the fact that research does not actually measure the neurotransmitter levels in the brain when coming to this conclusion. Secondly, it is not the case that everyone with these chemical imbalances will experience depression; it is likely that other factors such as genes, stressful life events and faulty mood regulation contribute too. Even if we could say that chemical imbalances cause depression that would simply describe the cause and not explain *why* or *how* that happens, it would not help to prevent depression. The other criticism levelled at biological psychologists is that their research only describes rather than explaining how things work. For example, we know that the **hippocampus, amygdala** and **cerebellum** are involved in memory. This has been discovered mostly through scanning human brains whilst conducting tasks that use memory and through case studies of people who have damage to those areas of the brain. However, we do not know *how* these structures work. We cannot see a physical trace of memory through our brain. Therefore, we are left with a description, and it can be argued that a description of the structures involved is rather limited.

Cognitive Psychology

Cognitive psychology, as outlined in Chapter 2, is a diverse perspective in psychology. It is also a perspective that overlaps with other perspectives such as social psychology to create sub disciplines such as social cognition. Here we are going to focus on the more core and traditional aspects of cognitive psychology.

Cognitive psychologists are concerned with the mental processes through which we think about the world around us, amongst other things. We mentioned in the previous section that biological psychologists may want to understand which structures are involved in memory, but for cognitive psychologists they may want to understand the impact memory strategies have on recall. To do so, they may ask participants in one group to remember a list of words through organising the information into categories and the other group are asked to use **mnemonics** (such as a song) to help them memorise the words. However, participants may decide to use their own strategies or use a range of strategies. Cognitive psychologists may not be concerned by this if it has the same potential impact on both groups as it won't systematically impact just one group (condition). However, say if participants in the category condition adopt a mnemonic-related strategy instead of the intended category strategy, then that is problematic because then you have a systematic issue. This illustrates that one issue cognitive psychologists have is that manipulating or controlling what we are thinking does not always work. This links to another related issue, the production of word lists. When cognitive psychologists are trying to test memory or learning they will often use word lists. These word lists need to contain unrelated words that have the same number of syllables. This is quite difficult to do, so when reading about any studies that have used word lists have a look at those word lists carefully to see if there are any issues that may impact the results. If you notice an issue though, it is important to state that it could have impacted the results and why. If it is unlikely to make a difference to the results, then it is best to not mention it as it won't be perceived as evidence of critical thinking.

Social Psychology

One of the key issues that social psychology faces is how to study behaviours in a way where clear conclusions can be drawn. Recall from Chapter 2 that whilst social psychology may be a diverse bunch, they do all agree that relational, situational, cultural and political contexts all need to be appreciated. Appreciating the importance of these factors make studying behaviour quite difficult.

If you use experiments, then you are studying behaviour away from the natural environment. However, by doing so you are controlling other variables that could occur in a natural environment, thereby enabling you to manipulate the variable of interest (the independent variable) to explore the effect on the dependent variable (DV). For example, experimental social psychologists may ask participants to read about someone or watch a video and then rate that person's personality characteristics such as likeability, credibility and so on. This process may be very different from the way that you judge people outside of that experiment where you have several other pieces of information that you can use. But experimental psychologists would argue that is the point, if they want to study the impact of accents on impressions of a speaker then they only want to manipulate the accent of the speaker in the video and keep all other information constant. So, when critically appraising experiments in social psychology be careful to not just say that the study was artificial so lacks **ecological validity** because whilst that may be true, you would need to be very clear in your argument as to why that it is an issue for the specific study you are evaluating and not just a generic evaluative point.

Conducting experiments enables you to be able to draw clearer inferences from the results compared with conducting observations. As we discuss later in this chapter, when observing we have to make inferences from what we see which then reduces our ability to determine cause and effect. Whilst it may be tempting to then suggest that we should not conduct experiments or observational research when we are exploring social phenomena, this would prevent us from learning about human behaviour. Instead, we can acknowledge the limitations of these different methods in social psychology but also recognise how the data and conclusions drawn from those studies can add to the existing research to construct a body of knowledge around that topic. No one study would, or should, ever claim that it has definitively answered a key question, but it does add a piece to the puzzle.

Developmental Psychology

As this perspective has moved away from focusing on child psychology (as discussed in Chapter 2) to explore psychological stability and change across the lifespan, this has presented several challenges. As outlined in Chapter 2, stage theories are used to explain the nature of human development, with expectations that each stage must be achieved before moving onto the next stage. However, development is a continuous and iterative process rather than a stepped process. Further, there are too many cross-cultural, situational and contextual changes and differences to have a rigid universal concept. If we think about how different life is now to what it was 50 years ago, without the internet and technology and other advances, it would be difficult to conceive that children today would move through a similar developmental trajectory to their grandparents or even parents. Another issue is how do these stage theories of development account for neurodiverse individuals whose development may be quite different from their neurotypical counterparts. Keep this in mind when you encounter these rigid developmental theories.

Whilst developmental theorists have tried to embrace the impact of culture and explore non-Western cultures, this is always going to be an ongoing consideration. As discussed in Chapter 2, coming from a Western society can mean that our assumptions are so intrinsic we are not even aware that they exist; so trying to overcome them and design studies that embrace cultural diversity is always going to be difficult. But adapting the researcher's toolkit to take account of cultural differences is critical.

Developmental psychologists conduct longitudinal studies that allow them to observe and assess behaviour and opinions over time and it is often the case that some participants will drop out over the course of the study, which will impact the validity of the data. The people that remain in the study may no longer be fully representative of the population of interest (see later in this chapter). It is easy to see that those that drop out may be potentially different from those that decide to remain in a study.

======= Key tip 5.1 =======

If you are reading a study that is using a longitudinal study over several years do look for the **attrition rate** and any commentary about participants that have dropped out as this could be a rich area for critical thinking.

CRITICAL THINKING IN RESEARCH METHODS AND STATISTICS

When applying critical thinking to research methods and statistics you need to think logically. You need to be asking questions that focus on understanding whether the research design was appropriate for the research question. If the research design is flawed, then you cannot make up for that in other aspects as the validity will be compromised. It is also important to assess the analysis that has been conducted and whether that analysis was appropriate given the data that was gathered. We will explore some issues with research methods and statistics to look out for when examining research in this next section. Also, there are some examples applied to journal articles in the next chapter.

Assessing Control Groups

When using experimental methods, control groups are often used. **Control groups** consist of a group of people who are the same as the treatment group except that they are not receiving treatment. They are important because they act as a point of comparison between doing nothing and doing something (or being treated with something or not treated). It is important that the control group matches the treatment or experimental group; otherwise clear comparisons cannot be made. The way to do this is by randomly allocating participants to conditions and if the sample is large enough then the assumption is that there should be no systematic differences across the two groups.

======= Key tip 5.2 =======

When you are reading about studies that have used a control group you need to be considering whether the samples were sufficiently large enough and whether participants were randomly allocated to conditions. If that is not the case then the research could be flawed.

Minimising Demand Characteristics

When conducting experiments or observations, demand characteristics need to be considered. If participants know that they are part of a study, they will often be more aware of their behaviour or responses. This can mean that their behaviour and responses are different from what they normally would be. In particular, if they know what the aim of the study is and what condition they are in then they may do what they think is expected of them (demand characteristics). This is human nature and difficult to not do. Therefore, it can be useful to employ single- or double-blind procedures. Single blind procedure is when participants don't know what group (condition) they are in, so they are unable to react to expectations because they have no knowledge (blind). A step further is to have double-blind procedures which is where the researcher also doesn't know what group (condition) the participant is in, so they also cannot then interpret behaviour in a way that suits the study. It also means that they won't change how they interact with the participant, even in subtle ways.

Due to the nature of the research, it is not always possible to have double- or even single-blind procedures, but it is good to be on the lookout for if they have been implemented or not. Even if it is not possible to implement these procedures then it is a good idea to try to minimise demand characteristics. This may be through only telling participants the information they really need to know. For example, it may mean not telling them what other participants are doing in the other groups (conditions) or not revealing the full aim of the study until the debrief, if that is ethically possible.

■■■■■■■■ Key tip 5.3 ■■■■■■■■

When critically evaluating other people's research it is always worth considering the part demand characteristics may have played in the results and what, if anything, the researchers did to try to reduce the impact. Sometimes demand characteristics are not relevant, but if they are then scrutinise what participants were informed prior to the taking part and whether this could have systematically impacted the results and conclusions.

Social Desirability

When researchers conduct research that requires self-report data there can be issues with social desirability. This is where people have the tendency to respond to questions in a way that they believe would meet the approval of others. The reason people display social desirability bias is due to two potential components (Paulhus, 1984). The first component relates to impression management, which is where people purposefully present themselves in such a way to meet the approval of others. The second component is more unconscious and is related to self-deception and motivation stems from wanting to main a positive self-concept. Social desirability is particularly prominent when the topic is socially sensitive.

For example, if you ask people how many units of alcohol they consume in a week they may suggest only 10 units to appear more socially acceptable rather than the 20 units they actually consume. If all, or the majority, of your respondents replied in that socially desirable way then you will come to the inaccurate conclusion that people's consumption of alcohol is low. This means that the validity of the survey will be reduced. This is something to consider when reading about surveys and questionnaires that have been conducted especially when you suspect impression management and/or self-deception could be at play. In this example, it may be that people want to appear healthier but also that they are deceiving themselves that they are light consumers of alcohol.

Social desirability bias is more likely to occur when data is collected face to face or over the phone. This is because they want to be viewed more favourably by the interviewer. If the information is collected online then social desirability is reduced, or at least the impression management component is.

■■■■■ Key tip 5.4 ■■■■■

When reading about self-report methods of data collection, keep in mind any issues related to social desirability. Think about whether issues of impression management and/or self-deception could be relevant and how this may have influenced the results and conclusions drawn from the research.

Inter-Rater Reliability

If you are critically reading a research paper that has included observational studies, then it is wise to take a very close look at the data and how it has been interpreted. It is very easy for a researcher to see what they may wish or hope to see, even if that may not have been their intention. They don't set out to be biased but knowing the past literature and what their study's aims are means they see the behaviour through a particular lens. Imagine, for example that a toddler is crying when a caregiver walks away, it would be easy to interpret that behaviour as separation anxiety. However, it could be that the child is hungry, tired or just having a bad day. But because the researcher is exploring separation anxiety in toddlers they jump to that conclusion. Therefore, it is useful for researchers to use multiple independent observers who have no idea of the aims of the research. These independent observers provide a useful check on the reliability of the data and interpretation. You can check then that the data obtained, and the interpretation matches between the independent observer(s) and the original researcher. Whilst having more than one researcher observing the behaviour is common, it is not always the case that one or more of those researchers is blind to the research aims.

■■■■■ Key tip 5.5 ■■■■■

It is a really good idea to scrutinise whether independent observers have been used in observational studies and if not, to then explore the potential impact of that omission.

Sampling and Critical Thinking

Selecting a **sample** requires careful consideration. The size of the sample is the first important consideration. The greater the number of participants the more likely it will represent the population. If larger samples are more likely to represent the population, then they are more likely to be generalisable to the population, compared with smaller samples. But collecting data from thousands of participants is time consuming and costly. So instead, researchers may use smaller samples but may have to be tentative when generalising their findings to the wider population. When evaluating studies, it is important to consider sample size but not to assume that it has impacted the findings just because the sample size was not in the thousands. Always ask yourself, would you expect the results to be different if more people were added to the sample? Why and how would the results differ? If they have found a clear significant difference then adding more participants is unlikely to change that, unless the sample was not representative.

This leads on to the next point about samples, obtaining a **representative sample**. Imagine that I am wanting to know about people's views of the education provided in mainstream secondary schools. Using this example, examine these different samples and think which one is most representative:

Sample 1

I choose 500 parents from across the country whose children are currently in mainstream secondary education. The survey includes roughly equal numbers from across the country.

Sample 2

I choose 500 parents from across the country whose children are currently in mainstream secondary education. The survey was balanced to ensure that more parents were included in parts of the country which had large populations and fewer were surveyed where populations were lower.

Sample 3

I choose 500 parents from across the country. The sample included some people whose children are in secondary education, some whose children are in primary education and others whose children left secondary education in the last five years.

Sample 4

I choose 500 adults from across the country ensuring that I include parents and non-parents. The sample was selected from every county, weighting the numbers so that more people were included from heavily populated areas.

You can see that each of these participants have been selected to reflect different considerations. Sample 1 is concerned with ensuring that geographical areas are represented equally, whereas Sample 2 is concerned with ensuring that the sample is representative of sample size. Both samples are focusing on surveying parents whose children are in secondary education. For Sample 3, the focus is still on parents but this time also including those parents whose children will soon be going to secondary school and others where their children have just left. The last sample is concerned about obtaining the opinions of parents and non-parents whilst ensuring that the sample reflects the size of the population.

Which of the four samples seems to be most representative? The answer will depend on the aim of the research. If you want to gain a cross section of people's views that represents the population, then Sample 4 should be chosen. But if the aim of the research is to understand parents' views of secondary education, then your population of interest is parents and then you must decide what factors are important within that population of interest. For example, is it important to only include those whose children are currently at secondary school?

Key tip 5.6

When reading the Methods section of research papers, check whether the most appropriate sampling method has been chosen given the aim of the research. Also check that the size and characteristics of the sample are appropriate.

Questionable Research Practices (QRPs)

In Chapter 3, we explored the concern that researchers may falsify their data to obtain statistically significant results, because of the publication bias and the pressure to secure research funding. To put this into context, imagine that you have applied and been successful in securing funding from a research council to run a series of experiments. You conduct your first experiment, analyse your data, and see there are no statistical differences. The rest of the experiments you have planned rest on there being differences in this first experiment. You are concerned that this could influence your ability to publish, your ability to secure funding in the future and therefore your promotional prospects. This is when researchers may turn to engaging in research practices that distort their results. These are known as Questionable Research Practices, or QRPs. A recent research integrity survey among academics across all disciplinary fields conducted in the Netherlands found that in the previous three years one in two researchers engaged frequently in at least one QRP (Gopalakrishna et al., 2022).

So what are these QRPs? They may include concealing results that contradict earlier findings, not publishing a study with negative results, hypothesising after the results are known (HARKing) and the stopping technique. They are not research misconduct, but they go against the principles of scientific integrity.

One of the QRPs that you may be able to spot is the stopping technique. An indication that this technique may have been applied is when the findings are only just statistically significant (i.e. just less than 0.05). This is because it could suggest that researchers have been analysing their findings as they go and deciding to stop collecting data when they reach statistical significance. Alternatively, the initial goal may have been to collect 100 participants but when that goal is reached the realisation is that the p value is 0.054

(or thereabouts) so they decide to 'top up' the sample until the probability is less than 5%. This is misleading because natural variation means that an apparent significant effect will appear at some point but if you collect more data again it is likely to disappear. If you have concerns about this technique being applied, you could look to see if the results have been replicated or whether calculations of statistical power have been conducted to determine sample sizes. We also explored in Chapter 3 how researchers can use open science to ensure their analysis plan; data and materials can be checked, so it is also useful to look for this in published work.

APPLYING CRITICAL THINKING WITH EXAMPLES

In this section, we are going to review some examples of critical thinking in psychology to demonstrate the ideas we have been exploring in this chapter. For each example we are going to present a student's response to a psychology essay question and ask you to consider some key questions about their response. This is to help you to critically engage with the response and start to think about how the response could be improved. Following that, we have produced an improved version of the response followed by some questions. We want you to use the questions following the improved version to get you to analyse why the second response is better. By doing so, we hope that you will be able to have a clear framework in your mind of what characteristics are present in a good response so that you can keep that in mind when you are writing.

Example 1

Essay question: 'Consideration of ethics means that experimental methods are of limited use in psychology'. Discuss this claim drawing on examples from psychological research.

Before we look at a student's response to this question, it would be good to break the question down to understand what the question is asking. This question is asking about a consideration of ethics but, importantly, that consideration is framed in the context of experimental methods. Therefore, it is important to not get sidetracked with describing or assessing ethical issues. Instead, the focus should be on the impact of ethics on research that uses the experimental methods. Asking questions such as 'has ethics prevented or changed experimental research?' 'if so, how, why, what is the impact' and 'is it possible to still do experimental research ethically and if so are there some examples?'. This will help to inform a discussion and that this is the key process word in the question. Discuss means to consider the arguments for different ideas and the strengths and weaknesses of evidence supporting them. It is not about asking you for your personal opinion; you need to provide evidence from psychological studies or theories to support your position.

If you have not come across ethical considerations before, then do look at the British Psychological Society (BPS) section on ethics here: bps.org.uk/guideline/code-ethics-and-conduct. The four main principles are related to: respect, competence, responsibility and integrity. There is the ethical code that can be downloaded from that webpage and the code outlines the ethical conduct and behaviour which the BPS expects of its members.

Part of the Student's Response to the Question

As ethics are put in place to both protect participants and the reputation of researchers, certain aspects of experimental methods are no longer viable as if the public perception is that researchers are doing unethical experiments, themselves and their research will no longer be trusted. Therefore, due to this, the research that is able to be conducted in modern day relies on experiments done before the consideration of ethics or getting consent from people who have the desired psychological phenomena naturally occurring or the phenomena is as a result of an incident in their everyday life and not imposed on them for the purpose of the experiment. This also means that there may be some topics that are not able to be researched by experimental methods due to the consideration of ethics. An example of a study that is no longer able to be replicated due to the consideration of ethics is the Stanford prison experiment (Zimbardo et al., 1971). This experiment focused on the effects of social roles on participants, which led to an increase in brutality between them. This was done by initially screening students at Stanford University to gather the most physically and mentally stable individuals and assign them role of prisoner or guard at random to see what would happen over the span of two weeks. The aim of the experiment was to discern if brutality was due to the sadistic personalities of prison guards or down to the prison environment. However due to the mental and physical effects of those assigned the role of prisoner as a result of those assigned guard the experiment was discontinued after six days due to multiple accounts of psychological trauma and abuse inflicted on prisoners by the guards. This is an example of a lab experiment; however, because of the psychological effects an experiment such as this caused to participants is deemed as unethical showing that ethics limits the scope of experimental methods such as a lab experiment lending them limited use.

━━━━━ Think 5.2 ━━━━━

Some key questions to think about here:

- Can you identify and note down the claim, evidence and warrant?
- Are there any qualifiers or rebuttals?
- Is all the information presented above necessary and focused on the question set?
- Could any information be cut and what would the benefit be of cutting out the information?
- Identify elements of a discussion here (this is the command term) – is there enough discussion here?
- How would you improve this paragraph?

We have had a go at improving this student's work using the points they are making but also adding an additional point. Have a read and consider the differences:

Improved Response

Ethical guidelines are there to protect participants and the reputation of researchers, so that the public can trust the research and the researchers. Without that trust, the public would be very reluctant to take part in psychological research and this would mean that research would be very difficult to conduct. However, by having ethical guidelines it can restrict what research can be conducted, especially when using experimental methods as often this means a level of deceit and exposure to certain situations that may go beyond what people would encounter in their everyday life. Previously, before such rigorous guidelines were introduced, it was possible to conduct research that today would not be met with ethical approval. One such study is the Stanford Prison Experiment, a laboratory experiment conducted by Zimbardo et al. (1971). In their study they wanted to investigate how readily people would conform to the roles of guard and prisoner in a role-playing exercise. To do so, they created a mock prison and assigned students at Stanford University to the roles of prisoners and guards. Although the experiment was originally due to run for two weeks it was halted after only 6 days due to multiple accounts of psychological trauma and abuse inflicted on prisoners by the guards. Due to the psychological harm and distress this laboratory experiment, and other studies like this, have the potential to cause, they are no longer permitted to take place. Therefore, this means that direct replications of this experiment and any very similar experiments planned to test the limits of the acceptance or abuse of social roles are not permitted, thereby limiting the scope of our knowledge of how social roles influence our behaviour, suggesting that the lab experiments are of limited use.

However, this does not mean that social roles cannot be explored experimentally using other techniques. For instance, Reicher and Haslam (2006) created a study which used the same basic set-up as Zimbardo but crucially, to reduce ethical concerns, the conditions were better and the researchers were not the prison superintendent as was the case in Zimbardo's study. Furthermore, Reicher and Haslam's study was overseen by clinical psychologists and an independent ethics committee chaired by an MP. Therefore, whilst an exact replication of Zimbardo et al.'s (1971) study has not been possible, it has still been possible to explore the conformity to social roles experimentally within the same prison environment and meeting ethical guidelines.

━━━━━━━━━━ Think 5.3 ━━━━━━━━━━

Some key questions to think about here:

- Can you identify the claim, evidence and warrant?
- Can you identify qualifiers and/or rebuttals?
- Is all the information needed?
- How has the second response improved on the first response?
- How does the above discussion differ to the student's discussion?

Example 2

Essay question: 'The presence of others is the main factor influencing whether we carry out anti-social behaviour'. Discuss this claim referring to psychological research.

This question is asking about how other people can change the way we behave. It is also suggesting that it is the *most important factor* in determining how we behave. So, the focus needs to be on using psychological research to illustrate whether other people's behaviour impacts our behaviour and also whether it is the main factor. More specifically, it is asking about how this influence may have a negative impact on us as it states antisocial behaviour. This is important as we may want to use these key words in our response to directly illustrate the link between other people's behaviour and our antisocial behaviour. We also need to be examining the psychological research carefully to see if it supports this link. As before, the process word is 'discuss' which means to consider the arguments for different ideas and the strengths and weaknesses of evidence supporting them. It is not about asking you for your personal opinion; you need to provide evidence from psychological studies or theories to support your position

Part of the Student's Response to the Question

Television is the biggest impact on children's behaviour as they idolise or copy what they see their favourite characters do. Robertson et al. (2013) conducted a study to investigate whether excessive TV viewing throughout childhood and adolescence is associated with increased antisocial behaviour in early adulthood. There were 1,037 individuals and they assessed hours spent watching television and the rate of criminal convictions and violent convictions and personality disorders between the ages of 5 to 15 years. Findings suggest that young adults who had spent more time watching TV during childhood and adolescence were significantly more likely to commit a crime, be diagnosed with antisocial personality disorder and have more aggressive personality traits compared with those who viewed less television. This was the same in both women and men. Society would say it is entirely in the hands of our parents how we turn out (nurture), and even though it is not fully their fault it is mainly based on the environment we are raised in.

Think 5.4

Some key questions to think about here:

- Can you identify and note down the claim, evidence and warrant?
- Are there any qualifiers or rebuttals?
- Is all the information presented above necessary and focused on the question set?
- Could any information be cut and what would the benefit be of cutting out the information?
- Identify elements of a discussion here (this is the command term) – is there enough discussion here?
- How would you improve this paragraph?

Improved Response

Television has the potential to impact children's behaviour because, as social learning theory has suggested, children can imitate what they see others do, especially if that person is seen as a role model (Bandura, 1977a). A longitudinal study by Robertson et al. (2013) investigated whether excessive television viewing during childhood and adolescence was associated with increased antisocial behaviour in early adulthood. They assessed a birth cohort of 1,037 participants at regular intervals from birth to 26 years. They used regression analysis to explore the associations between the amount of television viewing from ages 5 to 15 years and criminal convictions, violent convictions, diagnosis of antisocial personality and aggressive traits. For both males and females, they found a positive association between hours watching television and likelihood of having a criminal conviction, diagnosis of antisocial personality disorder and more aggressive personality traits. This suggests that increased television viewing is more likely to lead to antisocial characteristics and behaviour. It seems that people do not need to be present for us to be influenced but just watching others over a period of time can have a negative impact.

However, it is important to recognise that the link between excessive television viewing in childhood and adolescence and increased antisocial behaviour in early adulthood is only an association and not causation. We cannot definitively suggest that it was the excessive television viewing that led to the negative behaviour as there was no manipulation of the independent variable (television viewing) and no randomisation to the amount of television watched. There was also no control over other key influences such as parental behaviour. There is strong evidence that children that grow up in antisocial families are more likely to become antisocial thorough poor monitoring, harsh and inconsistent discipline and hostility (e.g. Conger et al., 2003; Thornberry et al., 2003). It may also be the case that antisocial parents are more likely to allow children to watch excessive television that contains violence. Therefore, whilst excessive television may influence our behaviour the more critical, or main, factor is the presence of parents that display aggression and antisocial behaviour.

▬▬▬▬▬▬ Think 5.5 ▬▬▬▬▬▬

Some key questions to think about here:

- Can you identify the claim, evidence and warrant?
- Can you identify qualifiers and/or rebuttals?
- Is all the information needed?
- How has the second response improved on the first response?
- How does the above discussion differ to the student's discussion?

Hopefully, these two examples have helped to illustrate how you can use critical thinking in psychology and demonstrate this skill in your writing.

We hope that exploring these two examples has demonstrated how making small changes to the way an argument is structured and *how* the research is used can have a really positive impact on the quality of the answer. There will be more examples to look at and explore in detail in Chapters 7 and 8.

KEY TAKEAWAYS

The first part of this chapter was concerned with exploring what is critical thinking by looking at critical thinking in our everyday lives and then applying that to critical thinking in academia. Critical thinking can be scary with many students believing it is beyond their capability and so avoid it, preferring to stick to description. Therefore, the next section was designed to show why critical thinking is important and how it can be achieved.

We then explored how developing critical reading skills allows you to recognise spurious and/or illogical reasoning which in turn helps you to develop your own critical writing. This is because learning to review work with a critical eye means that you will apply that same critical eye to your own writing, making your writing stronger and more convincing.

We then explored what makes an argument and how to recognise and evaluate an argument. We did this by using a framework in which to dissect the argument through some clear and helpful steps. The questions presented acted as prompts to harness a critical mindset and help to tease out some of the potential issues with the argument presented. This was followed by a discussion of common fallacies that can be found in people's writing such as slippery slope and false dilemmas. We ended this section by exploring how to evaluate an argument, with emphasis on how evidence is used to support an argument.

The next section was concerned with exploring critical thinking in psychology by applying critical thinking to the four core perspectives you were introduced to in Chapter 2, followed by an exploration of critical thinking in research methods and statistics. This enabled you to see how you can use critical thinking skills within psychology. The last section reviewed some examples of critical evaluation that had been written by students in response to psychology essay questions. Here we explored evidence of their critical thinking, relating back to the concepts introduced in the chapter. We then explored how their responses could have been improved.

6

GUIDANCE ON READING PSYCHOLOGICAL RESEARCH

Key goals for this chapter

- Understand how to read and take notes from the method section of a research report.
- Understand how to read and take notes from the results section of a research report.

WHY DO I NEED TO READ PRIMARY SOURCES?

You are over halfway through this book now and we have spent a lot of time explaining the importance of research in the field of psychology. In Chapter 1, we explored the difference between an opinion and a claim and the need to have claims which are evidence based. This involved briefly covering the most common ways of designing and conducting research in psychology. As you learnt in the previous chapter, critical thinking is crucial in psychology and one area where you can apply critical thinking is to the methodology and design utilised in research. In Chapter 3, you were introduced to how researchers disseminate their findings, whilst you will be familiar with reading research findings from textbooks and in lectures. In Chapter 4, you learnt how you could access the original write up (or report) of research. The benefit of reading the full report is that you gain a lot more detail on the way the study was conducted and how the data was analysed. This in turn allows you to engage with a more sophisticated critical analysis of the research. The purpose of this chapter is to provide you with some guidance, and a framework to assist you in reading full research reports.

When you begin reading a full research report it can be quite daunting. Firstly, they can be quite long, particularly in comparison to the concise summaries of research you will be familiar with from lectures and textbooks. Secondly, they can include a lot of terminology. The more you read research papers the more familiar you will become with some of this terminology, but initially it can be overwhelming. It can be tempting when you are new to studying psychology to try and avoid reading a full paper, relying only on the abstract. Whilst in some cases the abstract is sufficient for your needs, there will be times where you will need to engage at a deeper level with the research.

You may be wondering why you need to engage at a deeper level, after all the most important part of research is the findings and these can be found in the abstract. Why go to the effort to read research at a deeper level? Chapter 5 explored critical thinking and it is integral to apply this skill to psychological research. Reading the abstract does not allow you to do this, as you do not have enough detail on how the study was conducted. In Chapter 3, you were introduced to the peer review process. This is crucial in helping to ensure that research published is of a high quality; however, you also learnt that some research in psychology fails to replicate which suggests there may be some issues around the method-ology and/or analysis of the research. To be able to apply the conclusions of research appropriately, we need to understand the limitations of the research.

We hope to make the transition from reading summaries of research to reading full research papers a little less daunting by providing you with some tools to support you with your reading. We will also demonstrate some examples in this chapter of how to apply these tools we have given you.

───────── Think 6.1 ─────────

To understand the importance of applying your newly learnt critical thinking skills to research, go to Ted.com and search for a talk by Ben Goldacre titled *Battling bad science* (Ben Goldacre: Battling bad science | TED Talk).

As you watch the talk, reflect on the following questions:

- Why do we need to be careful when relying on news reporting of research findings?
- Why do we need to think carefully about who has funded the research?
- In what ways might research findings be manipulated?

Whilst we need to keep these points in mind, that is not to say that research should not be trusted. Indeed, this is one of the reasons that open sciences (which you were introduced to in Chapter 3) are gaining momentum: to reduce the likelihood of bias influencing the research process.

How to Read Research Papers

There is no 'set' or 'right' way to read research papers, but what we aim to do in this chapter is to provide you with some guidance to support you in reading research papers. The more you read, the more familiar you will become with this task, and you will gradually develop your own approach to reading research. However, as you begin you are likely to find it useful to have a framework to follow to support you in identifying key information. Of course, the key information will vary depending on the reason you are reading the research. We aim to give you a generic framework that you can tailor to your needs.

A Framework for Reading Research

The 'framework' mentioned previously is essentially a checklist of information that you can summarise as you work through the research paper. You will recall from Chapter 3, that a research paper follows a set format comprising of the title, abstract, introduction, method, results, discussion and references. All these sections are important when reading research; however, our checklist focuses on the method and results. This is because it is these two sections that are integral for considering the quality of the research, which in turn allows you to interpret the discussion with a clear understanding of the potential shortcomings of the conclusions. You will need to read both the introduction and discussion (and you may make your own checklist for reading these as you progress in your studies) but having a strong grasp of the method and results will make it easier for you to read and understand both the introduction and discussion. It is important to note that the checklist we have provided you with is not meant to be exhaustive and you may find you need to make additional notes depending on the research you are reading.

━━━━━ Stop 6.1 ━━━━━

It is important to engage with a research paper as you read it and not simply skim over the information.

Checklist for Reading Research

Here we include the checklist that we recommend you use when reading a research paper. Some of the points in the checklist refer specifically to quantitative or qualitative research, and thus not all points will be relevant to all research papers that you read. Ideally you will need to have an electronic version of this, which you can amend to suit the paper you are reading. Note how the checklist starts with the title of the paper and the reference. This is important, to allow you to find the paper again should you need to refer back to it and to ensure you are citing research properly in your work; more on this in Chapter 9.

Table 6.1 A checklist to apply when reading the method section of a report

	Method section	Why is this information necessary?

Participants	• How were participants recruited? Is there a potential for bias in how participants were recruited?
	• If quantitative data has been gathered:
	  - Was a power analysis conducted to determine the sample size?
	  - Is the target population clearly identified?
	  - Is the sample representative of the target population?
	  - Are demographic details of the sample reported?
	  - Are inclusion and exclusion criteria clearly stated?
	• If qualitative data has been gathered:
	  - Is detail provided on the participant/s and their life circumstances?
		Studies which take a nomothetic approach seek to make generalisations about their findings. This requires a representative sample, if the sample is biased in any way it reduces the external validity of the sample.
		
		Studies which take an idiographic approach require us to understand more about the sample, as the unique experience of the participant/s is important to be able to contextualise the findings.

Design	• Does the design of the study address the aims and hypotheses/research question (as identified in the introduction)?
	• Quantitative – If an experiment has been conducted:
	  - Does the operationalisation of the independent variable (IV) and dependent variable (DV) adequately address the variables of interest?
	  - How well do the IV and DV reflect the concepts in everyday settings?
	  - Is there a control group? Do the experimental groups offer a
		If the design of the study does not accurately test the hypothesis/research questions, this is a major issue as the study is not telling us what we are asking.
		
		In an experiment, we must decide how we are going to represent the IV and DV we are interested in. There are many ways to do this, and some ways better reflect the variables of interest than others. If the way the variables are operationalised does not reflect the variables of interest very well, it limits external validity.

Table 6.1 A checklist to apply when reading the method section of a report *(Continued)*

Method section	Why is this information necessary?
suitable comparison to each other? - What controls are put in place? - Were participants randomly allocated to conditions? - Was a double- or single-blind procedure followed? • If an observation was conducted (which can give quantitative or qualitative data): - Was the analysis checked by another rater for inter-rater reliability? • If a qualitative study was conducted: - Were a range of data collection methods used to allow for triangulation? - Is there detailed justification of the choice of methods used?	We cannot draw firm causal conclusions without a control group to compare to. Random allocation is important in an experiment to reduce any potential bias that the participants bring to the condition they participate in. As you learnt in Chapter 5, double- and single-blind procedures reduce the likelihood of bias occurring during the study. Observations are versatile, as it is how you analyse the behaviour viewed that determines whether it is qualitative or quantitative. Regardless, either way there is the potential for subjectivity in the interpretation of the data. For this reason, it is good practice to have another researcher check a sample to see if they are interpreting the behaviour in the same way. Due to the potential for subjectivity when analysing qualitative data, it is important to collect data via a variety of measures to allow us to see if similar conclusions can be drawn across all measures. There are no 'rights' and 'wrongs' when designing qualitative research. But, as the researcher's own perspective and beliefs can influence the design of the study, it is important to understand the justification for the decisions made.
Materials	• Quantitative – If an experiment has been conducted: - Do the materials adequately measure the DV/s? • Quantitative – If self-report measures are used: - Are they based on previously validated scales? - Are they assessed for reliability? • If a qualitative study was conducted: - Were detailed notes kept of the content, e.g. diary records, interview transcript?	It is important to reflect on the way the variables have been measured and if they are measured in a way that reflects the concept we are interested in. Self-report measures are prone to response bias from participants. There can also be issues with the questions that are asked and how they are worded. Using previously validated scales helps to ensure that the measures are as robust as possible. Key to qualitative data is depth and keeping this detail requires extensive

(Continued)

Table 6.1 A checklist to apply when reading the method section of a report *(Continued)*

	Method section	**Why is this information necessary?**
	- Is there sufficient detail on how data was collected? - Is the reader provided with the questions that were asked in the interview/focus group?	notes. Without these, the researcher may impose bias on the data before the analysis stage is reached. It is also important to know what questions were asked (if applicable), as this allows us to put any quotes/themes into context.
Procedure	• Is there sufficient detail that another researcher could carry out the same procedure? • If quantitative data is gathered: - If applicable, was the study conducted for a long enough period of time to be meaningful? - If testing a treatment/intervention, was there a follow up to measure the long-term effects? - Are the stages of the procedure standardised across participants?	As you learnt in Chapter 3, it is important to be able to replicate research – thus a detailed procedure is necessary. A detailed procedure also allows us to understand exactly what happened and to think about any potential issues with the way the study was conducted that may have influenced the results in some way.

You will notice the previous table was for the method section; whilst we have separated the checklist for the results section, you would want to apply both checklists to a research paper.

Table 6.2 A checklist to apply when reading the results section of a report

	Results section	**Why is this information necessary?**
General points	• Does the analysis address the hypothesis/research question?	The first point is relatively self-explanatory. Each piece of research has a specific focus; it is this we need to be testing in the results section. The focus throughout the report should be on the hypothesis/research question identified in the introduction.
Statistical analysis	• Has data cleaning been explained? E.g. outliers, non-normal distributions, missing values. • Have the statistical tests been described? Are they appropriate for the type of data gathered? • Has the data been checked to ensure it meets the assumptions for the statistical test being conducted? • Are potential confounding variables considered in the analysis? • Has an appropriate significance level been used?	Numerical data is usually not ready to be analysed as it is. It requires some preliminary 'cleaning'. It is important this is explained, as decisions made at this point can influence the results that are produced from the subsequent statistical tests. There are multiple ways to analyse both quantitative and qualitative data. Some ways are only suited to certain types of data and certain research questions. If an appropriate way to analyse data has not been used, any conclusions drawn are unlikely to be meaningful. The data gathered also influences which test can be used, as does the preliminary analysis, e.g. data usually needs to be checked to see, if it is normally distributed.

Table 6.2 A checklist to apply when reading the results section of a report *(Continued)*

Results section		Why is this information necessary?
		If data is not normally distributed, certain tests cannot be conducted. Researchers need to report this so that we can be certain the appropriate statistical tests have been conducted.
		Many statistical tests allow you to include 'covariates' in the analysis. These are additional variables that may affect the DV. If they are included in the analysis and the IV is still impacting the DV, we can be more confident that a causal relationship is present.
		The minimum acceptable significance level is usually 0.05, if a more stringent significant level is used that is not an issue (and is in fact even better). However, if a more lenient significant level is used, e.g. 0.10 we may find false positives; known as a Type I error.

Qualitative analysis	• Does the author identify their own stance, experiences and beliefs on the topic?
	• Are examples from the data included, e.g. quotes?
	• Does the analysis consider how the context that the research was conducted in may influence the data?
	• Is the credibility of the interpretation of the data checked, e.g.
	  - Asking participants to check the interpretations.
	  - Using triangulation of different data collection methods.
	  - Having a sample of the data double checked by another trained researcher.
	• Is the researcher open to alternative interpretations of the data?
		The nature of qualitative data means that different researchers can interpret the same information in different ways. Researchers are human and their own beliefs can influence their interpretations; this is why it is important that the researcher is transparent as to what these beliefs are.
		
		To be able to understand how the researcher came to their interpretation, we need examples/evidence from the data. Without another researcher double checking the data interpretation, we cannot determine how logical the interpretations are.
		
		Carrying out checks on the data reduces the potential for bias in the analysis. As does being open to alternatives, it shows the researchers are not led by any preconceived assumptions.

EXAMPLE: READING THE METHOD SECTION

Now that you have been introduced to the checklist, it would be beneficial to practise applying this checklist with an example before you start applying it to your own research.

An Example with Quantitative Research

We will start by looking at a method section in a quantitative paper and then repeat this task for a qualitative paper.

━━━━━━━ Think 6.2 ━━━━━━━

The quantitative paper we are going to apply the checklist to for the method section is:

Van der Zanden, T., Schouten, A. P., Mos, M. B. J., & Krahmer, E. J. (2020). Impression formation on online dating sites: Effects of language errors in profile texts on perceptions of profile owners' attractiveness. *Journal of Social and Personal Relationships, 37*(3), 758–778. https://doi.org/10.1177/0265407519878787

Before we look at the method section together, you need to use the reference above to locate this paper (either through your university library or Google Scholar). Once you have downloaded the paper, you should do the following:

- Read the abstract to gain a general understanding of the study.
- There are two experiments in this publication; we will focus on the first study. In the introduction section read the paragraph which starts '*The goal of the first study...*'. It is the fifth paragraph in the introduction.
- Read the two hypotheses for Study 1, labelled H1 and H2 in the Introduction.
- Read the method section for Study 1.

Having engaged in the previous task, you should understand what Study 1 was seeking to test and how the first experiment was designed to achieve this. We will now apply each of the relevant criteria in our checklist to this study.

Note at the beginning of the method section, the researchers state that they pre-registered their study as part of open science. This ensures that the researchers follow their original plans and do not amend them during the process (this is a positive).

Table 6.3 Applying the checklist for the method to a quantitative research paper

	Method section	Application to Van der Zanden et al. (2020)
Participants	• How were participants recruited? Is there a potential for bias in how participants were recruited?	Volunteer sampling was used to find participants which may mean we end up with a biased sample. Those who did not respond to the email from Parship about participation may have different characteristics than those who did.

	• If quantitative data has been gathered:
	  - Was a power analysis conducted to determine the sample size?
	  - Is the target population clearly identified?
		There is no reference to a power analysis being conducted.
		
		The population of interest are users of a dating site (Parship) in the Netherlands.
		
		Recruited participants were those who were already signed up to the dating site. The benefits of this are

Table 6.3 Applying the checklist for the method to a quantitative research paper *(Continued)*

Method section	Application to Van der Zanden et al. (2020)
- Is the sample representative of the target population? - Are demographic details of the sample reported? - Are inclusion and exclusion criteria clearly stated?	that it means the data gathered is likely to be truer to users of dating sites, which is integral to the hypotheses. The paper includes the gender and education of the sample; there is reference to the sample being mostly older adults, but we are not given precise details on the spread of age in the sample. The paper states the inclusion criteria as anyone registered on the dating website over the age of 18 and excludes anyone who is bisexual or does not disclose their sexuality. Anyone who did not fully complete the experiment was also excluded. The hypothesis refers to dating sites generally, but the study has not included bisexual users. Additionally, the sample is restricted to one country and one dating site. Characteristics of individuals are likely to influence which dating site they choose to use, which may create a bias in the sample. There may also be cultural differences around the importance of language errors on dating profiles.

Design
 	
• Does the design of the study address the aims and hypotheses/research question (as identified in the introduction)?
• If an experiment has been conducted:
  - Does the operationalisation of the IV and DV adequately address the variables of interest?
  - How well do the IV and DV reflect the concepts in everyday settings?
  - Is there a control group? Do the experimental groups offer a suitable comparison to each other?
  - What controls are put in place?
  - Were participants randomly allocated to conditions?
	There are two hypotheses the first predicts that when there are language errors on a profile, it will be rated lower for attractiveness and dating intention than profiles without language errors. The second specifies that this effect will be stronger when the profile includes a blurred picture than a visible picture.
	
	The design states a 2×2 design was used, which means there were two IVs each with two levels/conditions.
	
	IV 1: language errors or no language errors.
	
	IV 2: visible or blurred profile picture.
	
	These two IVs clearly address both hypotheses.
	
	When present, there were ten language errors. The researchers state that this number is consistent with the number of errors seen in a previous analysis of real dating profiles. The text used was also amended from real profiles, thus reflecting language errors in the real world.
	
	In the participants section, the researchers state that on the Parship dating site the photos are kept blurred until a mutual match occurs. Thus, the blurring of the photos also reflects this concept in the real world.
	
	The DV is explained in more detail in the 'measures' section. Based on the hypotheses we would expect the DV to measure perceived attractiveness and dating intention. As stated in the 'measures' section, the study did measure perceived attractiveness across three dimensions and

(Continued)

Table 6.3 Applying the checklist for the method to a quantitative research paper *(Continued)*

Method section	Application to Van der Zanden et al. (2020)
	measured dating intention. Whilst in real life the dating website would not directly ask these questions, it is likely that these are questions that users ask themselves when viewing profiles, so to some extent it does reflect real use of dating sites.
	Whilst there are two levels to each IV, strictly speaking there is no control group where nothing is manipulated. For the visible and blurred image ideally, we would want a condition where there was no image. For the language error and no language error, we would probably want a condition where no language was used. However, by adding the two control groups in this manner, it does move away a little from a realistic dating profile where both would be present.
	As one of the DVs is perceived attractiveness, it is important that the images are of people of average attractiveness. Otherwise, it is unlikely the language errors will have an effect. The researchers controlled this through a pre-test with 10 images of each sex. In doing so, this allowed them to select the two most averagely rated photos for each sex. A further control was in the content of the text; too extreme interests may influence perceived attractiveness regardless of language errors. As control for this, the researchers selected neutral text and kept the same text for both sexes. Due to the study being conducted online, researchers could not control for the testing environment. But this is also realistic to how dating profiles are ordinarily viewed (rather than in a laboratory), which retains some external validity.
	As a between-participants variable, the design states that participants were randomly allocated to whether they viewed a blurred or visible picture. The language errors were a within-participants variable, which means all participants saw a profile with and without language errors; however, it was randomised as to which profile they viewed first. This reduces any effects of the order that participants view the stimuli.
Materials	• If an experiment has been conducted: - Do the materials adequately measure the DV/s? • If self-report measures are used: - Are they based on previously validated scales? - Are they assessed for reliability?	The DV is measured via self-report. As we want to know whether participants perceive the person as attractive and whether they intend to date them, we can only find this out by asking participants. Participants recorded their responses on a Likert scale, which gives us more detail than simply asking yes or no. However, it does not allow participants to elaborate on what about the profile they may have found attractive (or not) and why they gave the rating that they did. Thus, we may know a rating of 4 was given but we are making assumptions as to the reason why.

Table 6.3 Applying the checklist for the method to a quantitative research paper *(Continued)*

Method section		Application to Van der Zanden et al. (2020)
		Most of the questions are taken from previous research, but it is not stated whether these have been previously validated or not. We could maybe find this out by reading the two papers that are cited.
		The authors report on Cronbach's alpha, which is a measure of internal consistency, i.e. reliability. It is measured between 0 and 1, the closer to 1 the higher the internal reliability. Thus, these measures do have internal reliability which is a positive.

Procedure	• Is there sufficient detail that another researcher could carry out the same procedure?
	• If quantitative data is gathered:
	  - If applicable, was the study conducted for a long enough period of time to be meaningful?
	  - If testing a treatment/ intervention, was there a follow up to measure the long-term effects?
	  - Are the stages of the procedure standardised across participants?
		The procedure is relatively brief, as a short online study, we do not need details of the setup. We are given detail on how the characteristics of the IV were chosen and the randomisation that occurred in the procedure. There is enough detail to allow for replication, particularly as on the Open Science Framework the materials have all been included. This means, we could replicate with the exact same materials.

An Example with Qualitative Research

We will now apply the checklist for the method section again, but this time with a piece of research which has taken a qualitative approach.

━━━━━━━━━ Think 6.3 ━━━━━━━━━

The qualitative paper we are going to apply the checklist to for the method section is:

Adamczyk, K., Janowicz, K., & Mrozowicz-Wrońska, M. (2022). Never-married single adults' experiences with online dating websites and mobile applications: A qualitative content analysis. *New Media & Society*, 1–24. https://doi.org/10.1177/14614448221097894

Before we look at the method section together, you need to use the reference above to locate this paper (either through your university library or Google Scholar). Once you have downloaded the paper, you should do the following:

• Read the abstract to gain a general understanding of the study.
• Read the paragraph which starts '*Recognizing the above-indicated gaps in the literature...*'. It is the ninth paragraph in the introduction. This will give you an

(Continued)

understanding of what it is the researchers were testing. Note the difference here to the quantitative paper which had fixed hypotheses.

- Read the following paragraph in the introduction which starts '*Finally, because traditional and online romantic...*' to understand the social context of the participants.
- Read the method section.

Table 6.4 Applying the checklist for the method to a qualitative research paper

	Method section	Application to Adamcyzk, Janowicz and Mrozowicz-Wrońska (2022)
Participants	• How were participants recruited? Is there a potential for bias in how participants were recruited? • If qualitative data has been gathered: - Is detail provided on the participant/s and their life circumstances?	We are told that participants were recruited via adverts on Facebook. There is the potential for bias in this recruitment method, as not all single, not married and childless people will use Facebook. Even those that do, not all will respond to the advert. It may be a certain type of single, never married, childless person who responds to an advert on social media. Whilst this is a qualitative study, it is not a detailed focus on one or two people thus we cannot expect in depth detail on the participants and their life circumstances. We are however given specific details on each individual participant in the table, including their gender, age and length of time being single, their desire to have a romantic partner and whether they currently use online dating services. In the text, we are also told each participant's sexuality. We are also referred to supplementary material which includes further detail on each participant including the type of place they live, educational attainment, employment and living arrangements. This gives us some context on everyone which might be useful in the results section when the interviews are analysed. Indeed, if you look to the results section, you will notice that next to the quotes included it states which participant the quote comes from. Thus, it is useful to have some context on each participant as this may help to understand the context of the quotes included. Note as well, that we are also given detail on the relevant cultural norms in Poland around relationships in the introduction section.
Design	• Does the design of the study address the aims and hypotheses/research question (as identified in the introduction)?	The introduction states that the research question is *How do never-married, single individuals experience dating services?* The introduction also states than a flexible approach was taken and that the research question was decided upon *after*

Table 6.4 Applying the checklist for the method to a qualitative research paper *(Continued)*

Method section	Application to Adamcyzk, Janowicz and Mrozowicz-Wrońska (2022)

• If a qualitative study was conducted:
  - Were a range of data collection methods used to allow for triangulation?
  - Is there detailed justification of the choice of methods used?
	completion of the interviews. We are told an interview took place with one key question which was focused on the experience of being single. This does directly address the question of interest; remember there is no mention of dating services in the question as this was decided in light of responses.
	
	There is very little detail on the interview procedure, however we are referred to the online supplementary file which covers in detail the interview procedure and lists the 12 questions asked.
	
	The study does not use triangulation and only utilises the interview to collect the data. We would need to keep this in mind when looking at the conclusions drawn from the interviews. In the supplementary materials, the authors note that triangulation occurred in the analysis as more than one researcher was involved in identifying themes.
	
	Another point that might be worth noting is that the interview was also conducted virtually rather than in person, which may influence how participants respond and the extent to which they open up. Given that dating is a personal and sensitive issue, it is important participants feel relaxed enough to be honest. For some, this may occur online whilst for others a face-to-face interview may help to build a rapport which allows the participant to speak more honestly about their personal dating experience.

Materials • If a qualitative study was conducted:
  - Were detailed notes kept of the content, e.g. diary records, interview transcript?
  - Is there sufficient detail on how data was collected?
  - Is the reader provided with the questions that were asked in the interview/focus group?
	We are told that the interviews were recorded and transcribed verbatim. As stated previously, the supplementary materials included sufficient detail on how the data was collected.

Procedure • Is there sufficient detail that another researcher could carry out the same procedure?	As the interview questions were provided we could, in theory, replicate the interview. However, as it is a semi-structured interview a direct replication would not be possible as some questions will occur in response to the participants' answers.

━━━━━━━━ Stop 6.2 ━━━━━━━━

It is important to not only take notes when reading a method section, but to also *think* critically about the way the study was conducted.

EXAMPLE: READING THE RESULTS SECTION

Now that you have practised applying the checklist to a method section in both a quantitative and qualitative paper, it would be beneficial to practise applying this checklist to a results section for each approach to research.

An Example with Quantitative Research

As before, we will start by looking at a results section in a quantitative paper and then repeat this task for a qualitative paper.

━━━━━━━━ Think 6.4 ━━━━━━━━

The quantitative paper we are going to apply the checklist to for the results section is:

Overdorf, V, Kollia, B, Makarec, K, Alleva Szeles, C. (2016). The relationship between physical activity and depressive symptoms in healthy older women. *Gerontology and Geriatric Medicine*, 2, 2333721415626859. https://doi.org/10.1177/2333721415626859

Before we look at the results section together, you need to use the reference above to locate this paper (either through your university library or Google Scholar). Once you have downloaded the paper, you should do the following:

- Read the abstract to gain a general understanding of the study.
- Identify the three hypotheses that this study sought to address.
- Read the method section of experiment 1, as this is the experiment we will focus on.
- Read the results section of experiment 1.

Table 6.5 Applying the results checklist to a quantitative research paper

	Results section	Application to Overdorf et al. (2016) – experiment 1
General points	• Does the analysis address the hypothesis/ research question?	The research tests two hypotheses in experiment 1, these were 1) that higher intensity physical exercise would be positively related to lower depressive symptoms and 2) that group exercise would have a greater benefit than individual exercise.
		Table 1 addresses both hypotheses and provides the means and standard deviations for all three levels of

Table 6.5 Applying the results checklist to a quantitative research paper *(Continued)*

Results section	Application to Overdorf et al. (2016) – experiment 1
	physical exercise intensity and both group and individual exercise, as well as depressive symptoms (BDI).
	The first hypothesis is tested via a regression between minutes of activity levels per week and score on the BDI. This peripherally tests the hypothesis but does not focus on each level of intensity, which is part of the hypotheses. Instead, the focus is on amount of exercise and depression, and amount is not equivalent to how intense the exercise was. This preliminary test allows the researchers to see if there is an association before focusing on the different levels of the physical exercise intensity.
	The next analysis in Table 2 addresses the first hypothesis more specifically via Spearman's Rho correlations. Specifically, the first row addresses hypothesis 1 by looking at the relationship between each level of exercise intensity and depressive symptoms.
	The second hypothesis is less clear than the first, as it states a *'greater benefit'* but is not explicit in telling the reader as to what the benefit is in. We can assume depressive symptoms based on the research questions in the introduction. This hypothesis was assessed in the correlation in Table 2 in the paper and using a *t*-test (Table 3 in the paper). However, the t-test compares *the amount of time spent exercising* across exercise intensity in both group and individual exercise. This does not assess depressive symptoms, which is what is stated in the research question. It is not clear why this additional analysis has been carried out and the relevance of it to the hypothesis.
Statistical analysis	<ul><li>Has data cleaning been explained? E.g., outliers, non-normal distributions, missing values,</li><li>Have the statistical tests been described? Are they appropriate for the type of data gathered?</li><li>Has the data been checked to ensure it meets the assumptions for the statistical test being conducted?</li><li>Are potential confounding variables considered in the analysis?</li></ul>	We are not given detail on any data cleaning that took place, but we are told that participants with missing data were excluded from the analysis and that participants who were taking antidepressants were removed from the analysis. We need to look at the type of data gathered to decide if appropriate analysis has been conducted. The IV in this study, intensity of physical exercise and group or lone exercise, were measured using the number of minutes spent in each type of exercise (either alone or in a group), giving continuous data. The DV, depressive symptoms, was measured via an inventory giving continuous data. The **regression analysis** is used with continuous data, thus appropriate for this data. The authors also state that the data underwent tests to check it met the assumptions necessary to conduct this analysis. A **Spearman's Rho** test is usually applied to ordinal data or continuous data that does not meet the assumptions for a parametric correlation. However, the researchers do not explain why a Spearman's Rho test was selected over Pearson's R as they already state the data met the requirements for a parametric test.

(Continued)

Table 6.5 Applying the results checklist to a quantitative research paper *(Continued)*

Results section	Application to Overdorf et al. (2016) – experiment 1
• Has an appropriate significance level been used?	A **t-test** is suitable for this data as different groups are being compared and the DV is continuous. We are not told the data is assessed to check it meets the assumptions for a t-test. In addition, multiple t-tests were conducted and the rationale for this has not been explained. Generally, the more tests you conduct the likelihood of a Type I error occurs. There are alternative tests, such as an ANOVA, which can assess multiple IVs and multiple levels which may have been more suitable.
	Potential confounding variables (covariates) have not been included in the analysis, which means we cannot rule out that other variables may be also playing a role.
	An appropriate significance level of 0.05 has been selected.

An Example with Qualitative Data

We will now apply the checklist for the results section again, but this time with a piece of research which has taken a qualitative approach.

━━━━━━ Think 6.5 ━━━━━━

The qualitative paper we are going to apply our results checklist to is:

Douglas, S., Stott, J., Spector, A., Brede, J., Hanratty, É., Charlesworth, G., ... Aguirre, E. (2022). Mindfulness-based cognitive therapy for depression in people with dementia: A qualitative study on participant, carer and facilitator experiences. *Dementia*, 21(2), 457–476. https://doi.org/10.1177/14713012211046150

Before we look at the results section together, you need to use the reference above to locate this paper (either through your university library or Google Scholar). Once you have downloaded the paper, you should do the following:

• Read the abstract to gain a general understanding of the study.
• Identify the five research questions that this study sought to address.
• Read the method section.
• Read the results section.

Table 6.6 Applying the results checklist to a qualitative paper

	Results section	Application to Douglas et al. (2022)
General points	• Does the analysis address the hypothesis/ research question?	We are told in the introduction that the study is exploring the perspectives of people with dementia, carers and facilitators on a **mindfulness-based cognitive therapy** (MBCT) course for depression in

Table 6.6 Applying the results checklist to a qualitative paper *(Continued)*

Results section	Application to Douglas et al. (2022)
	dementia. Specifically, there were five areas addressed:
	- How do the people with depression in dementia experience the MBCT course?
	- Which aspects of the MBCT course are perceived as useful.
	- How do the individuals with depression in dementia, the carers and facilitators perceive the effects of the MBCT course?
	- How do carers support home practice?
	- What changes are required to make MBCT suitable for individuals with depression in dementia?
	The analysis is a thematic analysis, which allows the researcher to identify themes in the data which relate to each of these five areas.
	The themes identified were:
	1 The experience of the MBCT programme and components within it.
	2 Outcomes experienced as a result of the course.
	3 Influences on the participants' engagement.
	4 Adaptations that were either used or suggested.
	It is not clear where carers supporting home practice would fit, but reading the analysis in more detail may help to explain this. Which it does, within the second theme. Therefore, the analysis does address the research questions.

Qualitative analysis	• Does the author identify their own stance, experiences and beliefs on the topic?
	• Are examples from the data included, e.g. quotes?
	• Does the analysis consider how the context that the research was conducted in may influence the data?
	• Is the credibility of the interpretation of the data checked, e.g.
	  - Asking participants to check the interpretations.
	  - Using triangulation of different data collection methods.
	  - Having a sample of the data double
		We are not told anything about the researcher who conducted the analysis; therefore we cannot consider how and if their own experiences and beliefs may have influenced the themes identified. Reflexivity is crucial in qualitative research; it involves acknowledging your role (and potential influence) on the research process. This influence can come from the researcher's assumptions, beliefs and prior experiences. All of which can influence how they may ask questions, the direction the research takes and the interpretation of the data.
		
		Each theme is broken down into several subsections and each of those is supported by direct quotes from the participants, carers or facilitators.
		
		The report identifies where the interviews were conducted and some detail on the MCBT, but it does not consider how the context may have influenced the data.
		
		One researcher analysed the data, but it is stated that another researcher analysed a sample of the data and compared the themes found. Changes were made based on differences in the themes
		(Continued)

Table 6.6 Applying the results checklist to a qualitative paper *(Continued)*

Results section	Application to Douglas et al. (2022)
checked by another trained researcher. • Is the researcher open to alternative interpretations of the data?	identified. This helps to control for some subjectivity in the themes. Whilst alternative interpretations/themes are not considered, in the discussion the researchers do identify that the small sample size has a potential issue with generating enough evidence for the themes.

━━━ Key tip 6.1 ━━━

Every research paper is different; therefore you cannot recreate the examples included in this chapter. However, the more you practise applying the checklist, the more familiar you will become with reading research.

─── Explore further ───

To further develop your skills in reading psychological research, you will be given some references that you can follow up and apply the checklist to. You can decide how many of the research papers you read, but regardless of how many you choose, apply the checklist to both the method and results section.

Bleske-Rechek, A., Gunseor, M. M., & Nguyen, K. (2023). I 'knew' they wouldn't last: Hindsight Bias in judgements of a dating couple. *Social Psychological Bulletin*, *18*, 1–22. https://doi.org/10.32872/spb.9967

Flint, S. W., & Reale, S. (2018). Weight stigma in frequent exercisers: Overt, demeaning and condescending. *Journal of Health Psychology*, *23*(5), 710–719. https://doi.org/10.1177/1359105316656232

Jessica, K., & Lee, A. J. (2023). Assortative preferences for personality and online dating apps: Individuals prefer profiles similar to themselves on agreeableness, openness, and extraversion. *Personality and Individual Differences*, *208*, 112185. https://doi.org/10.1016/j.paid.2023.112185

Mills, L., Lee, J. C., Boakes, R., & Colagiuri, B. (2023). Reduction in caffeine withdrawal after open-label decaffeinated coffee. *Journal of Psychopharmacology*, 02698811221147152. https://doi.org/10.1016/j.paid.2023.112185

Thompson, L., Pennay, A., Zimmermann, A., Cox, M., & Lubman, D. I. (2014). 'Clozapine makes me quite drowsy, so when I wake up in the morning those first cups of coffee are really handy': An exploratory qualitative study of excessive caffeine consumption among individuals with schizophrenia. *BMC psychiatry*, *14*, 1–10. https://doi.org/10.1186/1471-244X-14-116

Vandeweerd, C., Myers, J., Coulter, M., Yalcin, A., & Corvin, J. (2016). Positives and negatives of online dating according to women 50+. *Journal of Women & Ageing*, *28*(3), 259–270. https://doi.org/10.1080/08952841.2015.1137435

KEY TAKEAWAYS

This chapter and the previous chapter have focused on critical thinking, both its importance and how to read with a critical eye. To assist you with the reading, this chapter has guided you on how to approach reading a research paper. As a student who is new to studying psychology reading full research reports can be daunting and rightly so. There is a lot of information to read and digest and you may not be familiar with a lot of the terms that you come across.

By providing you with a checklist that you can apply to any research paper, you now have a framework to help to guide your reading. This should help to make the task of reading research papers a little more manageable and to guide you in where you can apply critical thinking.

Throughout this chapter we worked through examples of this checklist applied to four different research papers, both quantitative and qualitative. We hope that this has given you some self-confidence in your ability to read research.

Please be assured that the more you read research papers the more you will become familiar with the terminology to use and what to expect.

As the focus of this book is to support you in using psychological research effectively in your academic writing, being able to read, interpret and think critically about relevant studies is crucial to this process. The following two chapters build on the skills from this chapter and Chapter 5 bringing these skills together to develop your academic writing. Specifically, we will look at how to utilise our critical reading to make effective use of research in our writing.

7

HOW TO USE PSYCHOLOGICAL RESEARCH IN AN ESSAY

──────── Key goals for this chapter ────────

- Recognise the importance of using research in essays.
- Identify and understand the purpose and structure of essays.
- Understand how to use research in essays.
- Understand how to use research for critical evaluation in essays.
- Understand why it is important to write in your own words.
- Know how to write in your own words using paraphrasing.

DO I NEED TO INCLUDE RESEARCH IN MY ESSAYS?

Students often ask about whether they need to include research in their essays and how much to include. It is important to state here that including research evidence in an essay is critical. Without evidence then you are simply making a series of unsubstantiated statements. It is a bit like a barrister prosecuting a case and deciding to describe why the accused is guilty of murder, but providing no evidence at all. If you were on the jury, you would be screaming in your head 'where is the evidence?' which is what your reader will be screaming if you present an essay with no research. As we have mentioned throughout this book, research evidence is key. It is not an extra or something to tack on to your essay; it is the crux of your essay.

Students sometimes think that theories and research are the same. They are not. Theories are ideas to explain a phenomenon. So going back to the barrister, they could present a theory of who committed the murder, but you would not simply accept that was sufficient; you would expect to see evidence. As we outlined in Chapter 3, when discussing the research cycle, you can either conduct research to support your theory or you can conduct research that then builds into a theory. However, you do not simply come up with a theory which everyone will accept without question.

Hopefully, we have convinced you that you need to include research in your essay. Unfortunately, it is not the case that any research that is vaguely in the area of the essay topic will suffice. It is important that the evidence you select is relevant (see Chapter 4) and is used in a way that directly and explicitly relates back to the essay question. In other words, it is important to use the research effectively. As demonstrated in the previous chapter, you can use the same research as another student but receive different marks because it is about *how* you use the research. In this chapter, we will be looking at how you use the research by exploring how best to summarise the research so that it is clear *and* concise. We will also look at how to use multiple pieces of research in the same paragraph to build a clear and coherent argument that is focused on the question.

Before we get into that, we need to briefly explore the purpose and structure of an essay.

Purpose and Structure of Essays

Essays need to have an introduction, a main body and a conclusion. As a rough guide, it is normally the case that the body of the essay constitutes 80% of the word count and the introduction and conclusion taking up 10% each.

Writing the Introduction

Before we cover what is included in the introduction to an essay, it is worth us pointing out that an introduction to an essay serves a different function to an introduction for a report (see Chapter 8 for reports). The introduction to an essay serves a few important functions. One of the functions is to outline the main question or issue. This is to focus the essay and to orientate the reader to the area being covered by the essay question. Another function is to outline the key terms in the question. For example, if the question was '*Discuss the strengths and limitations of social identity theory to explain discrimination*' it may be useful to define **social identity theory** and **discrimination**. The final function is to signpost the content of the essay. This is because it is not possible to cover everything in your essay, so it is important to signpost to the reader the key points that will be covered. In this example, you may want to state what strengths and limitations you are focusing on in your essay when exploring social identity theory as an explanation for why discrimination occurs. For strengths this may include research to support social identity theory as an explanation for discrimination and for limitations this may include issues with the research that supports social identity theory as an explanation. You would want to signpost what research is going to be covered and some of the limitations of that research. Narrowing the focus and giving the reader a 'heads-up' to what is coming up in your essay helps the reader orientate themselves to what is coming up. It is a bit like when you watch the news on television. Often, they will give you the headlines at the start of the news and then give you the detail of each story (headline) after that. The detail for you is the main body of your essay, which we will look at now.

Writing the Main Body

In the main body of the essay, you start to unpack those points you have signposted in your introduction. It is a good idea in essays to ensure that you cover a point in depth, rather than trying to make lots of different points at the same time. Many students fall into the trap of thinking a scattergun approach to essay writing will ensure that they will hit the target at some point; a way of 'spreading their bets'. However, what actually happens is that each point the student makes is not well explained and the implication of the point is not clear. It can be confusing and hard work to read an essay where the point being made is constantly changing. Instead, just one clear point (and possibly a counterargument where appropriate) is best. This does not limit the paragraph to containing only one piece of research; it just means that the research should be on the same point (see later in this chapter for examples).

When structuring your paragraphs in your essay, it is important to:

1 Begin by making your point clearly and explicitly and ensuring that it is clear how it relates to the question. This may be by using wording from the question.
2 Following this, you then need to provide key information and evidence from a study to support your point.
3 The next stage is to present further evidence (or could be counter-evidence) or an example to help bolster the point being made.
4 The last stage involves ensuring that the relevance to the question is clear by linking back to the essay question and then starting a link to the next point where this process is repeated.

This structure is often referred to as PEEL (point, evidence/example, evidence/example and link).

Whilst the above process may seem long-winded and time-consuming, removing any of the critical steps means that the point is either lacking the required evidence or its relevance to the essay question becomes unclear. We see lots of student essays where the linking back to the question is not included and this means that it is difficult to see how the evidence relates to the question. One way to think about this is when writing your essay ask yourself, 'why is this important?' and 'how is this relevant to the essay question?'.

To go back to the example of the barrister, if they are presenting evidence to the jury the barrister may show the phone tracking of where the accused was around the time of the murder using a map on a screen, but they will also then outline why this is important and what it means in terms of whether the accused could have committed the murder. They do not leave it up to the jury to make that link.

When putting together the main body of your essay it is important to consider not just what you will include but also the order in which the points will appear so that your essay flows nicely. This means really thinking about how the ideas may relate to each other. Ask yourself, 'what is the characteristic of this idea?' and think about how you can signpost this at the end of the paragraph to then make a clear link to the start of the next paragraph. Some points will 'hang together' better than others and so thinking about the characteristics of each of your points is helpful. Do remember that most essays are relatively short (around 1500 words or so). This means you will only be including a handful of paragraphs, as you need to leave around 20% of your word count for the introduction and the conclusion.

Writing the Conclusion

The final part of your essay is your conclusion. Conclusions can be tricky. This is because you tend to leave the conclusion until last and at this point you may be fed up with writing and just want to hand it in and forget about it. However, remember that the conclusion will be the last thing your tutor/lecturer will read, and this will be in their mind when they are trying to assign a mark. Therefore, you want this part of your essay to shine just as much as the rest of it. It is important in your essay to summarise the points you have made in the main body. In our example about social identity theory, the conclusions of the research included in the main body should be referred to in the conclusion alongside the limitation(s). Be careful not to include too much detail though, as it should be a summary only. Another important aspect to consider is to make your conclusion specific to *your* essay. We always say to our students, if you could pick up your conclusion and place it at the end of another student's essay that answers the same question then your conclusion is not specific. It needs to summarise the specific points of *your* essay, not *any* essay on that topic. Keep that in mind when reading your conclusion. Also, think about how it links with your introduction. If the two don't relate then something has gone awry. You need to ensure that the conclusion reflects the argument that you have been making throughout your essay, including in the introduction. It is also important to answer the question in the conclusion using the arguments that you have presented to shape that stance.

It is also important to make reference to key words from the essay question, so you make it clear how you have answered the question. So in our example, it needs to be clear how social identity theory can (or cannot) explain discrimination. Lastly, do not include new points in your discussion. There should be no surprises for your reader. In the example of the prosecuting barrister, the conclusion is where the barrister sums the case for why the defendant should be found guilty and reminds the jury of the evidence presented to support the conclusion. You would not therefore expect the barrister to suddenly introduce new evidence here.

How to Use Research in Your Essays

Including the right amount, and type, of information about the research in your essay is a skill but is one that can be fairly easily acquired. The best way to think about it is to think about telling a story of what happened to you on a night out to your friends who were not there. You are not going to tell them every little detail, such as what the bar looked like, how clean the toilets were and how busy it was, unless these things are relevant to what happened. Instead, you pick out the relevant parts so that they can follow what happened and understand the point you are trying to make. Similarly, when discussing research, you will pick out the relevant aspects from the method (what they did) and then outline the results (what they found). If you provide too much unnecessary detail concerning the night out, then your friends will lose interest; but provide too little information then your friends will have to ask lots of questions to understand your point. This is similar when outlining the research, too much information and the reader is wondering why all the detail is included and the essay will lose focus, but too little information will leave the reader scratching their head wanting more information to understand your point.

One of the aims of this chapter is to help illustrate how to get the balance right when using studies in your essay. It will also help to illustrate what parts of the method and results to use and what parts you can miss out. Whilst there are some general rules about what information is important to report, it will also depend on the essay question and any evaluative points you may want to include. So, for example if you think the sample is limited in some way and may make generalisation to the population of interest difficult, then including details of the sample would be critical when describing the study. For some writers, including us, it may be that the amount of detail included changes as the essay goes through the drafting process. At first, it is often the case that you may put in more detail than is needed and once the essay takes shape you can then trim parts as you realise they are not important to telling the research 'story'. However, sometimes you may realise that some details need to be added because when you read your essay to others you realise that they are frowning and do not understand (yes, it is true that family members may also feel like they are doing a psychology degree at times!). This is why it is important to leave enough time to rewrite and edit your essay before handing it in. Ideally, it is best to leave sufficient time between drafts to ensure that you come at it 'fresh' otherwise it is difficult to see the issues. Reading it aloud and getting others to read it can be very useful, as then it is easier to spot any issues. It is also useful when reading to others or getting them to read your essay to hide the essay title and ask them to say what they think the essay question is as this helps to spot whether you are answering the question. This can also help to identify when you may have gone off track with the research you have included in your essay.

Examples of How to Use Research in Essays

Let us now look at some examples of how to use research effectively in essays. In this chapter, we will include different approaches that students could use and discuss the merits of each. By using these examples, we can identify some guidance and general principles that you can apply to your own writing. We are also going to offer places to practice this skill along the way.

Our first example includes the following essay question that students have been asked to answer. The essay is fairly short (1,500 words) which means there will be about 1,200 words for the main body and 150 words each for the introduction and conclusion.

Essay question:

> Using psychological research, discuss how group membership influences our
> responses to group-based messages (1,500 words)

Firstly, let us provide some background to this research area. When we think about group membership and how it influences our thoughts and behaviours, we tend to think about social identity theory. Social identity theory is the idea that who we are, in part, is encapsulated by the groups to which we belong and that part of our self-concept comes from being in a social group. Further, this sense of belonging and how it ties into our self-concept means that the groups we belong to, whether voluntarily or ascribed, contains some emotional significance associated to that group membership. We can belong to groups of various size and category, from being a supporter of Arsenal Football Club to a member of a university society.

Alongside this, the question is asking about our response to group-based messages. One of the research areas that would be useful here is research exploring the **intergroup sensitivity effect** (ISE), which was first named by Hornsey et al. (2002). The intergroup sensitivity effect is when people tolerate criticism from in-group members (those that belong to the group) more than criticism from out-group member (those that do not belong to the group). One of the reasons suggested that people tolerate in-group criticism better than out-group criticism is to do with social identity concerns; those inside the group are perceived more positively than those outside of the group due to their group membership. Put simply, in-group critics are 'one of us'.

In the next section, we are going to look at the first paper that explored the intergroup sensitivity effect and examine two students' attempts at summarising the first study from that paper.

Therefore, read the following two students' summaries of Hornsey et al.'s (2002) Experiment 1A below and answer the questions. In the paper they are exploring the intergroup sensitivity effect, and after exploring different approaches to summarising the paper you can then obtain the paper yourself from the full reference we will provide. This is the first student's approach.

Hornsey et al. (2002) conducted a series of studies using scenarios to examine whether people are more sensitive to in-group or out-group criticism. Results suggest that there were no differences when the comments were positive but when they were negative, they preferred the in-group speaker to the out-group speaker. This is the intergroup sensitivity effect.

━━━━━━━━━ Think 7.1 ━━━━━━━━━

Having read the above summary, consider the following questions:

- Can you understand the research from the summary provided?
- Is all the information needed in the summary or can some information be cut?
- Can the student evaluate the study from the description provided or is more information needed?
- Is the length of description appropriate for the word count of the essay?

Now consider a second student's approach to summarising the same study.

Hornsey et al. (2002) carried out a series of experiments to look at the intergroup sensitivity effect (ISE). In the first study, they had 168 participants take part and they were all Australian psychology students. Each participant was randomly allocated to one of the four conditions: positive in-group speaker, positive out-group speaker, negative in-group speaker or negative out-group speaker. In the study there were two scripts with two sections. In the first the speaker was introduced as being 22 years old and coming from one of the five countries: Australia, Canada, America, New Zealand or England. In the second section, there was a biography of the speaker with information about their hobbies, occupations of the speaker's family and then the speaker's opinions of Australia, which was either positive or negative. In the negative condition the speaker described Australians as being fairly racist, intolerant of Asians and not as cultured as other societies. In the positive condition, the speaker said that Australians were fairly friendly and warm people, very educated and having a very good sense of humour. Following this, the participants were then presented with a questionnaire that assessed participants' evaluations of the speaker and their comments. This included evaluating the speaker's personality (eight questions) and other questions around the positivity of the comments and perceived fairness. The researchers then analysed the questionnaires using ANOVA, examining the comment type and speaker group membership as the independent variables. They found that there was a statistically significant interaction between comment type (positive or negative) and speaker group membership (in-group or out-group). Further analysis shows that when the comments were positive there was no significant difference between whether the speaker was presented as an out-group or an in-group member. However, when the comments were negative, participants rated criticisms from the out-group speaker to be less positive than criticism from the in-group speaker. They also found that for evaluations of the speaker as the dependent variables there was also a significant interaction. When out-group speakers criticised Australians, they were evaluated more harshly than in-group members who made the same criticisms. But when the comments were positive there was no difference in speaker evaluations. This suggests that in-group members are more comfortable receiving criticisms from in-group members than from out-group members, thereby showing the intergroup sensitivity effect.

Think 7.2

Having read the second summary, consider the following questions:

- Can you understand the research from the summary provided?
- Is all the information needed in the summary or can some information be cut?
- Can the student evaluate the study from the description provided or is more information needed?
- Is the length of description appropriate for the word count of the essay?

When reading the first student's response, it is quite hard to understand what the researchers did in the study. It leaves the reader with several unanswered questions (e.g. what were these scenarios – written down, acted out or seen on a screen? what was the group membership? what information was presented in the scenarios? who were the participants? how, and what, precisely did they measure?). It is also difficult for Student 1 to then critically evaluate the method used when not much information has been provided.

In contrast, the second student's response is quite lengthy, and this reduces the words available to offer critical evaluation. It also means less research can be covered across the essay. The reader also feels a little 'bogged down' in the detail contained in that summary and it can be difficult to know the point the student is trying to make and how it is relevant to the essay question.

Therefore, it is important to try to strike a happy medium between the two approaches. Now consider our attempt to strike that happy medium.

Hornsey et al. (2002) carried out a series of experiments to explore the importance of group membership when responding to group-based messages. In the first study, Australian psychology students were randomly allocated to one of the four conditions: positive in-group speaker, positive out-group speaker, negative in-group speaker or negative out-group speaker. In the study, the speaker was introduced as being an in-group member (i.e. Australian) or an out-group member (e.g. Canadian). Participants then read a biography of the speaker and their opinions of Australian, which was positive or negative. In the negative conditions the speaker described Australians as being fairly racist and not as cultured as other societies. In the positive conditions, the speaker said that Australians were fairly friendly, very educated with a very good sense of humour. The participants were then presented with a questionnaire that assessed participants' evaluations of the speaker. The researchers found that when the out-group speaker criticised Australians, their personality was evaluated more harshly than in-group members who made the same criticisms. But when the comments were positive there was no difference in speaker evaluations. This suggests that in-group members are more comfortable receiving criticisms from in-group members than from out-group members, thereby showing that group membership influences responses to group-based messages.

▬▬▬ Think 7.3 ▬▬▬

Now that you have considered both responses and our attempt to summarise the study, use the reference below to locate the original paper (either through your university library or Google Scholar).
    Reference:

Hornsey, M. J., Oppes., T., & Svensson, A. (2002). 'It's OK if we say it, but you can't': Responses to intergroup and intragroup criticism. *European Journal of Social Psychology*, *32*, 293–307 https://doi.org/10.1002/ejsp.90

Read what Hornsey et al. (2002) did in Experiment 1A and compare it to the three summaries that have been presented. Think about the following questions:

- How well do all three summaries provide an accurate and clear reflection of what happened in Experiment 1A?
- What has been taken out of the second summary to produce our attempt?
- Why do you think that material has been taken out?
- Could any more information be taken out of our attempt without compromising the clarity?

As we have mentioned earlier, often you want to include more than one piece of research in the same paragraph to demonstrate breadth of support for the point you are making. It helps to show that the findings of that study are not just a one off. Depending on the type of research, you can also progress the point being made by showing that the effect occurs under different conditions or why the effect is happening. Due to the amount of psychology research that is easily accessible, there will be other research that can be included. For example, even though Hornsey and colleagues were the first to label the intergroup sensitivity effect (ISE), there was research that explored threats to social identity which is in a similar area; you can read about this in Hornsey et al.'s (2002) introduction. Since the 2002 article, there has also been further research exploring the ISE by Hornsey and colleagues and other researchers too. This is how the discipline develops. If you go back to Chapter 4, you can see how to find research that has been cited by others. In this example, you could go to Google Scholar and conduct a cited reference search on Hornsey, Oppes and Svensson (2002).

Now that we have fully explained how the seminal work of Hornsey et al. (2002) was conducted, let us now explore how you would then follow on from this using more research in this area. Fortunately, we can demonstrate this by looking at a paper published by Elder et al. (2005) which shows how multiple research findings can be used in one paragraph.

In Table 7.1, Elder et al. (2005) end their discussion of the method and results of Hornsey et al.'s (2002) study (as we have done above) and then move the discussion on to the explanation of why the intergroup sensitivity effect occurs (Table 7.1).

Table 7.1   Example of how multiple pieces of research can be discussed together with commentary

Elder et al.'s (2005) description of the research	Comments on the description
...Hornsey et al. (2002) found this intergroup sensitivity effect (ISE) to be mediated by perceptions that intergroup criticism is better informed and intentioned than intergroup criticism.	Here the writers have linked the two paragraphs together. By ending the paragraph with a mention of why the ISE occurs, it then opens the door for the next paragraph which explores the reasons for the ISE in more detail, using research to support.
These findings were mirrored by those published more or less simultaneously by O'Dwyer, Berkowitz, and Alfeld-Johnson (2002). These revealed greater hostility towards the critic, higher levels of anger and less agreement with the criticism when the critic was a member of the out-group rather than an in-group member. Subsequently, Hornsey, Trembath and Gunthorpe (2004) have shown that criticisms are only welcomed from in-group members who are highly identified with or committed to their group. This result underscores the importance of the motives that are perceived to underlie criticisms. Similarly, Hornsey and Imani (2004) found that out-group critics were not tolerated even when they were as knowledgeable about the group as in-group members, suggesting that motives and not experience is strongly predictive of sensitivity.	Here, O'Dwyer et al. (2002) is included to show that Hornsey et al.'s (2002) findings are not a one off.
	These two further pieces of research are presented as they explain *why* the intergroup sensitivity effect occurs. Notice that for each result there follows an interpretation to ensure that the reader understands what the result means in terms of the reasons why the ISE occurs. This is useful because otherwise the writers would just be listing the research findings and it would be difficult to follow the line of argument.

The example above shows how you can use multiple pieces of research when you are trying to make a collective point. In this instance, the main purpose of the paragraph was to demonstrate the importance of motives in explaining the intergroup sensitivity effect. Therefore, there was no need to include details of the method and lots of details about the results. This illustrates the need to think about *why* you are including the research and *how* you need to use it. It was important to include more detail of Hornsey et al.'s (2002) original work in our first example so that the reader could understand the way that group membership was manipulated. But following this, explaining the method of each study in detail is not needed. There are other times when you may need to explore the method and results in more detail which is what we are going to explore next.

Using Research to Critically Evaluate in Essays

When you are writing in an essay, you may feel like you need to provide more details of the study so that you can then offer a critique. If that is the case, then the example above would need to be amended to include more details of the method for the critique to make sense. The same goes with the results of the study. In some instances, it is important to include the results in more detail if they are quite nuanced or there was an issue with the interpretation of the results that you may want to discuss.

In the next example, we will look at how we can include research in discussion points within an essay. This is where we are taking the research beyond the description to evaluation. It is important to remember that critically evaluating research is not about simply finding fault, it is about really engaging with the research and thinking critically. You can do this by asking critical questions as you came across in both Chapters 5 and 6. Specifically, in Chapter 6 you were provided with a framework to think critically about the method section of different pieces of research. We are now going to take that framework and apply it in the context of writing about research in an essay.

Let us take the research in Chapter 6 that explored impression formation on online dating sites. This was a quantitative paper that can be found using this information:

Van der Zanden, T., Schouten, A. P., Mos, M. B. J., & Krahmer, E. J. (2020). Impression formation on online dating sites: Effects of language errors in profile texts on perceptions of profile owners' attractiveness. *Journal of Social and Personal Relationships, 37*(3), 758–778. https://doi.org/10.1177/0265407519878787

In this example, we are looking to use the above research in this essay:

Critically evaluate the impact of impression formation in online dating.

Van der Zanden et al. (2020) is relevant to this essay question and we can use the critical thinking framework demonstrated in Chapter 6 to now evaluate the research. Below we have demonstrated some ways that the research could be evaluated (they are other points you could raise) (Table 7.2).

Table 7.2   Example of how to evaluate research with commentary

Description and evaluation of Van der Zanden et al. (2020)	Commentary
Van der Zanden et al. (2020) examined the impact of language errors on impression formation using online dating profiles. They manipulated language errors in dating profiles to see the effect on ratings of attraction and dating intention. There were 373 participants recruited by Parship (online dating site in the Netherlands) with a mean age of 56 years. The results indicated that profiles with text errors were evaluated as less socially and romantically attractive than profiles without errors. However, this effect was only in those that noticed the errors, which was a third of participants. Whilst these findings suggest language errors reduce the dating potential for their owners, it is important to note that for the majority those language errors went unnoticed. Further, as the dating site's overall age is significantly younger than this study, and dating sites in general, it is possible that errors in language may not be so detrimental to a younger demographic who have grown up with more informal language (e.g. text speech). Another potential issue with the sample is that whilst the researchers reported the education level of the participants (over 66% had a college degree) there was no reporting of the effect of education level on whether errors were noticed and/or the effect on ratings of attraction and dating intention. It could be that those without a college degree are less likely to notice, or be bothered by, language errors but this was not investigated. Therefore, caution may need to be applied when suggesting that language errors impact impression formation in online dating given these limitations.	This detail is needed to make it clear what was manipulated in the study and how. Details of the participants are included as this becomes relevant later. The researchers also manipulated the picture (visible vs blurred) but we have not reported this here as the effect of picture was not significant. This is unpicking the results and presenting the counterargument that language errors may not have that much impact. This is to demonstrate that the mean age is high and higher than for most dating sites which impacts the generalisability of the results. This is making the point that researchers could have analysed the findings using education level (degree versus no degree) to see if there was an impact and this has either not been analysed or not reported. Notice here in this last sentence that we are using words from the essay question and from the manipulation (language error) to illustrate the impact and relevance to the question.

Whilst this is quite a lengthy paragraph, it is important to remember that we are not just describing in this paragraph we are also critically evaluating too. If this was solely description, then we would need to consider whether to reduce the content. When evaluating, as can be seen in the example above, it is important not to just state a single sentence which could be classed as generic evaluation; so using stock phrases such as 'it was a lab experiment so lacks ecological validity' or 'the sample size is small and consists of psychology students so lacks population validity' should be avoided. In the next activity we are going to explore the different ways the same research and points can be made, and how they compare with the example above.

━━━━━━━ Think 7.4 ━━━━━━━━━━━━━━━━━━━━━━━━━

Imagine that a student has been given the same essay title as above:

Critically evaluate the impact of impression formation in online dating.

They also choose to use the Van der Zanden et al. (2020) article and write the following:

Van der Zanden et al. (2020) looked at the impact of language errors on impression formation using online dating profiles by seeing the effect on ratings of attraction and dating intention. Participants were 373 participants with a mean age of 56 years. The results were that language errors meant they were evaluated as less socially and romantically attractive than those without errors. However, this effect was only in those that noticed the errors, a third of the participants. This suggests language errors reduce the dating potential for their owners, but most do not notice. It is important to note that the participants were quite old and so the results may not be generalisable. Also, many of the participants had college degrees but the rest didn't which is something the researchers should explore as this could impact the results.

Questions to ask whilst comparing our paragraph with the students:

- Which of the two paragraphs is clearer and why?
- What are the differences in the detail provided when describing the study? Does it matter?
- Is the evaluation in each paragraph clear?
- Is the impact and importance of the evaluation clear and easy to understand?
- Is the paragraph linked back to the essay question?

By answering the questions above, you hopefully recognised that although the student's summary was shorter and more concise it lacked the detail in the description and evaluation to truly appreciate the impact of the comments. For example, by not providing the details about how the participants were recruited and the average age of the participants it meant that a comparison to the normal age of people on the dating site was omitted. It was not clear *why* age and education level may be important in the student's example and the impact it may have on the results and the conclusions drawn. It is also not clear what the essay might be from the student's paragraph, unlike in the previous example. Finally, our example included an important link back to the essay question which was not included in the student's paragraph.

What we are hoping that this example demonstrates is that you can use the same study and even make the same points, but it is *how* you do this that counts and has a big impact on your grade. Unfortunately, this is an issue that students do not always fully appreciate or only come to really understand later in their studies. Students tend to think that as long as they have used relevant studies and made evaluative points, they will achieve a high mark but it is about using research *effectively*. Please don't worry if you have done this in the past too, as it is a learning process and we did the same, which is why we wanted to write this book.

━━━━━━━ **Key tip 7.1** ━━━━━━━━━━━━━━━━━━━━━━━

As a writer you need to think about the 'so what?' principle – in the example above you would be saying 'so what if they have got an older demographic in their example, why could that impact the results?' or 'how may the results differ if they had a younger demographic?'. This is about showing the reader that you have really thought about the issue you are raising and the potential implications.

─────── **Explore further** ───────

If you have an essay you have completed, read each paragraph where you have included research and answer the following questions:

- Is the purpose of the paragraph clear (remember the P for PEEL)?
- Is the summary of research you have provided clear and appropriately detailed (where needed) without redundant words?
- Is there any evaluation and if there is, is the impact and implications specific to the study and relevant to the question?
- Is the evidence/study linked back to the question (remember the L).
- Has the person who marked your work made any comments about your use of evidence? Can you apply that feedback to enhance your use of research?

It is always important to thoroughly examine the feedback you have been given and to do that whilst reading through your essay again. It is remarkable how coming back to your essay will help you to see its strengths and limitations; in effect you are critically evaluating your work. This period of self-reflection alongside reading the feedback will give you the best opportunity to improve. Even if the mark is pleasing, there are always elements that can be improved. You also need to understand what earned you that pleasing mark, so you know what to repeat. Remember that academics also receive feedback (peer review, see Chapter 3) which can be quite negative, but is essential to engage with. It can be difficult to read a critique of your work, particularly if it feels quite negative, but do remember that it is essential for self-improvement and is not a personal attack. Those that are commenting on your work are doing so to help you to understand how to improve and to also point out where you did well. They are seeing your potential and trying to harness that so that you can achieve your goals. If you have not understood the feedback, then don't hesitate to get in contact with your tutor/ lecturer so that you can have a chat about it. We have all been in the position of receiving feedback and not quite understanding what it means and what to do next.

Writing in Your Own Words

In our everyday lives, we often copy material without thinking. We find a funny image on the internet and post it on social media to make someone laugh. Did we consider the original authorship of the material? Probably not and most of the time there are no consequences. But we have all heard of cases in the media where copyright holders of music (or other work) have sued people for using their material without permission and passing it off as their own work. This non-academic plagiarism raises the issue of the difference between using other people's content that may be permissible, especially if you are not passing it off as your own, and using material that is someone else's and passing it off as your own. This difference is important as it has moral, and legal, implications.

In this next section, we are going to explore writing in your own words which is a key skill to acquire to avoid potential plagiarism, which is an act of academic dishonesty and academic misconduct. Plagiarism is about presenting ideas and presenting them as your own, whether that is intentional or not. Even if you include a reference to the original source, you cannot simply copy what they have written and put a reference at the end. Many students think this means they have not plagiarised. Alternatively, they think that using a series of quotes is the fix but that is not ideal either (see later).

Let us now think about plagiarism and why it is important to avoid plagiarism. You will often hear in higher education that it is vital to ensure that the work produced reflects your academic abilities. Let us now consider what this means.

━━━━━━━━━ Think 7.5 ━━━━━━━━━

Why is it important to ensure that the work you produce reflects your true academic ability?

_____

You may have suggested that work should reflect your understanding of the topic and demonstrate how you are progressing in the subject. It means that the feedback you receive will be more helpful as it will be specific to the needs you have. It will help your tutor/lecturer to identify what you are doing well at and what you may need help with. It will help you to develop and will mean that you are able to pinpoint what is needed to help you to improve – to come up with a clear and personalised action plan. If you think of it another way, if the feedback is provided for work that you did not write that feedback is not going to be meaningful for you.

The other reason you may have come up with is about fairness. Here you are probably thinking about ensuring that students receive a grade that reflects their ability and not someone else's. It is not fair if a student is given a grade for a piece of work that has been largely written by someone else. It does not reflect their actual knowledge and understanding.

Therefore, we can all acknowledge that it is important to show understanding through writing in your own words and to credit those who had the original idea. Sometimes when students are concerned with avoiding plagiarism, they can then think that as long as they reference they can still directly copy another person's work or they think they can just put in lots of quotations. Using quotations is where you repeat the words of the original author and acknowledge them by using quotation marks and a reference. It is important to remember that using quotations means you are replacing your own words with someone else's and, as such, that does not demonstrate understanding either. Whilst we are not suggesting that you can never use quotes, we are suggesting that if you need to use them, they should be used to *support* rather than *replace* your argument and they should be used sparingly. We have both encountered students' work where there are lines upon lines of quotations and our hearts sink because we then have no idea if the student has understood those ideas presented. This means their mark is significantly reduced, which is such a shame.

Having read and considered *why* it is important to write in your own words, you may be concerned about *how* to write in your own words. We will be covering that now. Often, one of the barriers to producing work in your own words is not feeling confident enough. It is quite common for students to feel that they are not academically able to present work in their words, particularly if they read another person's work and think that it is written extremely well. Hopefully, this next section will help you to recognise that it is possible to do so, no matter how inexperienced or under confident you are. We have both been there and know how you feel.

The Art of Paraphrasing

Paraphrasing is all about expressing the meaning of someone else's work but in your own words. This means that you will be changing the structure and how you use the idea to create your own argument and to ensure that it fits with the essay question you are answering. You don't want to change the meaning of the original, but you need to shape it and reconstruct it so that it shows your understanding, and it connects to other material you are presenting. The material you are using is not written directly and explicitly to answer the specific essay question you are answering; so this is another reason why writing in your own words is critical.

Sometimes students will misunderstand what paraphrasing is and just think that it means changing some words here and there. This leads to them using a thesaurus to replace a few words with a synonym. This is quite easy to do in Word, so can be very tempting. However, if you swap out words but keep everything else the same, you are then left with a sentence that is quite strange and can lack the precision and accuracy of the original. It also means that you have not really paraphrased, which means that you are still too close to the original work. Swapping out words does not show understanding and it often means that it is unlikely to have the flow and clear argument that you need to really address the essay question.

We will demonstrate this now by swapping out words using synonyms and you will see what we mean. You may remember in Chapter 5 we looked at this essay question:

> 'Consideration of ethics means that experimental methods are of limited use in psychology'. Discuss this claim drawing on examples from psychological research.

Below Is Part of the Response We Provided

Ethical guidelines are there to protect participants and the reputation of researchers, so that the public can trust the research and the researchers. Without that trust, the public would be very reluctant to take part in psychological research and this would mean that research would be very difficult to conduct. However, by having ethical guidelines it can restrict what research can be conducted, especially when using experimental methods as often this means a level of deceit and exposure to certain situations that may go beyond what people would encounter in their everyday life.

Previously, before such rigorous guidelines were introduced, it was possible to conduct research that today would not be met with ethical approval.

The words in grey above are the words that we are going to substitute with synonyms so you can see whether using that as a strategy is an effective way to write in your own words. Have a read and see what you think about:

1 Whether this avoids plagiarism
2 Whether the argument retains the clarity and flow by using synonyms.

Example of Word Substitution

Ethical guidelines are there to shield participants and the character of researchers, so that people can rely on the research and the scientists. Without that reliance, everyone would be very hesitant to take part in psychological research and this would indicate that research would be very tough to conduct. However, by partaking in ethical guidelines it can limit what research can be done, especially when using experimental means as repeatedly this means a level of dishonesty and acquaintance to certain states that may go outside what people would encounter in their way of life. Previously, before such severe strategies were proposed, it was feasible to conduct research that nowadays would not be encountered with ethical agreement.

Can you see here that there are several issues? The first is that ultimately the work is still a little too close to the original. Also, the style of writing means that it lacks flow and clarity which means that the strength of the argument is weakened. Finally, some of the technical terms have been replaced are of concern. For example, experimental method being replaced by experimental means does not have the same level of accuracy and precision as method is a very specific technical term used in psychology.

How to Paraphrase

Hopefully we have convinced you that replacing words alone does not work. So let us now concentrate on how to paragraph well using focussed note taking that is tailored to your assignment. Let us now examine the steps you can take to go from reading the source material to producing the words in your assignment.

- Start by reading the material through carefully. It may take several readings to ensure that you fully understand the material. Do not be tempted to read through quickly and then paraphrase because it is likely you have not understood fully and be tempted to copy from the source more. If you do not understand some terms, then look them up.
- Put the source away so you cannot see it. Then start to write down the key terms and ideas; this may be in lists or in note form. You may even want to do it as a spider diagram. It is important to find the style that works for you. This may be to use different coloured pens for different key ideas, it could be to tackle it electronically using notes on your tablet or laptop or it could be to use a flip chart or a wipe board. The key is to do it in a way that brings some joy to the process.

- Once you have the key terms you can then start to build up from those into sentences that express the key arguments from the source. Don't be tempted to look back at the original source. If you are struggling then it may be best to stop, have a break and then start this process again.
- Once you have completed your note taking, then look back at the original source and check to see if your notes capture the content/argument of the source. If not, you will need to start the process again. If it has, then check that you have included the reference from the original source alongside your notes.

━━━━━━━━━ **Stop 7.1** ━━━━━━━━━

When writing your notes do not copy from the source with the intention to then change it when you are typing up your essay. There have been cases when students have had this intention but because they left a gap between the note taking and the writing up, they forgot that was their intention. Instead, they believed their notes were their own words and typed it up. When their work was put through the plagiarism detection software they were picked up for plagiarism and their university imposed a penalty. Whilst there was no intention to deceive, because there were significant chunks of copied text the penalty had to be applied.

How to Take Notes to Help Your Paraphrasing

You may be concerned about what you are looking for when writing your notes. Let us return to our paragraph above and let us ask some important questions to help us really understand the content before we try to paraphrase it (Table 7.3).

Table 7.3   Key questions to ask when reading to help with paraphrasing

Original paragraph	Key questions to ask
Ethical guidelines are there to protect participants and the reputation of researchers, so that the public can trust the research and the researchers. Without that trust, the public would be very reluctant to take part in psychological research and this would mean that research would be very difficult to conduct. However, by having ethical guidelines it can restrict what research can be conducted, especially when using experimental methods as often this means a level of deceit and exposure to certain situations that may go beyond what people would encounter in their everyday life. Previously, before such rigorous guidelines were introduced, it was possible to conduct research that today would not be met with ethical approval.	What is the content about? It is about the purpose of ethical guidelines and how they have changed over time, with the impact on research considered. What is the argument? The argument is that strict ethical guidelines are needed to protect (potential) participants and researchers but that having these strict guidelines can reduce what research can be conducted. It is also argued that this impact is felt more for some methods (i.e. experiments deceit is often needed). Is there a counterargument? There is still an element of deceit that is permitted within the guidelines today as long as it is low level, justified and a full debrief provided. So not all research that involves deception is blocked.

It is useful to consider any counterarguments alongside your notes as it can help you to think about how you can build your essay and link points together to build a clear and cohesive argument. It is also useful to add any points that could be used for critical evaluation. These may be points that come to mind which will need further exploration later but if you do not note them down, you may not remember them later. Table 7.4 shows how we have paraphrased the original paragraph having asked the questions above.

Table 7.4   Taking the original paragraph and showing how it can be paraphrased

Original paragraph	Paraphrased
Ethical guidelines are there to protect participants and the reputation of researchers, so that the public can trust the research and the researchers. Without that trust, the public would be very reluctant to take part in psychological research and this would mean that research would be very difficult to conduct. However, by having ethical guidelines it can restrict what research can be conducted, especially when using experimental methods as often this means a level of deceit and exposure to certain situations that may go beyond what people would encounter in their everyday life. Previously, before such rigorous guidelines were introduced, it was possible to conduct research that today would not be met with ethical approval.	Ethical guidelines are important because they are there to protect participants from potential harm, and having the guidelines in place means that the public are more willing to take part in research, making it easier for researchers to obtain participants. It can also be reassuring for researchers to know that their research has been scrutinised by others and meets the ethical requirements. However, ethical guidelines can restrict what can happen in research, and this is particularly the case with experimental methods where an element of deception and exposure to less-than-ideal situations may be needed. As such, these studies would not be possible now as they would not gain ethical approval due to stricter guidelines that are in place.

Hopefully, you can see how we have taken the same argument but paraphrased it into our own words. It is not a simple case of just using synonyms, it has gone beyond that. It really helps to answer the questions we have provided in the previous table because it gets you to think deeply about the point being made in the original source as you are breaking that point down into the different elements and then in your paraphrasing building it back up. If you don't break it down, then you will find it difficult to put the point into your own words and will find the words and the phrasing from the original source creeping into your work.

--- Explore further ---

If you would like to explore psychology essay writing in more detail, you may find Paul Dickerson's book on essay writing in psychology particularly helpful (reference below). In the book, Paul takes you through how to write effective and compelling academic psychology essays using practical tips and exercises to help you succeed.

Dickerson, P. (2021). *How to write brilliant psychology essays*. SAGE.

KEY TAKEAWAYS

This chapter has explored how to use psychological research in your essay writing. We did this by first exploring the importance of including research in your essay and how it should be the crux of your essay. We then moved to exploring the structure of essays and how you should be looking to have about 80% of your word count as the main body with 10% each for the introduction and conclusion. We also covered the importance of using less points but, in more detail, and how using PEEL for every paragraph in your main body can help to achieve this. PEEL stands for Point, Evidence, further Evidence and then Linking back. Using this method means that you are ensuring your reader is clear on the point you are making and how it directly and explicitly links back to the essay question. We also explored how to write a good introduction and conclusion for your essay ensuring that they are specific and link together to bookend your essay.

The next section of this chapter was concerned with using examples of how research can be used effectively by really understanding what level of detail is needed. For example, if a piece of research is seminal then you may want to include more detail regarding the method and results to ensure the way the research was conducted is understood before discussing variations to the method and results following that. You can then spend less words outlining research that has followed that seminal paper. We also explored how you may include more details on some aspects of the method if you are then going to critically evaluate the method alongside the description. We looked at student examples to illustrate these important considerations.

The last section of this chapter explored the importance of writing in your own words and how to do that. We explained the art of paraphrasing and how to achieve this through note taking by asking yourself some critical questions. We also distinguished between using synonyms and paraphrasing.

8

HOW TO USE PSYCHOLOGICAL RESEARCH IN A REPORT

Key goals for this chapter

- Understand the difference between an essay and a research report.
- Understand how to use research in the introduction section of a research report.
- Understand how to use research in the discussion section of a research report.

WHY DO I NEED TO LEARN HOW TO USE RESEARCH AGAIN?

You may well be asking yourself this question, especially if you are reading this chapter directly after reading Chapter 7. The focus of Chapter 7 was explaining how to use psychological research when writing essays. As you will be aware from having read Chapters 3 and 4, research is disseminated via research reports which are published in academic journals. As a psychology student, you will be required to write both essays and research reports as part of your studies. The purpose of a research report differs to that of an essay; therefore the way in which you utilise psychological research also differs. So, whilst you may now be feeling rather confident about how to use research when writing an essay, you also need to learn the nuances of how to use research in a report. Having already developed important skills in critical thinking and how to apply this to reading research papers in Chapters 5 and 6, you are already well equipped with the skills necessary to use research when writing research papers. In this chapter, we will guide you on the purpose of research in the introduction and discussion section of a research paper and show you how you can apply the skills you have already developed in the earlier chapters of this book.

HOW DO WE USE RESEARCH DIFFERENTLY IN AN ESSAY TO A REPORT?

Before we look at how research is used differently in an essay to a report, we will begin by reminding ourselves how research is used in an essay. When you write an essay, you are usually given a title from your lecturer, and you use psychological research to help to answer this question. An undergraduate essay in psychology will usually involve critical thinking and will ask you to discuss or evaluate a specific concept or claim. Let's imagine you have been given the following essay question *Discuss what factors might influence eyewitnesses' ability to identify a perpetrator accurately in a line-up*. When approaching an essay question, you initially need to identify the concept/claim that you are being asked to discuss. Here, you are being asked to discuss the factors that might hinder the ability of an eyewitness to accurately identify the perpetrator of a crime that they have witnessed. To be able to discuss this claim, you will need to consider what claims you wish to make to address this question. If you have studied eyewitness testimony as part of your studies, you may already have some ideas as to what factors may influence accurate identification in a line-up. If you have not studied eyewitness testimony or have not studied line-up identification as part of the topic you may need some ideas here! There are many factors which may influence how accurate an eyewitness is in a line-up; some of these include how close the witness was to the perpetrator during the crime, the level of anxiety the witness experienced during the crime, whether the perpetrator was wearing a disguise during the crime and the race of both the witness and perpetrator. If you were writing this essay, it is unlikely you would want to (or need to) cover all these points. Let's pick one factor, whether the perpetrator was wearing a disguise. If we were going to address this in the essay, we would want research to support the suggestion that if a perpetrator has a disguise on during the crime that it can reduce the accuracy of identification in a line-up. As the essay asks for a discussion, we would need to consider some of limitations of the research which may impact the conclusions drawn. This could lead us to bring in research which has explored some of these limitations and whether this leads to different findings or not. To present a counter argument, we may also want to look for evidence which finds that a disguise does not always reduce accuracy, for example in super recognisers (people who are uniquely skilled in identifying faces).

Think 8.1

In Chapter 4, we explored how to find research for the following essay title *Discuss the relationship between phubbing and mental health*. As we have just done, think about how you would need to use research to address this issue. You may find it useful to revisit this part of Chapter 4 to help you to think about the claims/lines of argument that you might follow. Use the following prompts to help you:

- What is the concept/claim that you are asked to evaluate/discuss?
- What claims will you need to find research to support/challenge?
- How might you make use of the research to address the question?

Having spent a bit of time revisiting how to use research in an essay, we can now begin to think about how a research report differs from an essay. Before moving on, you may find it useful to revisit Chapter 3 where research reports and their structure were explained to you.

The main difference between an essay and a research report is that an essay uses secondary research to develop an answer to a specific question. A research report tests a very precise research question, and often a hypothesis, by gathering **primary data** through carefully designed research. If we return to our earlier example of the essay question – *Discuss what factors might influence eyewitnesses' ability to identify a perpetrator accurately in a line-up*, a research report would not be able to address this as it is too broad and each piece of research has a very specific focus. Of course, research does investigate what factors may influence an eyewitnesses' ability to accurately identify a perpetrator in a line-up, but a research report would test a very precise factor that may be involved. Let's look at an example using the research by Jones et al. (2020). In their study they were interested in factors influencing line-up identification, but specifically they were testing whether the perpetrator having a distinctive feature (a black eye) on their face affects the accuracy of correct identification in a line-up. They also tested whether having the distinctive feature present or absent in all the line-up photos had an effect on accuracy of identification and whether confidence was related to accurate identification. If we compare this to our brief essay plan, hopefully you can see the difference between the two. In a report we are not answering a question but testing something very narrow, because of this difference we do not use research in quite the same way in a research report as an essay. Before we move on to explore how research is used in a research report, it is important that you review the structure of a report in Chapter 3, specifically the introduction and the discussion section. It is in these sections where you will bring in the bulk of the research used in a research report.

THE INTRODUCTION SECTION OF A REPORT

As you will recall, the introduction section is at the beginning of the report after the title and abstract. The purpose of the introduction is to explain to the reader why the specific research question is being tested. Studies which explore the same broad area of psychology, such as identification in a line-up, will all test different elements of that area. The introduction will need to draw on why the specific factor is being studied, drawing on past research to develop the rationale for the present study.

━━━━━━━━━ Think 8.2 ━━━━━━━━━

One area of psychology that we have touched on in this book is obesity in children and how sugary drinks may contribute to this (see Chapter 5). Each of the studies below has investigated this area, but each has a different focus.

Your task is to skim read the introduction of each piece of research to identify what exactly the piece of research was testing, i.e. what was their specific research question/s? In most instances you are likely to find this in the final paragraph of the introduction section.

Cantoral, A., Téllez-Rojo, M. M., Ettinger, A. S., Hu, H., Hernández-Ávila, M., & Peterson, K. (2016). Early introduction and cumulative consumption of sugar-sweetened beverages during the pre-school period and risk of obesity at 8–14 years of age. *Paediatric Obesity*, *11*(1), 68–74. https://doi.org/10.1111%2Fijpo.12023

Katzmarzyk, P. T., Broyles, S. T., Champagne, C. M., Chaput, J. P., Fogelholm, M., Hu, G., … Zhao, P. (2016). Relationship between soft drink consumption and obesity in 9–11 years old children in a multi-national study. *Nutrients*, *8*(12), 770. https://doi.org/10.3390/nu8120770

Munsell, C. R., Harris, J. L., Sarda, V., & Schwartz, M. B. (2016). Parents' beliefs about the healthfulness of sugary drink options: opportunities to address misperceptions. *Public Health Nutrition*, *19*(1), 46–54. https://doi.org/10.1017%2FS1368980015000397

Zheng, M., Rangan, A., Allman-Farinelli, M., Rohde, J. F., Olsen, N. J., & Heitmann, B. L. (2015). Replacing sugary drinks with milk is inversely associated with weight gain among young obesity-predisposed children. *British Journal of Nutrition*, *114*(9), 1448–1455. https://doi.org/10.1017/S0007114515002974

By completing the previous task, you hopefully are beginning to see how a research report differs to an essay; specifically, how narrow and focused a research report is in comparison to an essay. Now you understand this, we can begin to explore how the introduction section of a report is structured and most importantly how research is used in the introduction. In Chapter 3, you were told how the introduction summarises theories and studies that are relevant to the study, leading to a rationale for the current study following a funnel format.

The Funnel Format

The funnel format involves starting by focusing broadly on the topic being studied and then becoming narrower and more focused, until eventually identifying the aim, research question and the hypothesis (if a quantitative study). The general funnel format is as follows (Table 8.1):

Table 8.1 An overview of the funnel format

Funnel format	Explanation	Example
Introduce the broader topic	The introduction needs to tell the reader what the main topic is that will be studied, but beyond this the reader needs to have some understanding of the need to study this topic. This can include telling the reader what effect the area/behaviour we are interested in may be having on people, or why the effects may be getting worse, or why the topic in question is becoming more important.	If we return to our sugary drinks and obesity example, here we might explain why the potential causes of obesity need studying. This could include explaining the effects of obesity on physical health and quality of life, it may also include looking at the prevalence of obesity and how it is increasing. If our study was testing children, we would also want some information specifically focused on children. This could include the prevalence of obesity in children or how sugary drinks are marketed towards children.
Explain the theory	Most of psychology is focused on *explaining* why something is happening. Having identified the topic that is being studied, the introduction can then begin to consider why this effect may be occurring. This explanation needs to be based on psychological theory. There are usually multiple theories that can explain the behaviour of interest, but to keep a narrow focus research may only test one theory although this is not always the case.	In our sugary drinks example, we may want to explain *why* children consume sugary drinks or we want to focus on why parents let their children consume sugary drinks. You can see here how the introduction is starting to become more focused towards the current study, as which explanation we put here would need to align with what we are testing. Let's say our study is focused on why children choose to consume sugary drinks. One theory we might want to include here is social learning theory. **Social learning theory** proposes that behaviour is learnt via observation and imitation. In this instance, we could explain how children may see their role models consuming sugary drinks, e.g. parents, older siblings, celebrities in advertisements and YouTubers, and view their role models receiving **vicarious reinforcement** when consuming the drink. This reinforcement may be looking 'cool', being refreshed or being energised (for example) which increases motivation in the child to also consume the drink.
Previous research	This is the key area this chapter is interested in. Here the author/s present studies which have tested the focus of the current study. This	If our study is exploring whether children consume sugary drinks because they are imitating role models, we would need to review research which has tested this. We might take the following approach:

(Continued)

Table 8.1 An overview of the funnel format *(Continued)*

Funnel format	Explanation	Example
	research is reviewed and summarised in the context of the theory presented. This section itself may follow a funnel format, reviewing studies that have explored that topic area leading to studies that have tested very similar, or the same, research question as the current study. The key here is to remember that you are explaining to the reader what we already know on the topic; this helps the reader to understand what is already known on the topic area. Crucially this also guides the reader to understand why this study has been conducted, and how it fits into what is already known. It can help to think of the research as one big puzzle, the previous research each being a piece of the puzzle and the current study will be a new piece of the puzzle. This is particularly important when it comes to summarising previous research; students often include a lot of unnecessary detail on each of the studies reviewed. This is partly because there is no rule on how much detail to include, as it all depends on what the research adds to the story and how much detail the reader requires to be able to understand how the study furthers our knowledge. If we return to our puzzle analogy, let's imagine you are completing a 1,000-piece puzzle of a landscape. If you were to describe the puzzle, how important would it be to describe each piece? It is possible that over 200 pieces could be purely for the sky, would it really be necessary to describe each piece	• Review research which shows that children do imitate role models (this is broader and more related to the theory generally; therefore it is likely that less focus would be required here). • Explore research which has tested imitation via specific role models/mediums. What we select here would depend on the focus of the study. If we were interested in advertising, we would need to review research which has tested whether children imitate role models they see in adverts. As we are focused on children, we would likely have a specific age range we are interested in. The research we review would need to have tested children in this age range to focus specifically on our study. Hopefully you can see how at each step we are shaping our 'story' and direction to lead to the research question that we will test. We would need to be careful here to not include related research that is not directly relevant to our study. It would be like taking a detour on a journey, we want to take the clearest route to our destination. • Following this we would need to narrow our focus onto the research question and review research which has tested whether children (who are the same age range that we are interested in) imitate role models in advertisements which promote sugary drinks. Specifically, we would want to know whether sugary drink consumption and/or intention to consume sugary drinks increased following viewing of an advertisement including a role model compared to no advertisement or an advertisement which does not include a role model. • To look in more detail in this area we may also want to consider what other factors may be involved in the relationship between observation and imitation. This could include whether the type of role model makes a difference, or the type of sugary drink, or the medium that the advertisement is presented through, the time between viewing the advertisement and when drink consumption was measured, whether the effects have been found long term and if there are any gender

Table 8.1 An overview of the funnel format *(Continued)*

Funnel format	Explanation	Example
	individually to get across that part of the picture is a blue sky or could this be summarised in a sentence or two? In terms of research, if there are multiple pieces of research which all show the same thing but in slightly different ways, it may not be necessary to describe every study individually but instead the same point can be made by stating that multiple studies have found the same outcome. This point can be substantiated with several in text citations to support that many studies have found similar findings. Back to our puzzle, let's say there is a dog with a bone in the puzzle. We might want a bit more detail on this in our description of the puzzle pieces, for example we might want to know what colour and breed the dog is. Returning to research, some studies may need more detail than others. You may include more detail if the method used differed to previous research, or it may be that the study included an additional variable that had not been tested before. It would not be pertinent to describe the *entire* study, but some additional details may be helpful to the reader. What is important as we are reviewing studies is that we are not simply describing study after study but that we are looking for general patterns across studies. This may involve considering how some studies might overcome limitations with others, as well as contradictory findings and why these contradictory findings may exist (often these can occur due to methodological differences across research).	differences. Of course, we would not explore all of these factors it would depend on the exact focus of our study; another instance of how we are narrowing down the introduction.

(Continued)

Table 8.1 An overview of the funnel format *(Continued)*

Funnel format	Explanation	Example
The rationale	This is probably the part of the introduction that students find most challenging to write and it is where you explain to the reader *why* the current study has devised the current research question. The rationale should follow on from the 'story' that was explored in the 'previous research' and should not appear out of the blue. Essentially your study is being conducted to address a gap in the research, or to keep to our puzzle analogy to fill in a missing piece of the puzzle. Often the rationale for carrying out a study is because that concept has not yet been studied, to add to or extend what we already know, to overcome methodological limitations in previous research or to replicate previous research. You will recall from Chapter 3 that scientific research follows a research cycle. One piece of research does not give us any definitive answers instead it creates further questions and gives direction to what else we need to study. The rationale tells the reader how the present study is adding to the field and continuing the cycle of enquiry. The rationale leads naturally onto the aim which tells the reader in a sentence or two exactly what the study is testing. If the study is testing hypotheses, these are stated after the aim and the predictions are based on the findings of the previous research stated in the introduction.	As we have not written the previous section, we cannot devise a rationale for our study here. However, we can look at the studies you were asked to look at in the previous activity and summarise the rationale in each study. • Cantoral et al. (2016) conducted their study to extend the findings of previous research. They cite research which shows that children who consumed sugary drinks in childhood were more likely to develop obesity, than children who did not consume sugary drinks. This study aimed to extend these findings by following children from birth to see the age sugary drinks are first consumed, and how this relates to later consumption and subsequent obesity. • Katzmarzyk et al. (2016) cite their rationale as extending previous findings by focusing on an under researched area, specifically by studying countries outside of North America and Europe to see whether the relationship between sugary drinks consumption and obesity in children occurs in countries of varying economic development. • Zheng et al.'s., (2015) rationale was to build on previous findings showing a relationship between children's sugary drink consumption and later obesity. It also extends the field by exploring whether non-sugary drinks may be suitable alternatives for weight management in children who are vulnerable to developing obesity.

Examples of How Research Is Used in the Introduction

Now that we have explained how research is used in the introduction of a research report, it would be helpful to look at some examples in published research. We will return to a topic area that falls under social psychology that we covered in Chapters 1 and 4, phubbing. You will recall that phubbing refers to someone using their mobile phone during a social interaction, a portmanteau of 'phone' and 'snubbing'. In previous chapters, we touched on the negative effects that this may have on the social partner who is being 'phubbed'. Phubbing is a form of **technoference**, whilst phubbing refers to mobile phone use technoference refers to disrupted interactions due to any form of technology.

Think 8.3

We are going to look at the introduction section of a research paper which has investigated the topic of phubbing, specifically during the Covid-19 pandemic. In the study we are going to look at, conducted by Zoppolat et al. (2022), the researchers were interested in whether the Covid-19 pandemic increased levels of technoference. Before we look at the example introduction, it would be beneficial to think about what we would *expect* to see in the introduction using what we already know about the funnel format. Using Figure 8.1, think about what you might expect to see in the introduction as it develops. Look back at our previous example of sugary drinks to help you if you are unsure. You are not expected to know exact theories or studies, but instead consider how the link between the pandemic and technoference may be explained and what the *studies* included may have investigated.

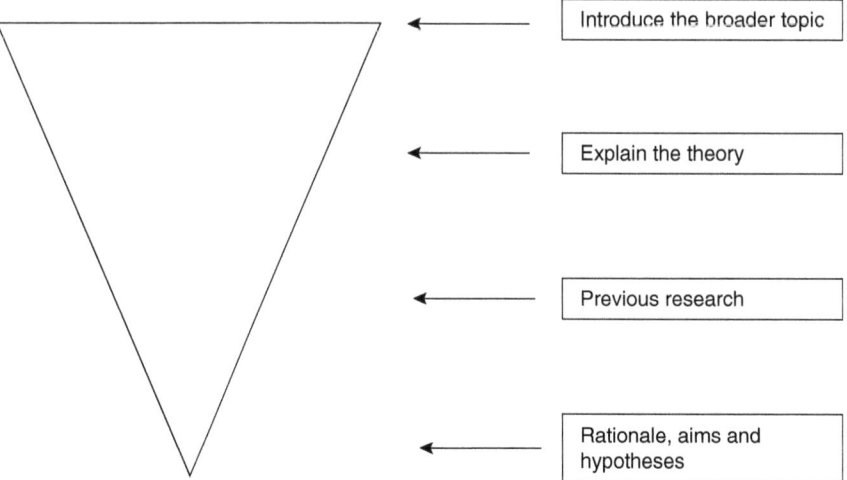

Figure 8.1   The funnel format

(Continued)

This figure represents the structure of the introduction section, which starts off broadly and becomes more specific. The figure includes an upside-down triangle on the left, representing a funnel, with four text boxes on the right. The first text box is next to the broadest part of the triangle and includes the words 'introduce the broader topic', followed by the second text box which says 'explain the theory'. This text box is below the first and has a text box underneath it which says 'previous research'. The final text box is at the bottom point of the triangle and says 'rationale, aims and hypotheses'. Each text box has an arrow which points to the upside-down triangle.

We will not read the full introduction in Zoppolat et al.'s (2022) research, but we will instead focus on some of the paragraphs where the authors have reviewed previous research. Below is an excerpt from Zoppolat et al.'s (2022) introduction. Read through it carefully and consider where you would place this in the funnel format, you may find it helpful to read our comments after you have thought about this.

In terms of where this paragraph fits in the introduction, it can help to think about what the study is testing – whether the Covid-19 pandemic affected technoference and what impact this had on relationship satisfaction. In the section we have reviewed, there is no mention yet of the Covid-19 pandemic and *how* lockdown could impact technoference. We would expect to see this further into the introduction as it becomes more focused. In Table 8.2 is a paragraph from Zoppolat et al.'s (2022) introduction that reviews research which addresses these elements.

Table 8.2 Reading an introduction

Zoppolat et al.'s (2022) introduction section	Comments on the introduction
While technology, such as the use of smartphones, can help people feel connected to others (Pettigrew, 2009) and provide support during stressful times (Holtzman et al., 2017), it can also interfere with relationships (McDaniel & Coyne, 2016) and render social interactions less enjoyable (Aagaard, 2016).	Here the authors identify the broader issue of smartphone use and both the potential benefits and negative consequences of smartphone use.
Part of the negative association between screen time and relationship quality has been attributed to a phenomenon called technoference, whereby the use of technology interferes with in-person social interactions (McDaniel & Coyne, 2014).	The use of research narrows slightly by homing in on screen time during social interactions and the effects this might have.
Technoference can occur through a variety of mediums, but phone use and time spent on social media in particular have been linked to poorer relationship dynamics and outcomes. In the context of romantic relationships, phone use can detract from meaningful in-person connection and take time away from engaging in enjoyable activities with one's partner (e.g. McDaniel et al., 2018). Partner 'phubbing' (i.e. snubbing the other by using one's phone), a form of technoference, occurs frequently, is felt as problematic by both the phubbed partner (e.g. Lenhart & Duggan, 2014) as well as the one doing the phubbing (Kushlev & Leitao, 2020), and is linked with	The introduction narrows further, moving from screen time in social interactions generally to phubbing, technoference

Table 8.2 Reading an introduction *(Continued)*

Zoppolat et al.'s (2022) introduction section	Comments on the introduction
greater conflict and, ultimately, poorer relationship satisfaction (e.g. McDaniel & Coyne, 2016; McDaniel et al., 2020; Roberts & David, 2016; Wang et al., 2017), both in the short and long term (Halpern & Katz, 2017). Social media use can also interfere with healthy relationship functioning by distracting partners from meaningful interactions (Hand et al., 2013), disrupting communication (Tong & Walther, 2011), and, like phubbing, can cause issues in the relationship (e.g. greater conflict, Lenhart & Duggan, 2014; jealousy, Muise et al., 2009; lower relationship satisfaction and commitment, Quiroz & Mickelson, 2021).	specifically due to phone use, and the impact that this has been found to have on romantic relationships. Notice the amount of detail on each study. There is not a copious amount of detail explaining exactly what happened in the study; instead we are just told what we need to know. In this case, what we need to know is what impact phubbing has on romantic relationships. The authors have simply stated these effects and added the citation, there is no need to give any further detail on the studies at this point in the introduction as each set of findings is adding an additional piece of information to the 'story' being told.
Given that social relationships are central to personal psychological and physical well-being (e.g. Holt-Lunstad et al., 2010), and can be particularly important during stressful times (e.g. Pietromonaco & Collins, 2017), such as during the Covid-19 pandemic (Pietromonaco & Overall, 2021), the worry that technology and screen time negatively affect people's relationships is legitimate. Indeed, frequent technology use can have cumulative social costs for people's relationships (Kushlev et al., 2019). Although people use technology for a variety of reasons, particularly to stay connected with others, thwart boredom and seek information (Stockdale & Coyne, 2020; Whiting & Williams, 2013), these reasons may have become even more important — and thus technoference potentially more present — within the Covid-19 pandemic. In this context, where people were suddenly cut off from their usual social lives, the drive to use technology may have been much stronger than before. For example, people have presumably been using technology more to cope with the worry and distress from the pandemic (Garfin, 2020). A recent study found that both adolescents and adults increased their technology and social media use during the pandemic to connect more with others and gather information, particularly when experiencing anxiety (Drouin et al., 2020). Thus, technology may have served as a replacement tool for the missing in-person social interactions (Drouin et al., 2018), as well as a means to manage worries (Lee & Hawkins, 2016; Juvonen et al., 2021), such as health, social isolation and financial preoccupations. Moreover, pandemic-related constraints elicited greater feelings of boredom (Boylan et al., 2020), and people who experience boredom engage in	Here the authors connect what has previously been covered to the specific focus of their study, the Covid-19 pandemic. Notice how the authors explain *why* Covid-19 may influence technoference and support this explanation with previous research. As the introduction becomes focused in on Covid-19 and technoference, the reader is given a little more detail on recent research by Drouin et al. (2020). This study is directly relevant to Zoppolat et al.'s (2022) investigation as it also studied how technology use changed during the pandemic and why. However, the information is still concise and does not include every detail of the procedure. For example, we cannot tell from this summary whether the data was gathered via surveys or interviews; however that point is not necessary hence why it is not included. If we really want to know, we can look to the reference list and read the full study.

(Continued)

Table 8.2 Reading an introduction *(Continued)*

Zoppolat et al.'s (2022) introduction section	Comments on the introduction
phubbing behaviour more frequently (Al-Saggaf et al., 2019), with potential consequences for their relationship well-being (e.g. McDaniel et al., 2020). Thus, the shift towards technology may have also replaced or distracted people from deeper off-line connections with romantic partners in a time in which a partner's support is particularly important as a buffer to the outside stressors (Balzarini et al. (in press)). In this way, pandemic-related stressors may have spilled over into people's most intimate relationships, both directly (Neff & Karney, 2017) and through the increased use of technology (Kushlev & Leitao, 2020).	Whilst Drouin et al.'s (2018) study tells us that technology use increased, the introduction then moves onto reviewing research which explains why this might be (boredom) and what effect this may have (on relationship well-being).

The segments of the introduction reviewed in Zoppolat et al.'s (2022) research paper give an example of how research has been used concisely to build a 'story' for the reader and to take the reader on a journey from the broader topic to the specific focus of the study. Whilst building this story, the introduction also begins to develop the rationale for the current study. Sometimes the writer interweaves the rationale throughout the introduction and sometimes the rationale is explained towards the end of the introduction. We will now look at an example of how a rationale is developed in an introduction. This time, we will look at a different way of understanding romantic relationships, through the exploration of shared problematic behaviours. A problematic behaviour refers to behaviours that we choose to engage in that are enjoyable in the short term but can be problematic long term, such as smoking. Research by Pauly et al. (2023) tested whether couples report higher relationship satisfaction when they both engage in the same problematic behaviours, e.g. they both engage in unhealthy eating. Pauly et al. (2023) cite symptom–system fit theory which suggests that a relationship is part of a family system and that because the shared behaviour fits in that system, it aids to create a sense of closeness when both partners engage in the behaviour together. To test this theory, Pauly et al. (2023) recruited couples who were either both smokers, who were both inactive or who both engaged in unhealthy eating. The researchers collected the data via daily diary entries where participants recorded their daily problematic behaviours, such as how many cigarettes smoked that day, and their feelings of closeness to their partner and their relationship satisfaction each day.

Think 8.4

We are going to look at the introduction in Pauly et al.'s (2023) research paper, specifically the rationale. Before we do this, it would be useful for you to have an overview of the introduction.

Read the brief overview of the introduction below, remind yourself of what Pauly et al. (2023) were trying to find out and how they did it and think about how the authors might develop the rationale from this research.

- The introduction begins with a description of symptom–system fit theory and applies this to problematic behaviours in couples.
- The introduction initially refers to a laboratory study which observed couples discussing alcohol consumption and found that alcohol had a positive effect on the relationship. The authors then cite a laboratory experiment which observed couples during an interaction in the laboratory where one, or both, members of the dyad engaged in smoking – finding that dual smoker couples reported more positive mood when both were smoking.
- Another laboratory study is then reviewed which observed and analysed couple's discussions and found that in couples with high relationship quality, shared problematic behaviour was related to BMI in women. However, in couples with poor relationship quality problematic behaviours were unrelated to BMI.

The above is a very brief overview of the introduction. Using this information, think about the following questions which will help to predict the rationale the authors may present.

- What do you notice about the methods that are used in the studies cited in the introduction and how do these differ to the method used in Pauly et al.'s (2023) study? Why might Pauly et al. (2023) have chosen to use a different method? What might the benefits of this be for the current topic?
- What do you notice about how the problematic behaviours were measured in the studies in the introduction and how that differs to Pauly et al.'s (2023) study? Why might Pauly et al. (2023) have chosen to measure the behaviours in this way? What might be the benefits of this in comparison to how the previous research measured the problematic health behaviours?

Having completed the previous task, you are likely to have a good idea as to how Pauly et al. (2023) developed the rationale for their study. Hopefully you felt that this task was achievable and could see how Pauly et al. (2023) built on the previous research. The idea of this task was to help you to see that there is a logical flow to developing the rationale and it builds throughout the introduction through the review of the research. Let's have a look at what Pauly et al. (2023) did write for their rationale (Table 8.3).

Table 8.3 Reading the rationale in a research paper

Pauly et al.'s (2023) rationale	Comments on the rationale
In brief, the above laboratory research indicates that shared problematic behaviours such as unhealthy eating or smoking might be maintained in couples due to their positive relationship functions, at least in the short term. However, positive relationship functioning has often been measured indirectly (e.g. as affective synchrony: Rohrbaugh et al., 2009; using we-talk: Skoyen et al., 2014), and when it was measured directly (e.g. relationship quality: Skoyen et al., 2018) it was assessed as a stable construct rather than on a time-varying level. This makes it difficult to examine whether for a given couple engaging in shared problematic behaviours goes	The rationale starts by bringing together what we know from the research cited so far. Here the rationale identifies a problem with how relationship outcomes have been measured, namely that participants are not directly asked how satisfied they are. Instead, it is inferred from other measures and in one study where couples are asked, they were only asked once. The problem with that being that satisfaction fluctuates, *(Continued)*

Table 8.3 Reading the rationale in a research paper *(Continued)*

Pauly et al.'s (2023) rationale	Comments on the rationale
along with more positive relationship functioning. It is also an open question whether symptom–system fit generalises across different shared problematic behaviours. There is some evidence that symptom–system fit exists for alcohol consumption (Rohrbaugh et al., 2002), smoking (Rohrbaugh et al., 2009) and shared unhealthy habits in general (Skoyen et al., 2018). Yet, it remains to be tested whether this phenomenon extends to established lifestyle factors that also carry chronic disease risk but appear less saliently risky such as sedentary behaviour and unhealthy diet (Roberts & Barnard, 2005). Third, previous research was laboratory-based, either prompting couples to engage in the shared problematic behaviour (smoking a cigarette together: Shoham et al., 2007) or by asking partners to talk about a certain topic and coding the conversation for shared problematic behaviours (e.g. Skoyen et al., 2018).	meaning that had you of asked participants on a different day then you may have received different results.

The rationale moves on to review gaps in the types of problematic behaviour studied.

Lastly, the rationale touches on the artificial nature of the studies cited as all were laboratory studies which manipulated engagement in the problematic behaviour. |
| Thus, the present research aims to move beyond existing work by taking the investigation of symptoms and systems out of the lab into daily life and by examining three different problematic behaviours (smoking, sedentary behaviour and unhealthy diet) and their time-varying associations with two indicators of positive relationship functioning (closeness and relationship satisfaction). | The rationale ends by taking the points made and explaining how these have been applied to the current study. |

━━━━━ Stop 8.1 ━━━━━

Research is used in the introduction of a research report to lead the reader to understand why the current study has been conducted.

THE DISCUSSION SECTION OF A REPORT

We have reviewed how research is used in the introduction section of a report, but as you have learnt previously a report has several sections: each with a different focus. The discussion section of a report also makes use of research, albeit to a lesser extent than the introduction. The discussion also utilises research to serve a different purpose to the introduction. We will now briefly remind ourselves of the purpose of a discussion section and how a discussion is structured, before moving our focus to how research is used in the discussion.

The purpose of the discussion is to 'discuss' the results of the study that has just been conducted, whereas the introduction takes the reader on a journey to review research and explain why the current study has been conducted using the funnel format; the discussion section instead follows a reverse funnel format. It starts with specific focus on the findings and becomes broader by discussing the findings in relation to what we already know and looks beyond the study to consider how future studies might build on the current study and how the findings might apply to everyday life. Figure 8.2 gives an overview of the discussion.

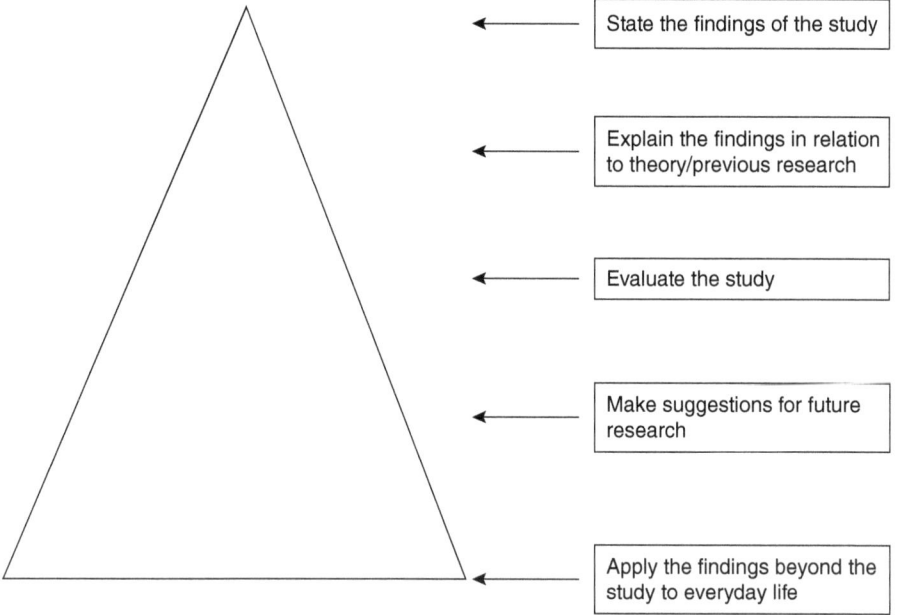

Figure 8.2   An overview of the discussion section

The figure represents the structure of a discussion section, which starts off narrow and becomes more broad. The figure includes a triangle on the left, with five text boxes on the right. The first text box is next to the point of the triangle and includes the words 'state the findings of the study', followed by the second text box which says 'explain the findings in relation to theory/previous research'. This text box is below the first and has a text box underneath it which says 'evaluate the study'. The fourth text box includes the words 'make suggestions for future research' and below is the final text box which says 'apply the findings beyond the study to everyday life'. Each text box has an arrow which points to the triangle.

As we are focused on how to use research, it is the second part of the discussion which is relevant to this chapter. Before we focus in more depth on this, it will be helpful to have a look at a full discussion in published work to give you an idea of how it flows from one part to another. We will utilise the discussion section in Zoppolat et al.'s (2022) research as an example, we came across this study earlier in the chapter.

Think 8.5

Use Google Scholar/your university library online search function to access the full paper, using the reference below.

Zoppolat, G., Righetti, F., Balzarini, R. N., Alonso-Ferres, M., Urganci, B., Rodrigues, D. L., … Slatcher, R. B. (2022). Relationship difficulties and 'technoference' during the COVID-19 pandemic. *Journal of Social and Personal Relationships*, *39*(11), 3204–3227. https://doi.org/10.1177/02654075221093611

(Continued)

Once you have the paper, read through the introduction (you have already read this earlier in the chapter) to remind yourself of the research that the authors reviewed. You should then read the discussion section. The next part of this chapter applies the discussion to the reverse funnel format. To get the most from this activity it would be useful to not only have read the discussion, but to also have it open so that you can follow along with our reflection on the discussion.

As you can see from Table 8.4, research is generally used in two key areas in the discussion. Primarily to explain the results and to discuss whether they align with the previous research in the field, but secondly to support strengths and limitations that the authors identify in the study. When researchers write a research report, they need to consider the strengths and limitations of the way the study was designed and conducted. As part of explaining these evaluative points, often research evidence is included to support the point made. For this chapter, we will focus on using research to explain the results as this is an area where students who are new to studying psychology tend to find challenging. We hope after finishing this chapter you will be a little more confident in your ability to discuss findings whilst referring to research previously identified in the introduction.

Table 8.4 How to structure the discussion section

Reverse funnel format	Explanation	A reflection on Zoppolat et al.'s (2022) discussion section
Explain the findings	The discussion begins with describing the results. Whilst the results section analyses the data and includes the findings, the discussion brings the findings together using easy to digest language. The reader should be able to read the beginning of the discussion and understand the key results without necessarily having to read the results section. Often this part of the discussion begins by restating what the study was aiming to find out and describes the findings in relation to the research question and/or hypotheses that were stated in the introduction.	Zoppolat et al.'s (2022) discussion begins by giving a very concise overview of the findings from both studies, followed by a little more detail on the specific findings from each study. This publication included two studies, both diary studies, one measured technoference and relationship outcomes before and during Covid-19 lockdown. The second study measured reasons for technoference during the pandemic and relationship outcomes. In the discussion, the authors described each set of findings separately. Study 1 found that relationships were rated more positively before lockdown. Study 2 found that social media was used more frequently when individuals had less face-to-face interactions and experienced boredom and this in turn predicted lower relationship quality.

Table 8.4 How to structure the discussion section *(Continued)*

Reverse funnel format	Explanation	A reflection on Zoppolat et al.'s (2022) discussion section
Explore the findings in relation to theory and previous research	The discussion then moves on to *discussing* the research. This may start with explaining the results from a theoretical perspective, specifically any theory/ies previously explained in the introduction. If the findings support the hypothesis/es it should be relatively straight forward to explain the findings using the theory. Usually, the author will also state what the findings add to what is already known on the topic. Next, the findings are discussed in relation to the most relevant studies that were cited in the introduction. This may include explaining how the results are similar to previous research, or a discussion as to why the findings may differ from previous research. The discussion does not have to refer to every study in the introduction, just those which are most relevant to the aim of the current study.	Zoppolat et al. (2022) go on to consider their findings in relation to some of the research summarised in the introduction. In discussing study 1, the authors refer to technoference and how technology can disrupt and interfere with social interactions. The discussion introduces some research that was not included in the introduction to explain the results. This includes research which has tested the effects of technoference in daily life overtime on relationship quality, supporting the current findings. The discussion then includes additional theoretical concepts to explain the findings, such as the stress spillover hypothesis which explains how stress can spillover into romantic relationships. The discussion also explores the specific context in which this study took place – during Covid-19 and how this may have impacted the results. The discussion goes on to explore the results in further detail by reviewing the differences at a between and within level between Study 1 and Study 2, with Study 2 only finding effects at the between person level.
Evaluating the study	The author will provide some limitations with the way in which the study was carried out. This is likely to draw on factors such as the method used, the procedure, the sample or how the variables were operationalised. In some discussions, the author/s will also explore some of the strengths in the way the study was carried out. The limitations are almost always present, as it is important that the reader is aware of the extent to which the findings are valid.	Zoppolat et al.'s (2022) discussion does refer to some of the strengths of the study, specifically in the methodology used and how the repeated measurements offer further detail beyond one off measurements in previous research in this field. To substantiate this point, the authors refer to other studies which have studied technoference in daily life, but only using one-time measurements. Limitations are also discussed, the first being potential issues with how phone use and social media use

(Continued)

Table 8.4 How to structure the discussion section *(Continued)*

Reverse funnel format	Explanation	A reflection on Zoppolat et al.'s (2022) discussion section
	Studies that were cited in the introduction, or research in addition to the introduction, may be cited here to support the lines of argument made.	were measured. Again, this is supported by research which has found that asking people about their phone use may not be a completely accurate measure. The second limitation identified is also related to how the variables were operationalised, this time it is technoference (in study 2) that is raised as a potential issue as the wording of the question may have led to answers that were not specifically technoference. Note that technoference occurs when technology interrupts an interaction, Zoppolat et al. (2022) did not specify whether social media use measured occurred in the presence of their partner or not. There is no research used to back up this point, this is not to say it is not possible to bring in research here. The authors could have found a study which has measured both general use and use around a partner to see if there is a difference. A final limitation discussed is around the lack of demographic data collected, Zoppolat et al. (2022) discuss differences in technology use depending on demographics and cite research to support this claim.
Directions for future research	Research does not complete the 'puzzle'; it gives us one piece of the puzzle and gives us an idea of where future research needs to go. In the discussion, the author will usually make suggestions that are based on the limitations of the current study. For example, if there is an issue with how one of the variables was operationalised, it might be suggested that future research operationalise the variable slightly differently. It is unlikely that any big changes will be suggested; usually these are smaller changes to see what effect these may have on the findings.	Zoppolat et al. (2022) identify several avenues for further research, notably ones that build on the limitations of their study. This includes research which collects detailed demographic data and comparing perceptions of technology use to objective measures of technology use.

Table 8.4 How to structure the discussion section *(Continued)*

Reverse funnel format	Explanation	A reflection on Zoppolat et al.'s (2022) discussion section
Application beyond the study	The purpose of psychological research is to explain behaviour in everyday life. Whilst the study being discussed is likely to have been manipulated in some way, it is important that the reader is made aware as to how the findings could be utilised beyond the study. This usually involves considering how the findings could be used to make positive changes to behaviour. For example, if phubbing does affect relationships, the research can be used to advise people as to how to try and reduce phubbing to improve relationship quality. Note that application to real life is not always included, as it may not be pertinent or there may not be enough research in the field yet to make recommendations.	Zoppolat et al. (2022) do not include this in their discussion. This may be for several reasons. Firstly, the study is specifically focused on the Covid-19 pandemic, which was a unique situation that is unlikely to occur again anytime soon. Secondly, as the study was an exploratory study, there is not enough previous research in the field which has also investigated similar behaviour in the pandemic. Therefore, it is difficult to draw any firm conclusions that we can use to advise people with.

Using Research in the Discussion to Interpret the Results

The introduction section of a research report will explain to the reader some of the key research in the field which has led to the design, and the predictions made, in the current study. Often, the findings in the study conducted will be in line with the previous findings and support the hypothesis. When interpreting the findings in the discussion it is tempting to write, *the findings supported previous research by XYZ, as the findings were the same.* Now, of course you would not necessarily be incorrect in saying this, but it is not really a *discussion*, more of a statement. The reader needs to understand *why* the findings of the current study were similar to previous studies. It is not enough to simply say they are, as a scientist you are seeking to explore why, as this will inform future research.

To aid your understanding of how a discussion uses research to explain the findings, we will look at some examples of sections of a discussion. Whilst the ideal place to look for examples is of course in published research, we will begin by looking at some examples from undergraduate students. Before we look at some examples, we first need to familiarise ourselves with the topic area.

The example we are going to look at is a study which investigates prosocial behaviour, specifically if computer games which contain prosocial content can increase prosocial behaviour. Prosocial behaviour involves actions which are intended to benefit others; this may include giving money to charity, providing emotional support, sharing or helping. There are multiple explanations as to what might cause people to engage in prosocial behaviour, one of which is that the behaviour is learnt. One way that behaviour can be learnt is via social learning theory. We touched on this theory earlier in the chapter, it is the suggestion that we learn via observing behaviour in a role model and imitating that behaviour. If we apply this to computer games, if the computer game includes a role model that engages in prosocial behaviour the person playing the game may later on imitate this behaviour, either in the game or in the real world. The students in the examples we will look at are writing the discussion for an experiment that allocated adults to play either a computer game that involved prosocial behaviour, specifically helping, as part of the game play or a neutral game that did not involve any social interactions. After playing the game, the experimenter 'accidentally' knocked some of their belongings off their desk. Helping behaviour was measured by whether the participant helped the experimenter to pick up the items and how quickly they helped. The hypothesis was that participants who played the prosocial game would be more likely to help the experimenter and quicker to help the experimenter than those who played the neutral game.

Using Research When the Findings Align with Previous Research

Let's imagine that the findings from the study described above support the hypothesis; the participants who played the prosocial game were more likely to help and were quicker to help, than participants who played the neutral game. In the discussion we would need to consider *why* these findings may have occurred drawing on previous research.

   Keeping in mind what you have just read about the study being discussed, please read the following excerpt of discussion sections written by the first student.

> This study tested whether prosocial behaviour can be learnt through playing prosocial video games. The key findings of the current study show that playing a prosocial game can increase levels of prosocial behaviour, above playing a neutral game, supporting the hypothesis. Participants who played the prosocial video game were more likely to help the experimenter pick up their belongings than the participants who played the neutral game. The findings of this study support previous findings that prosocial behaviour is influenced by video games. In a similar study, Greitemeyer and Osswald (2010) also had some participants play a prosocial game, whilst other participants played either a neutral game or an aggressive game. The participants who played the prosocial game were more likely to pick up the pencils than those who played either the neutral or aggressive game. Gentile et al. (2009) also investigated prosocial behaviour and found similar findings to the current study. They used a range of methods and samples, which shows that the results of the current study are generalisable. Whilst we studied

adults, other studies report similar findings in children aged 9–14 (Saleem et al., 2012) and 3–6 using a tablet rather than computer (Shoshani et al., 2022). In another study, participants were also more prosocial after playing a prosocial game, compared to playing a non-prosocial game but interestingly there was no difference in prosocial behaviours after game play regardless of whether they were rewarded for prosocial behaviour or punished for not being prosocial in the game (Yin et al., 2022).

Think 8.6

Having read the example paragraph from Student 1, think about the following questions:

- Has the student been explicit in stating if, and how, the current findings support previous studies?
- Are all the studies cited directly relevant to the focus of the current study?
- Has the student provided an appropriate amount of detail for each study cited?
- Has the student explained potential reasons *why* the results of the current study are similar to previous findings?

Now consider a second student's attempt to link the findings of the same study to previous research in a discussion.

The findings of the current study are consistent with previous studies which also found that participants engage in more prosocial behaviour after playing a prosocial game compared to a neutral game in both adults (Greitemeyer & Osswald, 2010; Yin et al., 2022) and children (Saleem et al., 2012; Shoshani et al., 2022). The similarity in findings can be partly explained due to the similarity in the methodology across studies which manipulated exposure to prosocial games. It is worth noting that operationalisation of prosocial behaviour varied across studies, which suggests the effect of prosocial games extends across various types of prosocial behaviour. Research from Gentile et al. (2009) report similar findings across three different countries and importantly utilising correlational and longitudinal methods as well as experimental. Indeed, a meta-analysis confirmed that prosocial games influence prosocial behaviour in the short and long term (Greitemeyer & Mügge, 2014). Together, these findings support the assumptions of social learning theory that human behaviour is shaped by observing and imitating the behaviour of others (Bandura, 1986). Children who observe adults modelling prosocial behaviour are more likely to be prosocial (Schuhmacher et al., 2019; Williamson et al., 2013). As the participants playing prosocial games observe prosocial behaviour during gameplay, the increase in prosocial behaviour may be due to modelling this behaviour.

━━━━━━━━ Think 8.7 ━━━━━━━━

Having read the example paragraph from Student 2, think about the following questions:

- Has the student been explicit in stating if, and how, the current findings support previous studies?
- Are all the studies cited directly relevant to the focus of the current study?
- Has the student provided an appropriate amount of detail for each study cited?
- Has the student explained potential reasons *why* the results of the current study are similar to previous findings?

You will notice that although Student 2 used fewer words than Student 1, they covered more research and more ideas. Both students were explicit in stating that the current findings supported previous research. Student 1, however, lost focus a little and begun to describe some of the research rather than focusing on explaining the similarity in results. Student 2 made a better attempt at this by using the references to previous research more concisely. Notice how Student 2 makes a point and adds in several citations, without needing to give further detail on the study in comparison to Student 1 who tended to redescribe the research. Both students have included research relevant to the current study, but the inclusion of Yin et al. (2022) by Student 1 is not directly relevant to the current study which was focused on social learning theory as an explanation rather than positive reinforcement. A core difference between Student 1 and Student 2 is that Student 2 explains the similarity in results, whereas Student 1 does not. This is important when you are writing a discussion, if there are similarities in findings this is likely to be due to similarities in methodology to previous research and due to the underlying mechanisms, which are influencing the behaviour.

━━━━━━━━ Stop 8.2 ━━━━━━━━

If you are explaining similarities in findings, consider methodological similarities and theoretical explanations for the similarities.

Using Research When the Findings Do Not Align with the Research in the Introduction

Sometimes when conducting research, we will not find what we expected to find, and our results will not align with the previous research cited in the introduction. It is crucial when this happens to consider why there might be these differences in findings.

Let's imagine that the findings from the study investigating prosocial behaviour (described previously) fail to support the hypothesis; the participants who played the pro-social game were not more likely to help than participants who played the neutral game. In the discussion, we would need to consider *why* these findings may have occurred drawing on previous research.

Now read the following excerpts from discussion sections written by students. This is the first student's approach.

> The current study found that playing a prosocial computer game did not increase prosocial behaviour in comparison to playing a neutral game. These findings fail to provide support for the relationship between playing prosocial games and increased prosocial behaviour in both adults (Greitemeyer & Osswald, 2010; Yin et al., 2022) and children (Saleem et al., 2012; Shoshani et al., 2022); thus the simple act of playing a prosocial game does not appear to increase subsequent prosocial behaviour.
>
> One possible explanation for this null effect is that the act of simply observing prosocial behaviour in computer game characters may be too simplistic to facilitate prosocial behaviour outside of the game. Indeed, for computer games to influence prosocial behaviour the game needs to influence cognitive processes and create scripts and schemas around prosocial acts (Gentile et al., 2009). If participants engaged in a more complex game, this may have changed cognitive processes and led to changes in prosocial behaviour.
>
> A second explanation may be that individual game play does not reflect the type of gameplay that participants are used to in their everyday lives. Online gaming allows players to interact with other players in the game cooperatively, and cooperative gameplay even in the predominantly violent game Fortnite has been found to increase prosocial behaviour, compared to non-cooperative play in the same game (Shoshani & Krauskopf, 2021). As this is likely to be the type of gameplay participants are familiar with, the solo gameplay in the current study may have lacked the social interactions necessary to influence prosocial behaviour.
>
> Third, the simplicity of the prosocial game may not have increased intrinsic motivation to be prosocial. This can be explained by the Player Experience of Need Satisfaction (PENS) model (Ryan et al., 2006) which suggests that the effects of playing video games are dependent on how the experience influences competence, autonomy and relatedness. Due to both the simplicity of the prosocial game used in this study and due to the short amount of time spent

playing the game, it is possible that the experience did not increase any of the three features identified by the PENS model.

━━━━━━━━ Think 8.8 ━━━━━━━━

Having read the example paragraph from Student 1, think about the following questions:

- Has the student been explicit in stating if, and how, the current findings conflict previous studies?
- Has the student explained *why* the findings may contradict the previous research?
- Are all the studies cited directly relevant to the focus of the current study?
- Has the student provided an appropriate amount of detail for each study cited?
- Has the student explained potential reasons *why* the results of the current study are similar to previous findings?

Now consider the excerpt from the second student.

The current study found that regardless of whether participants played a prosocial game or a neutral game, there was no difference in subsequent prosocial behaviour. These findings differ to previous studies such as Greitemeyer and Osswald (2010) who found that when participants played the prosocial game of Lemmings, they were more likely to engage in a spontaneous prosocial act than the participants who played the neutral game of Tetris or the aggressive game of Lamers. The difference in findings is surprising as prosocial behaviour was measured similarly in both studies; by picking up items the experimenter had knocked over. Possibly the difference in the game played may have influenced the findings, the current study involved a game where the player observes characters helping each other, whereas Greitemeyer and Osswald (2010) had participants play Lemmings, which involves directly helping the lemmings to safety. Perhaps being actively involved in prosocial behaviour in the game is what caused the subsequent prosocial behaviour, rather than learning via imitating the prosocial behaviour of other game characters. Social learning theory (Bandura, 1986) may be too simplistic to explain the relationship between playing video games and prosocial behaviour.

Another explanation for the difference in findings in the current study and previous research could be in whether the prosocial game changed the cognitions in the participants. Previous research has found that playing prosocial games can increase the accessibility of prosocial thoughts (Greitemeyer & Osswald, 2011). As the current study did not measure prosocial thoughts, it is possible that the lack of significance in the findings is because the game play did not affect prosocial thoughts.

Lastly, the prosocial behaviour observed in the game did not map onto real life behaviour. The prosocial behaviour observed was specific to the storyline and characters in the game; the act of helping someone pick up dropped items was not depicted in the game played. Possibly if the gameplay involved actions that were more easily relatable to everyday life the results would differ, for example when players worked together cooperatively with a teammate, prosocial cooperative behaviour was higher than in the participants who played alone (Greitemeyer & Cox, 2013). Greitemeyer and Cox (2013) measured the same prosocial behaviour that the participants engaged in during the prosocial game, which may explain why significant effects were found in their study but not the current study.

▬▬▬ Think 8.9 ▬▬▬

Having read the example paragraph from Student 1, think about the following questions:

- Has the student been explicit in stating if, and how, the current findings conflict previous studies?
- Has the student explained *why* the findings may contradict the previous research?
- Are all the studies cited directly relevant to the focus of the current study?
- Has the student provided an appropriate amount of detail for each study cited?
- Has the student explained potential reasons *why* the results of the current study are similar to previous findings?

Both students do explain how the current findings differ from previous research. Student 2 draws on one study at a time to explain the differences in findings from a methodological perspective whereas Student 1 makes use of more studies and focuses on broader ideas around both theory and research. Student 2 also tends to restate the findings of research which is not necessary if these studies were already reviewed in the introduction. Student 1 is much more concise in applying the findings to previous research. Notice how Student 1 brings in additional research from Shoshani and Krauskopf (2021) and Student 2 brings in research from Greitemeyer and Cox (2013). When the findings do not support previous research, the author needs to find evidence to explain the difference in findings; you can see how both students bring in different research to offer an explanation. Both students utilise findings which are directly relevant to the current study and both students offer explanations beyond social learning theory which is to be expected as the findings did not align with the prediction based on social learning theory. Notice how both students also offer more than one possible explanation for the non-significant findings; this is because we cannot say with certainty why the findings do not support the hypothesis and therefore must consider a range of explanations. Presenting several explanations also feeds into the research cycle, as other researchers who read the discussion can consider these explanations in the design of their studies. Note that we have only included an excerpt of a discussion from each student here, but if we were to include the full discussion, we would see suggestions for future research For example, Student 2 refers to not measuring prosocial cognitions therefore it would be logical for Student 2 to suggest that future research measures this. This is a useful tip for when you are exploring limitations in a discussion, if appropriate follow the limitation with a suggestion as to how the limitation can be addressed in future research.

▄▄▄▄▄ Stop 8.3 ▄▄▄▄▄

If you are explaining differences in findings, consider methodological differences and alternative theoretical explanations for the differences.

⸻ Explore further ⸻

To further develop your skills in using psychological research when writing a research report, it is important that you engage with reading published research and look at how these sections are written. The more you familiarise yourself with academic writing, the easier it will be for you when you come to write your own introduction and discussion sections. Below is a list of published research papers that are related to the topics covered in this chapter (phubbing and prosocial behaviour), your task is to read the introduction and discussion section of the paper to familiarise yourself with how the authors make use of research. You can decide how many of the research papers you read, but whichever you choose remember to focus on how research is used and how much detail is given on each study.

Coyne, S. M., Jensen, A. C., Smith, N. J., & Erickson, D. H. (2016). Super Mario brothers and sisters: Associations between coplaying video games and sibling conflict and affection. *Journal of adolescence, 47*, 48–59. https://doi.org/10.1016/j.adolescence.2015.12.001

Kim, S. S., Huang-Isherwood, K. M., Zheng, W., & Williams, D. (2022). The art of being together: How group play can increase reciprocity, social capital, and social status in a multiplayer online game. *Computers in Human Behavior, 133*, 107291. https://doi.org/10.1016/j.chb.2022.107291

Schneider, F. M., & Hitzfeld, S. (2021). I ought to put down that phone but I phub nevertheless: Examining the predictors of phubbing behavior. *Social Science Computer Review, 39*(6), 1075–1088. https://doi.org/10.1177/0894439319882365

Shoshani, A. (2023). From virtual to prosocial reality: The effects of prosocial virtual reality games on preschool Children's prosocial tendencies in real life environments. *Computers in Human Behavior, 139*, 107546. https://doi.org/10.1016/j.chb.2022.107546

Sun, J., & Samp, J. A. (2022). 'Phubbing is happening to you': Examining predictors and effects of phubbing behaviour in friendships. *Behaviour & Information Technology*, *41*(12), 2691–2704. https://doi.org/10.1080/0144929X.2021.1943711

Thomas, T. T., Carnelley, K. B., & Hart, C. M. (2022). Phubbing in romantic relationships and retaliation: A daily diary study. *Computers in Human Behavior*, *137*, 107398. https://doi.org/10.1016/j.chb.2022.107398

Verheijen, G. P., Stoltz, S. E., van den Berg, Y. H., & Cillessen, A. H. (2019). The influence of competitive and cooperative video games on behavior during play and friendship quality in adolescence. *Computers in Human Behavior, 91*, 297–304. https://doi.org/10.1016/j.chb.2018.10.023

Zhan, S., Shrestha, S., & Zhong, N. (2022). Romantic relationship satisfaction and phubbing: The role of loneliness and empathy. *Frontiers in Psychology, 13*, 967339. https://doi.org/10.3389/fpsyg.2022.967339

KEY TAKEAWAYS

This chapter and the previous chapter have both explored how to use psychological research in your writing. Whilst Chapter 7 focused on essay writing, this chapter has focused on how to make use of psychological research when writing a research report. This chapter is not an exhaustive guide and working with the feedback you are provided with on your written work is crucial to improving your writing, but we hope that this chapter provides you with some pointers that avoid you becoming sidetracked with overly long descriptions of studies.

We began the chapter by considering how a research report differs to an essay. It is important you understand this, because each has a different focus which in turn influences how you utilise research. An essay makes use of research findings to discuss a set question, whereas a research report involves carrying out a study and writing it up.

A research report includes different sections, each with a specific focus. In this chapter, we focused specifically on the introduction and discussion section of a research report as psychological research is crucial to writing these sections effectively. The introduction and discussion section each follow a different structure and whilst both will utilise many of the same studies, they will use them differently. The introduction uses research to explain to the reader why the current study is being conducted; this involves reviewing what is already known on that topic and where there are gaps in the literature. The discussion explains the findings of the current study in relation to the research reviewed in the introduction. The discussion will take a different direction depending on whether the findings of the current study support the research included in the introduction or not. If the findings are not significant, the discussion will need to include additional research to explain potential reasons for these differences.

The examples included in this chapter from published studies and students should provide you with some guidance as to how research is used. However, there are no rules here and you will need to consider how the literature fits in with the study that you are writing about. Rest assured that this takes time, and you are not expected to be able to do this successfully just because you have read this chapter. You will need to read published research papers with a specific focus on how authors make use of research in the introduction and discussion sections and actively work on trying to apply this style of writing to your own work.

9

REFERENCING

─────── Key goals for this chapter ───────

- Understand the importance of referencing.
- Understand the difference between primary and secondary referencing.
- Understand how to structure references.
- Know about referencing management software.

The focus of this book has been on how to use research and so it makes sense now to spend the last chapter discussing why and how you reference the research that you have used in your assignment. If you have spent all that time researching a topic and ensuring that you have used it appropriately in your essay (see Chapter 7) or report (see Chapter 8) then you do not want to fall at the final hurdle and not reference the sources correctly (or not at all). Ensuring you include all the necessary citations in your work and making sure the formatting is accurate may seem like an unimportant task, but it is surprising how jarring it can be to read a piece of work that does not follow the correct conventions for referencing sources. Spending time getting this skill perfected is time well spent and will come as second nature to you fairly quickly. Students always worry about referencing, but it really is not that bad and once you are in the practice of doing it, you will not even have to think about it (like walking on a familiar route and when arriving not remembering anything about the journey).

This chapter is first going to explain what referencing is, why it is important and what is the difference between primary and secondary referencing before going through the mechanics of how to reference.

WHAT IS REFERENCING?

Referencing is about acknowledging other people's contribution to your work. It is about ensuring that you provide details of the sources you have used so that anyone reading your work can then find those sources. In this chapter, we will be exploring both *why* you need to use citations and referencing in your work and *how* to create those citations and references.

WHY IS REFERENCING IMPORTANT?

Including citations and a reference list may seem like a bit of a burden and another hurdle to jump over that takes time, but referencing other people's work is important for several reasons. We explored some of these reasons in Chapter 7, but it is important to understand why we reference before looking at the mechanics of referencing. Firstly, it is important that you give the authors the credit for their ideas. We all have experienced a time in our lives when someone says they have had a great idea and as they outline the details you realise that it was actually your idea. This may have happened in school, college or even with friends and family. It is not pleasant when it happens, especially if they receive some form of accolades for the idea that was yours. The same can be said for ideas in academia. If you have acquired knowledge from a source and you are using that knowledge in your assignment, then give them the credit they deserve by citing their work. If you do not cite the source of knowledge, then you run the risk of being accused of plagiarism which is defined as using other people's ideas, words or other material in your work without the proper acknowledgement.

If, having read the paragraph above, you are now concerned about accidentally plagiarising someone else's work, do go back to Chapter 7. In that chapter, we explored how to paraphrase by taking notes in your own words whilst being careful to ensure that you indicate in your notes the source of the content/argument (e.g. if it is a journal article carefully indicating the author(s) and the date). Getting into the habit of doing this will mean that when you come back to your notes you can recall the origin of the ideas so that you can cite them in your assignment and ensure the reference appears in your reference list (see later in this chapter on how to do this).

The second reason to include citations and a list of references is to ensure that the reader of your assignment can find that source for themselves. Providing the surname and date means the reader can then go to the reference list at the back and search alphabetically to find the full reference. Using that reference the reader can then track down that original source and read it for themselves. As outlined in Chapters 7 and 8, you often can only provide an overview of the research methodology and findings; so by providing the citation you are giving your reader the opportunity to find out more. Similarly, you will find that turning to the reference list of a paper or a book you are reading to track down the original source is extremely useful if you want to know more about the research. It is really satisfying as a reader to track down the original source to be able to answer questions you may have such as 'were there any other dependent variables in their study' or 'what other questions were the participants asked' or 'did they control for X variable' and so on (see Chapter 6 for more information about reading research).

Another reason to include citations is to show your reader/marker that you have researched the area and not just stated your opinion. Students can mistakenly think that when writing assessments in psychology they need to state their opinion and so including references is seen as a negative. This is not the case. You need to demonstrate that you have read and understood past research and show how it relates to the assessment you have been set. Therefore, using citations and including a reference list is essential.

Hopefully, we have convinced you to use citations and include a reference list. But before we look at the mechanics of using citations and referencing, we need to explore the different sources you can use – primary and secondary sources.

WHAT ARE PRIMARY AND SECONDARY SOURCES?

Primary sources are the original source of the information. In psychology, they are normally original research articles and often the work covered in those articles are referred to as empirical studies. They are written by the researchers who have conducted the research. A **secondary source** in psychology are those articles, books or lecture slides that summarise and provide interpretations of original research. As such, secondary sources can be often easier and quicker to read as they are condensed versions of the original and highlight the main results. However, because they are interpretations of the original and provide only the main results, they can sometimes be missing details and even a bit misleading at times. To provide an example, it is often the case with experimental research that researchers will conduct several studies and report them in the one article. However, due to issues of brevity, the secondary source may only report on one of those studies or just a few sentences about the overall pattern of results. If you were to obtain the primary source, you may discover that the effect that is being reported in the secondary source was only actually found in certain conditions, but this nuance is lost in the summary. Therefore, wherever possible, it is a good idea to go back to the primary source, particularly if that source is key to your argument. Secondary sources are often a good place to start if you want to get an overall summary of what research has found in a given area, and then you can track down the key primary sources using their reference list.

Whether you are using a primary or secondary source impacts the way you present the citation (see later for how to reference primary and secondary sources). Importantly, you should only cite a primary source when you have accessed and read that source. If you have read about the research from another source, then you need to cite the secondary source. This demonstrates to the reader that you have only read the secondary source and not the primary source.

WHEN DON'T YOU NEED TO REFERENCE?

You don't need to reference what is common knowledge. For example, you would not need to reference who the President of the United States is or that Facebook is an example of social media. It is considered common knowledge because a) most people know these things and b) they are easy to verify using several sources (written or verbal). Common knowledge may be subject-specific and depend on the level of study, so the audience needs to be considered when deciding what is 'common knowledge'. When you are writing your assessments you can assume that your reader has some understanding of psychology so you need not provide citations for all concepts.

HOW DO I STRUCTURE REFERENCES?

To ensure consistency, references follow a standardised structure. There are slightly different structures to follow depending on your discipline. In psychology the most used referencing system is APA Style, developed by the American Psychological Association. The guidance is updated periodically and at the time of writing, APA Style is in its 7th edition. The guidance given here, therefore, refers to APA 7th style referencing.

When you are writing an assignment, there are two places you will need to reference. The first is within the text itself. Whenever you refer to someone else's ideas, research and theoretical ideas you will need to provide a citation that tells the reader whose work you are referring to. The second place you will reference is at the end of the assignment in the reference list. The reference list includes the full details of the reference, which allows the reader to follow the reference up if necessary. Crucial is that the citations within the assignment match those in the reference list. Every citation in the assignment should appear in the reference list, and every reference in the reference list should appear within the assignment as a citation. The purpose of this is to allow the reader to know exactly where you used the information you are referencing and to allow them to find the sources you used (if they want to).

In-Text Citations

We will begin with the citations that appear in the assignment and you will be pleased to read that the format for these is relatively straightforward. The first piece of information you need to know when you are writing an in-text citation is whether you are using a primary or secondary source. The format for each is slightly different, and thus we will explain each separately below.

Primary Sources

For a primary source the in-text citation follows the author-date format. The exact structure depends on where in the sentence you put the citation and on how many authors there are.

You can either place your citation so that it forms part of the sentence, or you can put it in parentheses at the end of the information you are using. Whether you decide to add the citation to the narrative or in parentheses is your decision, you will need to think about what works best in the sentence you are writing.

The Citation as Part of the Narrative

> Wu and Cai (2023) found that when children were exposed to peers' beliefs that boys are better at maths than girls, boys' subsequent maths performance improved whereas girls' subsequent math performance declined.

We can tell from the citation that there are two authors to the piece of work being cited. Notice as well that each author is only referred to by their surname and no initials are included. When you use an in-text citation as part of the narrative, the year of publication should be in parentheses directly after the author's surname. In this example, we can see that the work was published in 2023.

The Citation in Parentheses

> If children are told that their peers perceive boys as better at maths than girls, boys' subsequent maths performance improves whereas girls' subsequent math performance declines. (Wu & Cai, 2023)

We have used the same study here so that you can see how a citation differs depending on whether it forms part of the narrative or not. You can see that the inclusion of the authors and the year remains, but when a reference is in parentheses and there is more than one author, we use the & (ampersand) symbol rather than writing 'and'. We also put the year in the parentheses, rather than separately.

Two Authors or Less

If the source you are citing has one or two authors, then both authors are named in the citation.

> Wang and Ziano (2023) found that if people give ambiguous answers, if affects how they are perceived, with people less likely to date or befriend people who provide ambiguous responses.

When people provide ambiguous responses to questions, they are perceived as less likeable. (Wang & Ziano, 2023)

Three or More Authors

When there are three or more authors, you only cite the first author and then add 'et al.' to signal that there are more than two authors. 'et al.' is the abbreviation for 'et alia', which is Latin for 'and other people'; thus it tells the reader that there are other authors.

> Townsend et al. (2023) found that women who perceived gender roles as malleable rather than fixed, anticipated experiencing less work-family conflict than women with fixed gender role perspectives.

> Women who perceive gender roles as malleable rather than fixed, anticipate experiencing less work-family conflict than women with fixed gender role perspectives. (Townsend et al., 2023)

The format of the citation is slightly different to one or two authors, as with the addition of 'et al.' we also have a bit of extra punctuation to include. Notice how in the narrative citation there is a full stop after 'al', whereas in the parentheses citation the 'al' is followed by a full stop and a comma. These little details are important in correctly applying the referencing system.

Secondary Sources

For a secondary source the principles are the same in that an author-date system is applied, but for a secondary source it needs to be clear from the citation that you have not read the original source. This is achieved by adding 'as cited in' to the citation, where you are essentially telling the reader you read the information via another source.

As with primary citations, you can write these either within the narrative or in parentheses and the same rules apply if there are more than two authors.

Secondary Citation as Part of the Narrative

> Patel and Hu (2008, as cited in Marks et al., 2021) found that shorter sleep duration in children was related to weight gain.

In the example above, we can see that the person writing has not read Patel and Hu's (2008) work but that they have read about Patel and Hu's (2008) work via Marks et al. (2021). If the reader wants to find out more about Patel and Hu's (2008) work, they know to look for Marks et al. (2021) in the reference list and not Patel and Hu (2008). Patel and Hu (2008) should not appear in the reference list, as the writer has not read this source.

Secondary Citation in Parentheses

> Children who sleep for shorter durations are more likely to gain weight. (Patel & Hu, 2008, as cited in Marks et al., 2021)

You can see that the same principles apply when using parentheses and that an ampersand is used instead of writing 'and' when there are two authors. The 'as cited in' is included in the same way, thus again it is clear to the reader that the writer of this piece has not read Patel and Hu's (2008) work directly.

Two Authors or Less

> Bandura (1977b, as cited in Marks et al., 2021) proposed the concept of self-efficacy, which is a trait that refers to having confidence in one's ability to carry out a particular action.

> Self-efficacy is a trait that refers to having confidence in one's ability to carry out a particular action. (Bandura, 1977b, as cited in Marks et al., 2021)

We can see from this example that the writer is referring to a concept that Bandura (1977b) proposed, but that they did not read Bandura's work and instead read about Bandura in Marks et al.'s (2021) work.

Three or More Authors

> Thompson et al. (2016, as cited in Marks et al., 2021) analysed an online forum for teenagers and young people with cancer and found that online users were more likely to use future tense and discuss emotion than in face-to-face support groups.

> Teenagers and young adults using an online support forum for cancer patients were more likely to use future tense and discuss emotion than in face-to-face support groups. (Thompson et al., 2016, as cited in Marks et al., 2021)

As with the previous examples, we still have 'as cited in'; we just have the addition of 'et al.' to the source being referred to with either a full stop or full stop and comma after the 'al' depending on whether the citation is in the narrative or parentheses.

━━━━━━━ Think 9.1 ━━━━━━━

Below are some examples of in-text citations, for each one identify any error or errors that you can spot:

a) Boers, E., Afzali, M. H., Newton, N., and Conrod, P. (2019) found that adolescents who spent more time on social media reported higher levels of depression.
b) Fourth year female college students who live with pets or were missing their pets have higher internalising symptoms than females who do not live with pets or do not report missing their pets (Barker et al., 2020).
c) Lee et al., 2014 found that children are less likely to lie if they hear a story that promotes the positive consequences of telling the truth as opposed to the negative consequences of dishonesty.

(Continued)

d) Boot and Simons et al. (2013) discuss why much of the research using active control groups to measure the placebo effect, rarely include active control groups which involve the same level of expectation as the treatment group.

e) Brief mindfulness sessions have been found to increase enjoyment of food and reduce calorie consumption (Arch et al., 2016).

The aim of this activity was to apply your understanding of how to format in-text citations.

Example (a) should not include the initials of the authors and as there are more than two authors 'et al.' should be used after the first author's name as follows: Boers et al. (2019).

Example (b) is missing the period and comma after the 'et al.'. The correct way to format the citation is (Barker et al., 2020).

Example (c) is missing the parentheses around the year and should read Lee et al. (2014).

Example (d) is a paper with more than two authors, thus only the first author should be named rather than the first two as in this example. The correct format is Boot et al. (2013).

In the final example, (e), the reference includes all of the correct elements, but it is placed outside of the sentence, in a sentence of its own. The full stop should not be before the parentheses, but only at the end of the citation.

Looking at how published work includes citations is a good way to develop your understanding of how to format citations. Doing this will also help you to identify any mistakes in your own in-text citations.

Reference List

The reference list comes at the end of the assignment and gives the full information for each of the in-text citations, to allow the reader to find the source being cited. The reference list should be in alphabetical order by surname. Also note that for APA 7th style, lines after the first line of each reference need to be indented. How each reference is structured depends on the format of the source: a journal article follows a different structure to a textbook, both of which follow a different format to a website. As you should be sourcing most of your material from journal articles, we will focus on how to structure these. If you need to reference a different type of source, there is ample guidance online which will show you how to reference different types of sources according to APA 7th style.

━━━━━ Stop 9.1 ━━━━━

When following APA 7th style, it is good practice to use the primary source to ensure there are no inaccuracies in your application of the style. You can read more on APA style here References (apa.org)

The reference for a journal article follows this format:

Surname, initial. (year). Title of the journal article. *Name of the journal, volume*(issue), page range. DOI link.

Each part of the reference must adhere to the following structure (see Table 9.1).

Table 9.1 Guidance on reference structure

Feature of reference	Key detail
Surname, initial	If there is more than one author, they should be listed in the same order that they appear in the publication.
	A comma should be placed after the surname and a full stop should follow each initial. A space should be left between each initial.
(Year).	The year of publication should be in parentheses and end with a full stop.
Title of the journal article.	A capital letter should be used for the first letter of the first word. The title should end with a full stop.
Name of the journal,	Each of the main words in the journal name should be capitalised. The name should be in italics and end with a comma.
Volume	The volume number should be in italics. There should be no space between the volume and issue number.
(issue),	The issue number should not be italicised and should follow directly from the volume and be followed by a comma. If there is no issue number, then this can be omitted.
Page range.	Use the page range for the article, separated with a dash, e.g. 67–89. The page range should be followed with a full stop.
DOI	Include the DOI link if the work has one, e.g. https://doi.org/xxxx
	The DOI link should not be followed by a full stop.

It is important to include all the necessary information for each source in the reference list, as it allows the reader to find the source they need to.

Here are some examples of full references for some of the sources mentioned in this chapter:

Patel, S. R., & Hu, F. B. (2008). Short sleep duration and weight gain: a systematic review. *Obesity, 16*(3), 643–653. https://doi.org/10.1038/oby.2007.118

Wu, S. J., & Cai, X. (2023). Adding Up Peer Beliefs: Experimental and Field Evidence on the Effect of Peer Influence on Math Performance. *Psychological Science, 34*(8), 851–862. https://doi.org/10.1177/09567976231180881

Notice the indentation after the first line for each reference and the exact punctuation as directed in Table 9.1.

===== **Think 9.2** =====

The best way to develop your referencing skills is to practise. Below are some references for a reference list, for each one identify the error that is present.

a) Boers, E., Afzali, M. H., Newton, N., & Conrod, P. (2019). Association of screen time and depression in adolescence. *JAMA Pediatrics, 173*(9), 853–859.

b) Barker, Schubert, C. M., Barker, R. T., Kuo, S. I. C., Kendler, K. S., & Dick, D. M. (2020). The relationship between pet ownership, social support, and internalizing symptoms in students from the first to fourth year of college. *Applied Developmental Science, 24*(3), 279–293. https://doi.org/10.1080/10888691.2018.1476148

c) Lee, K., Talwar, V., McCarthy, A., Ross, I., Evans, A., & Arruda, C. (2014). Can classic moral stories promote honesty in children? *Psychological Science*, 1630–1636. https://doi.org/10.1177/0956797614536401

d) Boot, W. R., Simons, D. J., Stothart, C., & Stutts, C. (2013). The pervasive problem with placebos in psychology: Why active control groups are not sufficient to rule out placebo effects. Perspectives on Psychological Science, 8(4), 445–454. https://doi.org/10.1177/1745691613491271

e) Arch, J. J., Brown, K. W., Goodman, R. J., Della Porta, M. D., Kiken, L. G., & Tillman, S. (2016). Enjoying food without caloric cost: The impact of brief mindfulness on laboratory eating outcomes. *Behaviour Research and Therapy, 79*, 23–34. https://doi.org/10.1016/j.brat.2016.02.002

Hopefully you were able to identify some of the issues in the examples above.

In (a) first reference, the DOI link was absent.

In the second reference (b) the initials are missing for the first author (Barker).

In reference (c) the volume and issue number are absent.

In the fourth reference (d) the title of the journal is not in italics.

In the final reference, all elements are present but there is no indentation.

USING REFERENCE MANAGEMENT SOFTWARE

Writing your references by hand is strongly recommended as you are learning how to structure references. However, once you have grasped this you might want to think about using reference management software. Reference management software are programmes that you can use to store your references and to import both in-text citations and a reference list into your assignment. The benefits of this are that as long as you have set the referencing management system to format the references following APA 7th (or whatever system your institution requires that you use), you will not have to manually write out each reference. This reduces the likelihood that mistakes will be made, but it relies on you initially inputting all of the necessary information correctly. This is why it is important that you understand how to accurately format references as it allows you to identify any errors that might occur due to incorrectly inputted information into reference management software.

What Is Reference Management Software?

This is a piece of software where you can store all of the research papers, and any other electronic sources that you read. There are various different referencing management software available; some are open access (such as Mendeley), and it is likely that your institution has a licence for one. You will usually be able to organise your stored electronic resources such as research papers or PDF copies of books/book chapters; you may want to organise them by topic or by module. When you upload a source to the reference management software, you will need to input key details of that source such as the title and journal (if it is a journal paper), that the software will use to format the reference. You will also need to tell the software what medium the source is, i.e. is it a book, a book chapter, website or journal article. Based on your selection, the software will guide you to input the relevant information for that type of source.

Once your reference library is built, you can sync that reference management software with the word processing software you are using. As you write your assignment and you come to a point where you need to include a citation, you can select the source to input from the reference management software. The software will then add the in-text citation and a corresponding reference to the reference list.

If you are considering using reference management software, you will need to dedicate some time initially to learning how to use the software you have selected. Once you have learnt how to use the software, it can save you a lot of time. However, it is not without its limitations, for example the software will not spot any errors in how you have inputted the source material, e.g. if you have included a typing error. The accuracy of the references formatted is only as good as the information inputted, which means you need to understand how to format each type of reference to ensure that you have included all of the necessary information.

Stop 9.2

Do not use reference management software to avoid learning how to reference. If you choose to use it, wait until you have a strong grasp of referencing. It is not until postgraduate study that referencing management software tends to be used, we are just alerting you to it early on!

Explore further

To further develop your understanding of the importance of referencing and how to reference, you need to engage with references! Below are a few suggestions to help to develop your referencing skills.

Suggestion one
To develop your understanding of how primary and secondary sources differ, take the summary of Hornsey et al.'s (2002) paper outlined in Chapter 7 (called 'our summary'), and see how that differs to the original paper listed below.

(Continued)

(Continued)

Hornsey, M. J., Oppes, T., & Svensson, A. (2002). 'It's OK if we say it, but you can't': responses to intergroup and intragroup criticism. *European Journal of Social Psychology, 32,* 293–307 https://doi.org/10.1002/ejsp.90

When comparing the summary with the original think about the following questions:

- Why was only Experiment 1A mentioned in the summary?
- Do you think the summary provided in Chapter 7 was accurate?
- What information do the subsequent experiments tell you about the intergroup sensitivity effect?
- If you wanted to present a summary of all the experiments in this paper, how could you do that? Chapter 7 may give you some ideas here. The general discussion in Hornsey et al.'s paper may also help here.

Suggestion two

One way for you to see the importance of referencing is by using reference lists from published work to find the source that is being referred to. Select a piece of research, or a textbook and go to the reference list. Choose two to three different entries in the reference list and use the internet to try to find the source. Think about *how* you will find the source, you could go to the journal and locate the volume that the article was published in, or you might want to input the article title into your university library search engine or Google Scholar.

Suggestion three

Write out a full reference for each of the sources below. You have been given the relevant information, but you need to structure the reference appropriately. To check whether you have referenced correctly, you can check your answer in a free online reference generator, e.g. https://www.mybib.com/tools/apa-citation-generator. We have also included the correct references in the reference list at the end of the book.

(a)
Source type: Journal
Author/s: Wiebke Bleidorn, Andre Kretzschmar, John Rauthmann, Ulrich Orth, Jaap, J. A. Denissen and Christopher J. Hopwood
Title: Self-Esteem and Income Over Time
Journal name: Psychological Science
Volume: 34
Issue: 10
Pages: 1163–1172
DOI: https://doi.org/10.1177/09567976231185129

(b)
Source type: Journal
Author/s: Paul Conner and Ellen R. K. Evers
Title: The Bias of Individuals (in Crowds): Why Implicit Bias Is Probably a Noisily Measured Individual-Level Construct
Journal name: Perspectives on Psychological Science
Volume: 15
Issue: 6
Pages: 1329–1345
DOI: https://doi.org/10.1177/1745691620931492

(c)
Source type: Journal
Author/s: Ian Anderson, Santiago Gil, Clay Gibson, Scott Wolf, Will Shapiro, Oguz Semerci and David M Greenberg
Title: 'Just the Way You Are': Linking Music Listening on Spotify and Personality
Journal name: Social Psychological and Personality Science
Volume: 12
Issue: 4
Pages: 561–572
DOI: https://doi.org/10.1177/1948550620923228

KEY TAKEAWAYS

The first part of this chapter focused on why it is essential to include in-text citations and a reference list. We explored how important it is to credit the sources you have read and that without doing so could mean you have plagiarised, even if that was not your intention. We also explored how providing both the citation and the full reference allows your reader to find the original source to gain more information. Lastly, we also suggested that providing citations and references shows that your work is informed by research in the field and not simply your own opinion. We then ended the first half of this chapter by looking at primary and secondary sources and how they differ.

This chapter also focused on how to structure in-text citations and a reference list according to APA 7th style. The key to mastering referencing is lots of practice, using the feedback you receive on your referencing and looking at how published papers reference. We understand that referencing can be daunting when you first start writing assignments, but trust us when we say that the more you practise the easier it will get.

Congratulations, you have made it to the end of the book. We hope we have achieved what we set out to which was to demystify, simplify and demonstrate how you can use research in your work so that it becomes second nature to you. It is likely that along the way you may have felt overwhelmed by the task at hand, but we sincerely hope that this book has helped to provide you with the practical guidance that you have needed so that you have gained confidence and achieved your goals. There may be times when you feel your grasp of research and how to use it effectively in your essays and reports starts to loosen. If that happens do not feel intimidated or under-confident (we have both been there) but set aside some time to sit down go through the feedback from your lecturer/tutor and dip into the relevant chapters so you can get back on track. Remember that your learning journey will not always take the most direct route and there may be detours on the way, but with some determination (and this book!), you will achieve your goals. Thank you for choosing this book on your learning journey and we would like to wish you all the best for your future endeavours.

Glossary

Addiction: A dependency on a substance or behaviour that dominates thoughts, feelings and behaviour.

Amygdala: A region of the brain that processes emotions, particularly fear and threat.

Anxiety: A feeling of worry about an uncertain outcome.

Attrition rate: The proportion of participants who discontinued with a study at defined points.

Between participants design: During an experiment, whereby different participants are studied in each level of the independent variable.

Brain scanning: An overarching term for a range of different neuroimaging techniques that allow researchers to see the activity and structure of the brain.

Causation: A systematic change in one variable leads to changes in another variable

Cerebellum: Located at the back of the head, the cerebellum plays an important role in directing movements and balance. It is also implicated in executive control, spatial cognition and emotional processing.

Cognitive behavioural therapy: A talking treatment which can be applied to a range of mental health problems.

Cognitive neuroscience: Explores the biological processes that are involved in cognition, with a particular emphasis on the relation between brain structures, activity and cognitive functions.

Computer simulation: The use of mathematical modelling to make predictions of real-world situations.

Confirmation bias: The tendency to seek out information that supports what we already believe and disregard information that does not align with our already held beliefs.

Control: A scientific approach will normally try to ensure that no other factors are influencing what is being measured other than the variables of interest.

Control group: A group of people who are the same as the treatment group except that they are not receiving treatment.

Controlled observation: A branch of observational technique which involves setting up a situation in which participants are observed.

Correlation: A statistical method that measures the relationship between two co-variables.

Correlation coefficient: A statistical measure of the strength of a correlation that is measured from −1 to +1.

Covert observation: A branch of observational technique where participants are not aware that they are being observed.

Demand characteristics: A change in the participant's behaviour during a study, where participants try to guess the aim of the study and act in a way they think the researcher wants them to act.

Dependent variable: A variable measured in an experiment, to see if it is affected by the independent variable.

Depression: A clinically diagnosable mental illness which is characterised of a range of symptoms including low mood and lack of motivation.

Descriptive statistics: Used to describe characteristics of a data set. Examples include the mean and standard deviation.

Discrimination: A negative action towards an individual due to their membership of a particular group.

Dispersion: In statistics, dispersion refers to describing how spread out a set of data is.

Ecological validity: The extent to which a study reflects naturally occurring or everyday situations.

Empirical evidence: Evidence that has been collected through the research process. This can come from different research methods including surveys, interviews, experiments or observations.

Episodic memory: A type of long-term memory that requires conscious recall, for personal memories that involve being able to recall the time and place they occurred.

Ethics: The rules of conduct that are necessary when carrying out research. They guide psychologists to behave responsibly and maintain professional client relationships.

Experiment: A way of conducting research that seeks to establish cause and effect between the independent and dependent variable(s).

Exposure therapy: A psychological therapy which involves gradually exposing a patient to the object, situation or place they are fearful of.

Eye tracking: A method which utilises technology to measure where a participant looks during a study.

Fallacy: An incorrect conclusion or a mistaken belief that is based on faulty or no evidence.

Falsifiability: The notion of seeking out evidence which can disprove our hypothesis. Popper suggested this is a key feature of science.

Field experiment: A research method that has some controlled aspects that you see in lab experiments but takes place in natural real-world settings.

Focus group: A form of self-report which involves a small group of participants being interviewed about a specific research question.

Groupthink: Due to the desire to conform to a group, group members can come to a group decision which does not account for individual beliefs or critique.

Hippocampus: A brain region in the forebrain involved in regulating emotion and memory

Hypothesis: A precise, testable statement of what researchers predict will be the outcome of the study.

Idiographic: An approach that aims to understand one person in detail and their unique experiences without seeking to apply what is found to everyone.

Independent variable: A key feature of an experiment, this is something that varies and is deemed as having a causal role on the dependent variable being measured.

Inferential statistics: Statistical tests that allow inferences to be made and conclusions to be drawn from quantitative data generated by research.

Interpersonal variables: Characteristics of people which influence how they feel, think and behave such as their age, personality or socioeconomic status.

Interview: A research method which involves a conversation between the researcher and participant.

Longitudinal studies: A research method where the same participants are tracked over time allowing the researcher to track any changes.

Measures of central tendency: Examples of descriptive statistics that illustrate an overall central point of a data set. The mean, median and mode are the most common measures of central tendency.

Mnemonics: Conscious strategies to help improve memory, which often involve associating the information with something that is easier to remember.

Mindfulness-based cognitive therapy: A type of talking (psychological) which includes features of mindfulness. Mindfulness is a technique that involves focusing on internal and external sensations as they happen.

Natural observation: A branch of observational technique where participants are involved in their natural environment.

Negative correlation: When one co-variable increases, the other co-variable decreases.

Neurotransmitters: Chemical messengers that enable communication within the nervous system, and between the nervous system and the rest of the body.

Nomophobia: Feelings of anxiety that occur at the thought of being without one's mobile phone.

Nomothetic: An approach to conducting research aims to discover general laws of behaviour that we can apply to most people.

Non-participant observation: A branch of observational technique where the researcher observes from a distance and is not part of the interaction being observed.

Objective: The absence of personal opinion or bias in the research process.

Observation: A way of conducting research that involves watching and recording how participants behave.

OCD: Obsessive-compulsive disorder. This is a clinically diagnosable disorder characterised by obsessive thoughts and/or compulsive, ritualised behaviours. Often the behaviours seek to manage the intrusive thoughts.

Open science: Involves transparency at all stages of research; this includes in the design and planning of the study as well as data collection and analysis.

Overt observation: A branch of observational technique where the participants are aware that they are being observed.

Participant observation: A branch of observational technique where the researcher is involved in the interaction that is being observed.

Peer-reviewed journal: A journal which uses experts in the field to review and comment on research submitted to the journal to assess its suitability for publication.

Phubbing: When one member of a social interaction uses their mobile phone during the interaction.

Positive correlation: When one co-variable increases, the other co-variable also increases.

Primary data: Data that is collected first hand by the researcher from the participants.

Primary source: The original source of the information. Usually used to refer to the original write ups of research.

Pseudoscience: Beliefs or practices that claim to be scientific but lack the key features of science.

Qualitative data: Data that is in words.

Quantitative data: Data that is numerical.

Random allocation: A technique used in an experiment which involves allocating participants to the different conditions of the independent variable based on chance, without any bias from the researcher.

Reliability: The consistency, or stability, of a measure or study. It is the extent to which it can produce the same results under similar circumstances.

Regression analysis: A technique used to analyse quantitative data, to examine the strength of the relationship between variables. There are many different types of regression analysis.

Replicate: Repeating a piece of research in the exact same way it was conducted originally.

Replication: When a result from a study found again in a subsequent study. Replications test reliability.

Representative sample: A subset of the population that accurately reflects the characteristics of a larger population.

Research cycle: The way in which the questions that research addresses are often derived from theories or explanations, and the findings of that research then generate new questions or refinements to theory or explanation.

Researcher bias: Usually unintentional, but occurs when the researcher's own beliefs, expectations and decision influence the research process.

Retroactive interference: A type of forgetting in our long-term memory, when new information that is learnt interferes with the recall of an existing memory. We can no longer recall the old information accurately, due to the interference of the new information.

Sample: Subset of the population of interest that is studied in a piece of research.

Schizophrenia: A mental health disorder characterised by continuing or relapsing episodes of psychosis. Symptoms of the disorder include disruptions in thought processes, perceptions, emotional responsiveness and social interactions.

Secondary source: A source which summarises and provides interpretations of the findings of research studies.

Self-report techniques: A research method where the participants report on themselves either through surveys, interviews or focus groups.

Semi-structured interview: A type of interview where some of the questions are planned, but the researcher will ask additional questions based on the participant's responses.

Social desirability: Occurs when participants give responses that they feel are more desirable to have.

Social identity theory: The idea that who we are, in part, is encapsulated by the groups to which we belong, and that part of our self-concept comes from being in a social group.

Social learning theory: A theory that suggests behaviour is learnt via observation and imitation of a role model.

Spearman's Rho: A statistical test used to measure correlational data. It is used when the data does not meet the assumptions for a parametric test.

Structured interview: A type of interview where all of the questions are planned and are not deviated from.

Subjective: The influence of a person's beliefs, feelings and opinions rather than fact.

Survey: A written set of questions that the participant can complete either within the researcher's presence or alone.

Technoference: Disruption to a social interaction caused by technology.

T-test: A statistical test used to compare the difference in the means between two different groups.

Thematic analysis: A way to analyse qualitative data that involves the researcher looking carefully through the text to draw out common themes in the data.

Unstructured interview: A type of interview where none of the questions are planned.

Validity: The extent to which a measure or study is measuring what it set out to measure.

Vicarious reinforcement: A concept used as part of social learning, whereby a role model is observed being rewarded for their behaviour.

Video conferencing: A meeting between two or more people in different locations which takes place over the internet.

Within-participants design: During an experiment, whereby the same participants are studied in each level of the independent variable.

References

Aagaard, J. (2016). Mobile devices, interaction, and distraction: A qualitative exploration of absent presence. *Artificial Intelligence & Society, 31*(2), 223–231. https://doi.org/10.1007/s00146-015-0638-z

Aagaard, J. (2020). Digital akrasia: A qualitative study of phubbing. *AI & Society, 35*, 237–244. https://doi.org/10.1007/s00146-019-00876-0

Aarts, A. A., Anderson, J. E., Anderson, C. J., Attridge, P.R., Attwood, A., Axt, J., Bable, M., Bahník, S., Baranski, E., Barnett-Cowan, M., Bartmess, E., Beer, J., Bell, R., Bentley, H., Beyan, L., Binion, G., Borsboom, D., Bosch, A., Bosco, F., & Zuni, K. (2015). Estimating the reproducibility of psychological science. *Science, 349*(6251). https://doi.org/10.1126/science.aac4716

Adair, J. G., & Vohra, N. (2003). The explosion of knowledge, references, and citations: Psychology's unique response to a crisis. *American Psychologist, 58*(1), 15–23. https://doi.org/10.1037/0003-066X.58.1.15

Adamczyk, K., Janowicz, K., & Mrozowicz-Wrońska, M. (2022). Never-married single adults' experiences with online dating websites and mobile applications: A qualitative content analysis. *New Media and Society*, 1–24. https://doi.org/10.1177/14614448221097894

Al-Saggaf, Y., MacCulloch, R., & Wiener, K. (2019). Trait boredom is a predictor of phubbing frequency. *Journal of Technology in Behavioral Science, 4*(3), 245–252. https://doi.org/10.1007/s41347-018-0080-4

American Psychological Association. (2023, February 02). *APA Dictionary of Psychology.* https://dictionary.apa.org/nomothetic

Anderson, I., Gil, S., Gibson, C., Wolf, S., Shapiro, W., Semerci, O., & Greenberg, D. M. (2021). 'Just the way you are': Linking music listening on Spotify and personality. *Social Psychological and Personality Science, 12*(4), 561–572. https://doi.org/10.1177/1948550620923228

Arch, J. J., Brown, K. W., Goodman, R. J., Della Porta, M. D., Kiken, L. G., & Tillman, S. (2016). Enjoying food without caloric cost: The impact of brief mindfulness on laboratory eating outcomes. *Behaviour Research and Therapy, 79*, 23–34. https://doi.org/10.1016/j.brat.2016.02.002

Arnett, J. J. (2008). The neglected 95%: Why American psychology needs to become less American. *American Psychologist, 63*(7), 602–614. https://doi.org/10.1037/0003-066X.63.7.602

Atkinson, R. C., & Shiffrin, R. M. (1968). Human memory: A proposed system and its controlled processes. In K. W. Spence (Ed.), *The psychology of learning and motivation: Advances in research and theory* (Vol. 2, pp. 89–195). Academic Press. https://doi.org/10.1016/S0079-7421(08)60422-3

Balzarini, R. N., Muise, A., Zoppolat, G., Di Bartolomeo, A., Rodrigues, D. L., Alonso- Ferres, M., Urganci, B., Debrok, A., Bock Pichayayothin, N., Dharma, C., Chi, P., Karremans, J., Schoebi, D., & Slatcher, R. B. (2023). Love in the time of Covid: Perceived partner responsiveness buffers people from lower relationship quality associated with Covid-related stressors. *Social Psychological and Personality Science, 14*(3), 342–355. https://doi.org/10.31234/osf.io/e3fh4

Bandura, A. (1977a). *Social learning theory.* Prentice-Hall.

Bandura, A. (1977b). Self-efficacy: Toward a unifying theory of behavioral change. *Psychological Review, 84*(2), 191–215. https://psycnet.apa.org/doi/10.1037/0033-295X.84.2.191

Bandura, A. (1986). *Social foundations of thought and action.* Prentice Hall.

Barker, S. B., Schubert, C. M., Barker, R. T., Kuo, S. I. C., Kendler, K. S., & Dick, D. M. (2020). The relationship between pet ownership, social support, and internalizing symptoms in students from the first to fourth year of college. *Applied Developmental Science, 24*(3), 279–293. https://doi.org/10.1080/10888691.2018.1476148

Berry, K., Barrowclough, C., & Wearden, A. (2008). Attachment theory: A framework for understanding symptoms and interpersonal relationships in psychosis. *Behaviour Research and Therapy, 46*(12), 1275–1282. https://doi.org/10.1016/j.brat.2008.08.009

Bhatia, S., & Priya, K. R. (2018). Decolonizing culture: Euro-American psychology and the shaping of neoliberal selves in India. *Theory and Psychology, 28*(5), 645–668. https://doi.org/10.1177/0959354318791315

Bleidorn, W., Kretzschmar, A., Rauthmann, J. F., Orth, U., Denissen, J. J., & Hopwood, C. J. (2023). Self-esteem and income over time. *Psychological Science, 34*(10), 1163–1172. https://doi.org/10.1177/09567976231185129

Bleske-Rechek, A., Gunseor, M. M., & Nguyen, K. (2023). I 'knew' they wouldn't last: Hindsight bias in judgments of a dating couple. *Social Psychological Bulletin, 18*, 1–22. https://doi.org/10.32872/spb.9967

Boers, E., Afzali, M. H., Newton, N., & Conrod, P. (2019). Association of screen time and depression in adolescence. *JAMA Pediatrics, 173*(9), 853–859. https://doi.org/10.1001/jamapediatrics.2019.1759

Boot, W. R., Simons, D. J., Stothart, C., & Stutts, C. (2013). The pervasive problem with placebos in psychology: Why active control groups are not sufficient to rule out placebo effects. *Perspectives on Psychological Science, 8*(4), 445–454. https://doi.org/10.1177/1745691613491271

Boylan, J., Seli, P., Scholer, A. A., & Danckert, J. (2020). Boredom in the COVID-19 pandemic: Trait boredom proneness, the desire to act, and rule-breaking. *Personality and Individual Differences, 171*, 110387. https://doi.org/10.1016/j.paid.2020.110387

Cantoral, A., Téllez-Rojo, M. M., Ettinger, A. S., Hu, H., Hernández-Ávila, M., & Peterson, K. (2016). Early introduction and cumulative consumption of sugar-sweetened beverages during the pre-school period and risk of obesity at 8–14 years of age. *Pediatric Obesity, 11*(1), 68–74. https://doi.org/10.1111%2Fijpo.12023

Chotpitayasunondh, V., & Douglas, K. M. (2018). The effects of 'phubbing' on social interaction. *Journal of Applied Social Psychology, 48*(6), 304–316. https://doi.org/10.1111/jasp.12506

Cipriani, A., Furukawa, T. A., Salanti, G., Chaimani, A., Atkinson, L. Z., & Geddes, J. R. (2018). Comparative efficacy and acceptability of 21 antidepressant drugs for the acute treatment of adults with major depressive disorder: A systematic review and network meta-analysis. *The Lancet, 391*(10128), 1357–1366. https://doi.org/10.1176/appi.focus.16407

Conger, R. D., Neppl, T., Kim, K., & Scarmella, L. (2003). Angry and aggressive behavior across three generations: A prospective longitudinal study of parents and children. *Journal of Abnormal Child Psychology, 31*, 143–160. http://doi.org/10.1023/a:1022570107457

Connor, P., & Evers, E. R. (2020). The bias of individuals (in crowds): Why implicit bias is probably a noisily measured individual-level construct. *Perspectives on Psychological Science, 15*(6), 1329–1345. https://doi.org/10.1177/1745691620931492

Coyne, S. M., Jensen, A. C., Smith, N. J., & Erickson, D. H. (2016). Super Mario brothers and sisters: Associations between coplaying video games and sibling conflict and affection. *Journal of Adolescence, 47,* 48-59. https://doi.org/10.1016/j.adolescence.2015.12.001

DeLoache, J. S., Pierroutsakos, S. L., Uttal, G. H., Rosengren, K. S., & Gottlieb, A. (1998). Grasping the nature of objects. *Psychological Science, 9*(3), 205-210. https://doi.org/10.1111/1467-9280.00039

Dickerson, P. (2021). *How to write brilliant psychology essays.* SAGE.

Douglas, S., Stott, J., Spector, A., Brede, J., Hanratty, É., Charlesworth, G., Noone, D., Payne, J., Patel, M., & Aguirre, E. (2022). Mindfulness-based cognitive therapy for depression in people with dementia: A qualitative study on participant, carer and facilitator experiences. *Dementia, 21*(2), 457-476. https://doi.org/10.1177/14713012211046150

Drouin, M., McDaniel, B. T., Pater, J., & Toscos, T. (2020). How parents and their children used social media and technology at the beginning of the COVID-19 pandemic and associations with anxiety. *Cyberpsychology, Behavior, and Social Networking, 23*(11), 727-736. https://doi.org/10.1089/cyber.2020.0284

Drouin, M., Reining, L., Flanagan, M., Carpenter, M., & Toscos, T. (2018). College students in distress: Can social media be a source of social support? *College Student Journal, 52*(4), 494-504.

Elder, T. J., Sutton, R. M., & Douglas, K. M. (2005). Keeping it to ourselves: Effects of audience size and composition on reactions to criticisms of the in group. *Group Processes and Intergroup Relations, 8*(3), 231-244. https://doi.org/10.1177/1368430205053940

Flint, S. W., & Reale, S. (2018). Weight stigma in frequent exercisers: Overt, demeaning and condescending. *Journal of Health Psychology, 23*(5), 710-719. https://doi.org/10.1177/1359105316656232

Garfin, D. R. (2020). Technology as a coping tool during the coronavirus disease 2019 (COVID-19) pandemic: Implications and recommendations. *Stress and Health, 36*(4), 555-559. https://doi.org/10.1002/smi.2975

Gentile, D. A., Anderson, C. A., Yukawa, S., Ihori, N., Saleem, M., Ming, L. K., Shibuya, A., Liau, A. K., Khoo, A., Bushman, B. J., Huesmann, L. R., & Sakamoto, A. (2009). The effects of prosocial video games on prosocial behaviors: International evidence from correlational, longitudinal, and experimental studies. *Personality and Social Psychology Bulletin, 35*(6), 752-763. https://doi.org/10.1177/0146167209333045

Gopalakrishna, G., ter Riet, G., Vink, G., Stoop, I., Wicherts, J. M., & Bouter, L. M. (2022). Prevalence of questionable research practices, research misconduct and their potential explanatory factors: A survey among academic researchers in the Netherlands. *PLoS One, 17*(2). https://doi.org/10.1371/journal.pone.0263023

Greitemeyer, T., & Cox, C. (2013). There's no 'I' in team: Effects of cooperative video games on cooperative behavior. *European Journal of Social Psychology, 43*(3), 224-228. https://doi.org/10.1002/ejsp.1940

Greitemeyer, T., & Mügge, D. O. (2014). Video games do affect social outcomes: A meta-analytic review of the effects of violent and prosocial video game play. *Personality and Social Psychology Bulletin, 40*(5), 578-589. https://doi.org/10.1177/0146167213520459

Greitemeyer, T., & Osswald, S. (2010). Effects of prosocial video games on prosocial behavior. *Journal of Personality and Social Psychology, 98*(2), 211. https://psycnet.apa.org/doi/10.1037/a0016997

Greitemeyer, T., & Osswald, S. (2011). Playing prosocial video games increases the accessibility of prosocial thoughts. *The Journal of Social Psychology, 151*(2), 121-128. https://doi.org/10.1080/00224540903365588

Halpern, D., & Katz, J. E. (2017). Texting's consequences for romantic relationships: A crosslagged analysis highlights its risks. *Computers in Human Behavior, 71*, 386-394. https://doi.org/10.1016/j.chb.2017.01.051

Hand, M. M., Thomas, D., Buboltz, W. C., Deemer, E. D., & Buyanjargal, M. (2013). Facebook and romantic relationships: Intimacy and couple satisfaction associated with online social network use. *Cyberpsychology, Behavior, and Social Networking, 16*(1), 8-13. http://doi.org/10.1089/cyber.2012.0038

Henrich, J., Heine, S. J., & Norenzayan, A. (2010). Most people are not WEIRD. *Nature, 466*, 29. https://doi.org/10.1038/466029a

Holt-Lunstad, J., Smith, T. B., & Layton, J. B. (2010). Social relationships and mortality risk: A meta-analytic review. *PLoS Medicine, 7*(7), e1000316. https://doi.org/10.1371/journal. pmed.1000316

Holtzman, S., DeClerck, D., Turcotte, K., Lisi, D., & Woodworth, M. (2017). Emotional support during times of stress: Can text messaging compete with in-person interactions? *Computers in Human Behavior, 71*, 130-139. https://doi.org/10.1016/j.chb.2017.01.043

Hornsey, M. J., & Imani, A. (2004). Criticizing groups from the inside and the outside: An identity perspective on the intergroup sensitivity effect. *Personality and Social Psychology Bulletin, 30*, 365-383. https://doi.org/10.1177/0146167203261295

Hornsey, M. J., Oppes, T., & Svensson, A. (2002). 'It's OK if we say it, but you can't': Responses to intergroup and intragroup criticism. *European Journal of Social Psychology, 32*, 293-307. https://doi.org/10.1002/ejsp.90

Hornsey, M. J., Trembath, M., & Gunthorpe, S. (2004). 'You can criticise because you care': Identity attachment, constructiveness, and the intergroup sensitivity effect. *European Journal of Social Psychology, 34*, 499-518. https://doi.org/10.1002/ejsp.212

Iyengar, S. S., Lepper, M. R., & Ross, L. (1999). Independence from whom? Interdependence with whom? Cultural perspectives on ingroups versus outgroups. In D. A. Prentice & D. T. Miller (Eds.), *Cultural divides: Understanding and overcoming group conflict* (pp. 273-301). Russell Sage Foundation.

Jackson, P. L., Meltzoff, A. N., & Decety, J. (2005). How do we perceive the pain of others: A window into the neural processes involved in empathy. *NeuroImage, 24*, 771-779. https://doi.org/10.1016/j.neuroimage.2004.09.006

Jessica, K., & Lee, A. J. (2023). Assortative preferences for personality and online dating apps: Individuals prefer profiles similar to themselves on agreeableness, openness, and extraversion. *Personality and Individual Differences, 208*, 112185. https://doi.org/10.1016/j.paid.2023.112185

Jones, A. R., Carlson, C. A., Lockamyeir, R. F., Hemby, J. A., Carlson, M. A., & Wooten, A. R. (2020). 'All I remember is the black eye': A distinctive facial feature harms eyewitness identification. *Applied Cognitive Psychology, 34*(6), 1379-1393. https://doi.org/10.1002/acp.3714

Juvonen, J., Schacter, H. L., & Lessard, L. M. (2021). Connecting electronically with friends to cope with isolation during COVID-19 pandemic. *Journal of Social and Personal Relationships, 38*(6), 1782-1799. https://doi.org/10.1177/0265407521998459

Katzmarzyk, P. T., Broyles, S. T., Champagne, C. M., Chaput, J. P., Fogelholm, M., Hu, G., Kuriyan, R., Kurpad, A., Lambert, E. V., Maia, J., Matsudo, V., Olds, T., Onywera, V., Sarmiento, O. L., Standage, M., Tremblay, M. S., Tudor-Locke, C., &, Zhao, P. (2016). Relationship between soft drink consumption and obesity in 9-11 years old children in a multi-national study. *Nutrients, 8*(12), 770. https://doi.org/10.3390/nu8120770

Kim, S. S., Huang-Isherwood, K. M., Zheng, W., & Williams, D. (2022). The art of being together: How group play can increase reciprocity, social capital, and social status in a multiplayer online game. *Computers in Human Behavior, 133*, 107291. https://doi.org/10.1016/j.chb.2022.107291

Klaming, R., Annese, J., Veltman, D. J., & Comijs, H. C. (2017). Episodic memory function is affected by lifestyle factors: A 14-year follow-up study in an elderly population. *Aging, Neuropsychology, and Cognition, 24*(5), 528–542. https://doi.org/10.1080/13825585.2016.1226746

Kohlberg, L. (1958). *The development of modes of moral thinking and choice in the years ten to sixteen.* Unpublished doctoral dissertation. University of Chicago.

Ku, K. Y. (2009). Assessing students' critical thinking performance: Urging for measurements using multiple-response format. *Thinking Skills and Creativity, 4*(1), 70–76. https://doi.org/10.1016/j.tsc.2009.02.001

Kushlev, K., Dwyer, R., & Dunn, E. W. (2019). The social price of constant connectivity: Smartphones impose subtle costs on well-being. *Current Directions in Psychological Science, 28*(4), 347–352. https://doi.org/10.1177/0963721419847200

Kushlev, K., & Leitao, M. R. (2020). The Effects of smartphones on well-being: Theoretical integration and research agenda. *Current Opinion in Psychology, 36*, 77–82. https://doi.org/10.1016/j.copsyc.2020.05.001

Lee, K., Talwar, V., McCarthy, A., Ross, I., Evans, A., & Arruda, C. (2014). Can classic moral stories promote honesty in children?. *Psychological Science, 25*(8), 1630–1636. https://doi.org/10.1177/0956797614536401

Lee, S. Y., & Hawkins, R. P. (2016). Worry as an uncertainty associated emotion: Exploring the role of worry in health information seeking, *Health Communication, 31*(8), 926–933. https://doi.org/10.1080/10410236.2015.1018701

Lenhart, A., & Duggan, M. (2014). *Couples, the internet, and social media.* Pew Research Center. http://www.pewinternet.org/2014/02/11/couples-the-internet-and-social-media

Lilienfeld, S. O. (2010). Can psychology become a science? *Personality and Individual Differences, 49*(4), 281–288. https://doi.org/10.1016/j.paid.2010.01.024

Lilienfeld, S. O., & Landfield, K. (2008). Science and pseudoscience in law enforcement: A user-friendly primer. *Criminal Justice and Behavior, 35*(10), 1215–1230. https://doi.org/10.1177/0093854808321526

Loftus, E. F. (2005). Planting misinformation in the human mind: A 30-year investigation of the malleability of memory. *Learning & Memory, 12*(4), 361–366. https://doi.org/10.1101/lm.94705

Loprinzi, P. D., Frith, E., & Crawford, L. (2020). The effects of acute exercise on retroactive memory interference. *American Journal of Health Promotion, 34*(1), 25–31. https://doi.org/10.1177/0890117119866138

Loprinzi, P. D., Loenneke, J. P., & Storm, B. C. (2021). Effects of acute aerobic and resistance exercise on episodic memory function. *Quarterly Journal of Experimental Psychology, 74*(7), 1264–1283. https://doi.org/10.1177/1747021821994576

Marks, D. F., Murray, M., & Estacio, E. V. (2021). *Health psychology: Theory, research, practice* (6th ed.). SAGE.

McDaniel, B. T., & Coyne, S. M. (2014). 'Technoference': The interference of technology in couple relationships and implications for women's personal and relational well-being. *Psychology of Popular Media Culture, 5*(1), 85–98. https://doi.org/10.1037/ppm0000065

McDaniel, B. T., & Coyne, S. M. (2016). 'Technoference': The interference of technology in couple relationships and implications for women's personal and relational well-being. *Psychology of Popular Media Culture, 5*(1), 85–98. https://psycnet.apa.org/doi/10.1037/ppm0000065

McDaniel, B. T., Galovan, A. M., Cravens, J. D., & Drouin, M. (2018). 'Technoference' and implications for mothers' and fathers' couple and coparenting relationship quality. *Computers in Human Behavior, 80*, 303-313. https://doi.org/10.1016/j.chb.2017.11.019

McDaniel, B. T., Galovan, A. M., & Drouin, M. (2020). Daily technoference, technology use during couple leisure time, and relationship quality. *Media Psychology, 24*(5), 637-665. https://doi.org/10.1080/15213269.2020.1783561

Miguel, E. C., Baer, L., Coffey, B. J., Rauch, S. L., Savage, C. R., O'Sullivan, R. O., Phillips, K., Moretti, C., Leckman, J. F., & Jenike, M. A. (1997). Phenomenological differences appearing with repetitive behaviours in obsessive-compulsive disorder and Gilles de la Tourette's syndrome. *British Journal of Psychiatry, 170*, 140-145. https://doi.org/10.1192/bjp.170.2.140

Mills, L., Lee, J. C., Boakes, R., & Colagiuri, B. (2023). Reduction in caffeine withdrawal after open-label decaffeinated coffee. *Journal of Psychopharmacology.* https://doi.org/10.1016/j.paid.2023.112185

Moseley, D., Elliott, J., Gregson, M., & Higgins, S. (2005). Thinking skills frameworks for use in education and training. *British Educational Research Journal, 31*, 367-390. https://doi.org/10.1080/01411920500082219

Muise, A., Christofides, E., & Desmarais, S. (2009). More information than you ever wanted: Does Facebook bring out the green-eyed monster of jealousy? *CyberPsychology and Behavior, 12*(4), 441-444. http://doi.org/10.1089/cpb.2008.0263

Munsell, C. R., Harris, J. L., Sarda, V., & Schwartz, M. B. (2016). Parents' beliefs about the healthfulness of sugary drink options: Opportunities to address misperceptions. *Public Health Nutrition, 19*(1), 46-54. https://doi.org/10.1017%2FS1368980015000397

Neff, L. A., & Karney, B. R. (2017). Acknowledging the elephant in the room: How stressful environmental contexts shape relationship dynamics. *Current Opinion in Psychology, 13*, 107-110. https://doi.org/10.1016/j.copsyc.2016.05.013

O'Dwyer, A., Berkowitz, N. H., & Alfeld-Johnson, D. (2002). Group and person attributions in response to criticism of the in-group. *British Journal of Social Psychology, 41*, 563-588. https://doi.org/10.1348/014466602321149885

Overdorf, V., Kollia, B., Makarec, K., & Alleva Szeles, C. (2016). The relationship between physical activity and depressive symptoms in healthy older women. *Gerontology and Geriatric Medicine, 2.* https://doi.org/10.1177/2333721415626859

Patel, S. R., & Hu, F. B. (2008). Short sleep duration and weight gain: A systematic review. *Obesity, 16*(3), 643-653. https://doi.org/10.1038/oby.2007.118

Paulhus, D. L. (1984). Two-component models of socially desirable responding. *Journal of Personality and Social Psychology, 46*(3), 598-609. https://psycnet.apa.org/doi/10.1037/0022-3514.46.3.598

Pauly, T., Lüscher, J., Berli, C., Hoppmann, C. A., Murphy, R. A., Ashe, M. C., Linden, W., Madden, K.M., Gerstorf, D., & Scholz, U. (2023). Let's enjoy an evening on the couch? A daily life investigation of shared problematic behaviors in three couple studies. *Personality and Social Psychology Bulletin.* https://doi.org/10.1177/01461672221143783

Pettigrew, J. (2009). Text messaging and connectedness within close interpersonal relationships. *Marriage & Family Review, 45*(6-8), 697-716. http://doi.org/10.1080/01494920903224269

Piaget, J. (1932). *The moral judgment of the child.* The Free Press.

Pietromonaco, P. R., & Collins, N. L. (2017). Interpersonal mechanisms linking close relationships to health. *American Psychologist, 72*(6), 531. http://doi.org/10.1037/amp0000129

Pietromonaco, P. R., & Overall, N. C. (2021). Applying relationship science to evaluate how the COVID-19 pandemic may impact couples' relationships. *American Psychologist, 76*(3), 438. http://doi.org/10.1037/amp0000714

Quiroz, S. I., & Mickelson, K. D. (2021). Are online behaviors damaging our in-person connections? Passive versus active social media use on romantic relationships. *Cyberpsychology: Journal of Psychosocial Research on Cyberspace, 15*(1). http://doi.org/10.5817/cp2021-1-1

Reicher, S., & Haslam, S. A. (2006). Rethinking the psychology of tyranny: The BBC prison study. *British Journal of Social Psychology, 45*, 1–40. https://doi.org/10.1348/014466605X48998

Riva, P., & Andrighetto, L. (2012). 'Everyone feels a broken bone, but only we can feel a broken heart': Group membership influences perceptions of targets' suffering. *European Journal of Social Psychology, 42*, 801–806. http://dx.doi.org/10.1002/ejsp.1918

Roberts, C. K., & Barnard, R. J. (2005). Effects of exercise and diet on chronic disease. *Journal of Applied Physiology, 98*(1), 3–30. https://doi.org/10.1152/japplphysiol.00852.2004

Roberts, J. A., & David, M. E. (2016). My life has become a major distraction from my cell phone: Partner phubbing and relationship satisfaction among romantic partners. *Computers in Human Behavior, 54*, 134–141. https://doi.org/10.1016/j.chb.2015.07.058

Robertson, L. A., McAnally, H. M., & Hancox, R. J. (2013). Childhood and adolescent television viewing and antisocial behaviour in early adulthood. *Pediatrics, 131*, 439–446. https://doi.org/10.1542/peds.2012-1582

Rohrbaugh, M. J., Shoham, V., Butler, E., Hasler, B. P., & Berman, J. S. (2009). Affective synchrony in dual- and single-smoker couples: Further evidence of 'symptom-system fit?' *Family Process, 48*(1), 55–67. https://doi.org/10.1111/j.1545-5300.2009.01267.x

Rohrbaugh, M. J., Shoham, V., & Racioppo, M. W. (2002). Toward family level attribute × treatment interaction research. In H. A. Liddle, D. A. Santisteban, R. F. Levant, & J. H. Bray (Eds.), *Family psychology: Science-based interventions* (pp. 215–237). American Psychological Association. https://doi.org/10.1037/10438-011

Rutter, M., Donuga-Barke, E. J., Beckett, C., Castle, J., Kreppner, J., Kumsta, R., & Bell, C. A. (2011). Deprivation-specific psychological patterns: Effects of institutional deprivation. *Monographs of the Society for Research in Child Development, 75*(1), 1–250. http://www.jstor.org/stable/40608153

Ryan, R. M., Rigby, C. S., & Przybylski, A. (2006). The motivational pull of video games: A self-determination theory approach. *Motivation and Emotion, 30*, 344–360. https://doi.org/10.1007/s11031-006-9051-8

Saleem, M., Anderson, C. A., & Gentile, D. A. (2012). Effects of prosocial, neutral, and violent video games on children's helpful and hurtful behaviors. *Aggressive Behavior, 38*(4), 281–287. https://doi.org/10.1002/ab.21428

Schneider, F. M., & Hitzfeld, S. (2021). I ought to put down that phone but I phub nevertheless: Examining the predictors of phubbing behavior. *Social Science Computer Review, 39*(6), 1075–1088. https://doi.org/10.1177/0894439319882365

Schuhmacher, N., Köster, M., & Kärtner, J. (2019). Modeling prosocial behavior increases helping in 16-month-olds. *Child Development, 90*(5), 1789–1801. https://doi.org/10.1111/cdev.13054

Segall, M. H., Lonner, W. J., & Berry, J. W. (1998). Cross-cultural psychology as a scholarly discipline: On the flowering of culture in behavioral research. *American Psychologist, 53*(10), 1101–1110. https://doi.org/10.1037/0003-066X.53.10.1101

Shoham, V., Butler, E. A., Rohrbaugh, M. J., & Trost, S. E. (2007). Symptom-system fit in couples: Emotion regulation when one or both partners smoke. *Journal of Abnormal Psychology*, *116*(4), 848-853. https://doi.org/10.1037/0021-843X.116.4.848

Shoshani, A. (2023). From virtual to prosocial reality: The effects of prosocial virtual reality games on preschool children's prosocial tendencies in real life environments. *Computers in Human Behavior*, *139*, 107546. https://doi.org/10.1016/j.chb.2022.107546

Shoshani, A., & Krauskopf, M. (2021). The Fortnite social paradox: The effects of violent-cooperative multi-player video games on children's basic psychological needs and prosocial behavior. *Computers in Human Behavior*, *116*, 106641. https://doi.org/10.1016/j.chb.2020.106641

Shoshani, A., Nelke, S., & Girtler, I. (2022). Tablet applications as socializing platforms: The effects of prosocial touch screen applications on young children's prosocial behavior. *Computers in Human Behavior*, *127*, 107077. https://doi.org/10.1016/j.chb.2021.107077

Skoyen, J. A., Randall, A. K., Mehl, M. R., & Butler, E. A. (2014). 'We' overeat, but 'I' can stay thin: Pronoun use and body weight in couples who eat to regulate emotion. *Journal of Social and Clinical Psychology*, *33*(8), 743-766. https://doi.org/10.1521/jscp.2014.33.8.743

Skoyen, J. A., Rentscher, K. E., & Butler, E. A. (2018). Relationship quality and couples' unhealthy behaviors predict body mass index in women. *Journal of Social and Personal Relationships*, *35*(2), 224-245. https://doi.org/10.1177/0265407516680909.

Stockdale, L. A., & Coyne, S. M. (2020). Bored and online: Reasons for using social media, problematic social networking site use, and behavioral outcomes across the transition from adolescence to emerging adulthood. *Journal of Adolescence*, *79*(1), 173-183. https://doi.org/10.1016/j.adolescence.2020.01.010

Squire, L. R., Ojemann, J. G., Miezin, F. M., Petersen, S. E., Videen, T. O., & Raichle, M. E. (1992). Activation of the hippocampus in normal humans: A functional anatomical study of memory. *Proceedings of the National Academy of Sciences*, *89*(5), 1837-1841. https://doi.org/10.1073/pnas.89.5.1837

Sun, J., & Samp, J. A. (2022). 'Phubbing is happening to you': Examining predictors and effects of phubbing behaviour in friendships. *Behaviour and Information Technology*, *41*(12), 2691-2704. https://doi.org/10.1080/0144929X.2021.1943711

Thomas, T. T., Carnelley, K. B., & Hart, C. M. (2022). Phubbing in romantic relationships and retaliation: A daily diary study. *Computers in Human Behavior*, *137*, 107398. https://doi.org/10.1016/j.chb.2022.107398

Thompson, L., Pennay, A., Zimmermann, A., Cox, M., & Lubman, D. I. (2014). 'Clozapine makes me quite drowsy, so when I wake up in the morning those first cups of coffee are really handy': An exploratory qualitative study of excessive caffeine consumption among individuals with schizophrenia. *BMC Psychiatry*, *14*, 1-10. https://doi.org/10.1186/1471-244X-14-116

Thornberry, T. P., Freeman-Gallant, A., Lizotte, A. J., Krohn, M. D., & Smith, C. A. (2003). Linked lives: The intergenerational transmission of antisocial behavior. *Journal of Abnormal Child Psychology*, *31*, 171-184. https://doi.org/10.1023/a:1022574208366

Tienari, P., Wynne, L. C., Sorri, A., Lahti, I., Läksy, K., Moring, J., Naarala, M., Nieminen, P., & Wahlberg, K. E. (2004). Genotype-environment interaction in schizophrenia-spectrum disorder. Long-term follow-up study of Finnish adoptees. *British Journal of Psychiatry*, *184*, 216-222. https://doi.org/10.1192/bjp.184.3.216

Tong, S., & Walther, J. B. (2011). Just say 'no thanks': Romantic rejection in computer-mediated communication. *Journal of Social and Personal Relationships, 28*(4), 488-506. http://doi.org/10.1177/0265407510384895

Toulmin, S. (1958). *The uses of argument.* Cambridge University Press. https://doi.org/10.1017/CBO9780511840005

Townsend, C. H., Kray, L. J., & Russell, A. G. (2023). Holding the belief that gender roles can change reduces women's work-family conflict. *Personality and Social Psychology Bulletin.* https://doi.org/10.1177/01461672231178349

Van der Zanden, T., Schouten, A. P., Mos, M. B. J., & Krahmer, E. J. (2020). Impression formation on online dating sites: Effects of language errors in profile texts on perceptions of profile owners' attractiveness. *Journal of Social and Personal Relationships, 37*(3), 758-778. https://doi.org/10.1177/0265407519878787

Vanden Abeele, M. M., Hendrickson, A. T., Pollmann, M. M., & Ling, R. (2019). Phubbing behavior in conversations and its relation to perceived conversation intimacy and distraction: An exploratory observation study. *Computers in Human Behavior, 100*, 35-47. https://doi.org/10.1016/j.chb.2019.06.004

Vandeweerd, C., Myers, J., Coulter, M., Yalcin, A., & Corvin, J. (2016). Positives and negatives of online dating according to women 50+. *Journal of Women and Aging, 28*(3), 259-270. https://doi.org/10.1080/08952841.2015.1137435

Verheijen, G. P., Stoltz, S. E., van den Berg, Y. H., & Cillessen, A. H. (2019). The influence of competitive and cooperative video games on behavior during play and friendship quality in adolescence. *Computers in Human Behavior, 91*, 297-304. https://doi.org/10.1016/j.chb.2018.10.023

Veronesi, C. (2014). Falsifications and scientific progress: Popper as sceptical optimist. *Lettera Matematica, 1*(4), 179-184. https://doi.org/10.1007/s40329-014-0031-7

Wang, X., Xie, X., Wang, Y., Wang, P., & Lei, L. (2017). Partner phubbing and depression among married Chinese adults: The roles of relationship satisfaction and relationship length. *Personality and Individual Differences, 110*, 12-17. https://doi.org/10.1016/j.paid.2017.01.014

Wang, D., & Ziano, I. (2023). Give me a straight answer: Response ambiguity diminishes likability. *Personality and Social Psychology Bulletin.* https://doi.org/10.1177/01461672231199161

Werner, C. M., Stoll, R., Birch, P., & White, P. H. (2002). Clinical validation and cognitive elaboration: Signs that encourage sustained recycling. *Basic and Applied Social Psychology, 24*(3), 185-203. https://doi.org/10.1207/S15324834BASP2403_2

Whiting, A., & Williams, D. (2013). Why people use social media: A uses and gratifications approach. *Qualitative Market Research: An International Journal, 16*(4), 362-369. https://doi.org/10.1108/QMR-06-2013-0041

Williamson, R. A., Donohue, M. R., & Tully, E. C. (2013). Learning how to help others: Two-year-olds' social learning of a prosocial act. *Journal of Experimental Child Psychology, 114*(4), 543-550. https://doi.org/10.1016/j.jecp.2012.11.004

Wu, S. J., & Cai, X. (2023). Adding up peer beliefs: Experimental and field evidence on the effect of peer influence on math performance. *Psychological Science, 34*(8), 851-862. https://doi.org/10.1177/09567976231180881

Yang, Y. T. C. (2015). Virtual CEOs: A blended approach to digital gaming for enhancing higher order thinking and academic achievement among vocational high school students. *Computers and Education, 81*, 281-295. https://doi.org/10.1016/j.compedu.2014.10.004

Yin, M., Qiu, B., He, X., Tao, Z., Zhuang, C., Xie, Q., Tian, Y., & Zhang, W. (2022). Effects of reward and punishment in prosocial video games on attentional bias and prosocial behaviors. *Computers in Human Behavior*, *137*, 107441. https://doi.org/10.1016/j.chb.2022.107441

Zhan, S., Shrestha, S., & Zhong, N. (2022). Romantic relationship satisfaction and phubbing: The role of loneliness and empathy. *Frontiers in Psychology*, *13*, 967339. https://doi.org/10.3389/fpsyg.2022.967339

Zheng, M., Rangan, A., Allman-Farinelli, M., Rohde, J. F., Olsen, N. J., & Heitmann, B. L. (2015). Replacing sugary drinks with milk is inversely associated with weight gain among young obesity-predisposed children. *British Journal of Nutrition*, *114*(9), 1448–1455. https://doi.org/10.1017/S0007114515002974

Zimbardo, P. G., Haney, C., Banks, W. C., & Jaffe, D. (1971). *The Stanford prison experiment*. Zimbardo, Incorporated.

Zoppolat, G., Righetti, F., Balzarini, R. N., Alonso-Ferres, M., Urganci, B., Rodrigues, D. L., Debrot, A., Wiwattanapantuwong, J., Dharma, C., Chi, P., Karremans, J. C., Schoebi, D., & Slatcher, R. B. (2022). Relationship difficulties and 'technoference' during the COVID-19 pandemic. *Journal of Social and Personal Relationships*, *39*(11), 3204–3227. https://doi.org/10.1177/02654075221093611

Index

Milton Keynes UK
Ingram Content Group UK Ltd.
UKHW051628021224
3319UKWH00047B/1527

9 781529 626216